This book is dedicated to all the girls I've loved before, my condolences.

To my wife, for putting up with me for this long.

To all my friends, family and anyone who's ever swung a hammer, spliced a wire, fastened a valve, laid con-crete, flipped a burger and/or dropped out of school to get a real job, this book is for you.

Oh. And to my adoptive father, Dennis Coles (a.k.a. Ghostface Killah), your words are like ziti. Everything I know I learned from listening to you.

Mom, now is a good time to stop reading.

VICE

SKINEMA

BY CHRIS NIERATKO

FIRST PUBLISHED IN THE UNITED STATES OF AMERICA IN 2007 BY
VICE BOOKS
97 North 10th Street, Suite 202
Brooklyn, NY 11211
viceland.com

chrisnieratko.com

Lyrics from "All That I Got Is You" and "Save Me Dear"
by Ghostface Killah Courtesy of Starks Enterprises
and Money Come First Management.

DISTRIBUTED BY
powerHouse Books
37 Main Street, Brooklyn, NY 11201
PHONE 212 604 9074   FAX 212 366 5247
powerHouseBooks.com

FIRST EDITION
2007 / 10 9 8 7 6 5 4 3 2 1

PRINTED AND BOUND IN CHINA

ISBN: 978-1-57687-384-7
Library of Congress Control Number: 2006940165

FOREWORD

by Johnny Knoxville

1

INTRODUCTION

by Dave Carnie

5

PREFACE

by Chris Nieratko

10

CHAPTER 1

"I Know It's Over and It Never Really Began"
(The old sex stories)

12

CHAPTER 2

"Sometimes I Look Up at the Stars and Analyze the Sky"
(Drug-induced rants and paranoia)

86

CHAPTER 3

"Even the Losers Get Lucky Sometimes"
(My poor wife)

168

CHAPTER 4

"Misty Water-Colored Memories"
(The photos)

260

"You wanna fight? Let's go outside and you and me fuckin' fight." These were the first words that were ever uttered between Chris Nieratko and me. He approached me in a bowling alley about seven years ago and asked me to step outside. Now I get this a lot. People often times challenge me to a round of fisticuffs. They want to prove themselves against my ill perceived "toughness." But Chris was different. He wasn't trying to test his measure against mine. He wasn't trying to prove anything. Chris is, simply put, an asshole.

What other man's idea of yuletide cheer is growing a Hitler mustache every December that he keeps until Christmas? An asshole; that's what type of man. Who else gets caught buggering a guy's girlfriend by the boyfriend (who is in a well-known emo band—the name of which will remain unnamed to protect the guilty) and tells the jilted lover in his thick jersey accent, "Hey you. Get da fuck outta here." The poor bastard just stood there and cried. (Sorry that one makes me laugh every time.) What other jerk gets a picture of themselves in *Sports Illustrated* sitting courtside at a Celtics / Nets game holding a sign that says, "Will someone please stab Paul Pierce?" (This, mind you, was after Paul Pierce had been stabbed in a bar fight 11 times in the face, neck, and back and almost died.) Who would do that? Nieratko, that's who. Puuurrre asshole.

We used Chris on the *Jackass* TV show a couple of times. He appeared in a bit called "The 50 Egg Challenge" to see if he could eat 50 boiled eggs in a sitting like Paul Newman in *Cool Hand Luke*. Luckily, he couldn't and the bit ended with Nieratko puking directly on Preston Lacy. He and Preston appeared in another bit called "The Egg Nog Challenge." This one was a drinking game. Chris was dressed as an elf and Preston was Frosty the snowman. Well, needless to say this one ended with Nieratko puking on Preston too. Actually, he puked into Frosty's top hat while Preston was face down on the table and then our little elf put the hat back atop Frosty's head. Wow, that was one mad snowman.

At the beginning of *Jackass* we were toying with the idea of having Chris interview a band every week so we sent him over to the House of Blues to interview Ronnie James Dio. To film it we sent over Spike Jonze, Rick Kosick and a couple of no-longer-employed producers to get releases. Both parties arrived on time and all the necessary papers were signed and given back to our producer.

The interview commences: Chris is slumped in a couch drinking Budweiser after Budweiser as Ronnie sits down beside him. Chris greets him, "Wow Rodney, you sure are a lot shorter in person." The first missile had been launched and Ronnie is visibly pissed (and I must say in Chris's defense, waaaaayyy shorter in person). Ronnie shoots back, "First of all, my name is Ronnie, not Rodney!! Secondly, you don't call someone short, you got it?!!"

"Oh sorry," Chris responds passive aggressively, "I'm totally sorry." Trying to get back into Ronnie's good graces, Chris asks, "So what was it like being in Black Sabbath with Ozzy Osbourne?" Ronnie is really perturbed now. "What? I am a lead singer and Ozzy is a lead singer. How could we both be in Black Sabbath at the same time?!!" Chris just shrugs his shoulders and chugs another beer. Ronnie continues, "I get it. You are trying to get a rise out of me. You want to fight me?! Well I'm not taking the bait. I am on to you." Ronnie (feeling like Sherlock Holmes for uncovering Chris's not-so-secret investigative strategy) smiles as if the pile of shit beside him is going to let up now that he has "figured out" his game. Well the pile of shit doesn't let up. He just strokes Ronnie's ego with a couple of meaningless inquiries and then slowly starts peppering in more and more contentious questions. It was beautiful watching Chris get Ronnie angry and then bring him back down. For 30 minutes Chris played Dio like a banjo missing a couple of strings. Drinking beer and smiling all the while. Finally, Nieratko finishes another beer, belches, and, while reaching for another brew, grabs Dio's arm and goes, "Wow you are a skinny little shit aren'tcha?" This is where Dio loses it. He yells "Okay, you want to fight? Let's fight," and he stands up over top of Chris. Nieratko remains seated (and still can look Ronnie in the eye by the way), smiles and says, "I would fucking kill you." At this point Ronnie's manager runs over to our producer, grabs the releases from her hands and rips them into pieces. Dio's security guards tackle our cameraman Kosick and choke him out to get his tape of the event. Spike sees what's going on and sprints out the back door escaping scot-free as usual. By this time Nieratko was hauling ass too, still carrying his beer of course, with two beefy security guards hot on his heels. Luckily the security guards were in worse shape than Nieratko and he made it to safety. The same can't be said for our footage of that evening because Dio's security successfully stole Kosick's tape. Spike made it out with his tape but he only had Chris's side of the interview. He got a little of Dio when the fight started but we couldn't show any of it because his manager seized the release forms.

So, that is Chris Nieratko in a nutshell. He is always running to or from a bar with a six-pack under his right arm like a football, and he is always, always starting some type of shit. He will start shit with a person or group of persons. "He will start shit with a wall. He will start shit in a hall. He will start shit in a mall . . ."

Had I known what kind of prick I was dealing with in the bowling alley all those years ago, I may have obliged him and stepped outside into the alley but nah, that would have only made his day. Instead we ended up ingesting lots of pills and lots of booze that night and ended up back at my house because the fucking jerk said, "You didn't fucking shoot yourself with a 0.38 while wearing a bulletproof vest in the *Big Brother* video. You're full of shit." Incensed, I produced the dented vest and flattened slug that slammed into it. All he said was, "Oh I guess you didn't fake it after all, bitch."

On that I called him a cab and told him to get the fuck out of my house. That was years ago. Chris Nieratko was an asshole then and he is an asshole now. Hell, I guess that's why we became friends.

—JOHNNY KNOXVILLE

was first introduced to Chris Nieratko's work in 1997 when he began freelancing for *Big Brother* magazine shortly after it was bought by Larry Flynt. I was managing editor at the time, but oddly enough I did very little editing and even less managing. That was left to Sean Cliver, who, unbeknownst to the rest of us, had somehow struck up a relationship with Chris. I believe Chris's first article to appear in the mag was an interview with the recently reunited EPMD in issue #31. It was obvious from the beginning of the interview that Chris was "one of us."

"So, being big, black men," he asked, "do you have big, black penises?"

They humbly admitted they did, and thus a good portion of the rest of the interview was devoted to the subject of big, black penises. He did, at one point, take a break from the big, black penis theme, but only to ask Eric Sermon if he was gay.

Chris's stupid questions continued into the next issue, where for his second interview he spoke with Angus Young from AC/DC. Toward the end, he wondered if Angus was pissed that Princess Diana was dead.

"I can't say either way," Angus replied. "I never met the woman before in my life, so it didn't really affect me."

"You weren't bummed that you never got to shag the old bugger?" Chris asked.

"What are you saying?" Angus asked. "Are you talking about necrophilia now? My, you really dig in to the bottom of the barrel, don't you? First Mongolians up the ass, now necrophilia with the Princess of Wales. What else have you got up your dirty sleeve?"

It wasn't until his third submission, an interview with Big Punisher, that I finally took notice. Like Chris, I don't pay much attention to what's going on around me, me, me. But after I read it, I had to ask, "Who is this kid, and how does he keep hooking up these big-name interviews?" Anyone can get lucky here and there, but three good interviews in a row was fairly uncommon among our stable of retarded freelancers.

"You carry that everywhere?" he asked Big Pun about the gun he was holding. "Even to the clubs?"

"Usually," the 400-pound Big Pun said. "I mean, most guys don't 'cause they get searched and hassled, but nobody searches me."

"I'm sure," Chris said. "Who has time for that? You've got hiding spots under hiding spots. They'd be searching for a week."

We were sold on Nieratko, and we wanted more. Although there was still the problem with his name. Chris spelled his name "Chri$." Sean, for some reason, and contrary to his aesthetics, allowed this nonsense into print. In hindsight, Sean was a bit skittish and I wonder if he allowed the dollar sign to continue for as long as it did because he was intimidated by the idea of a confrontation with anyone who was thuggy enough to have a dollar sign in his name (Chri$, at the time, claimed to be a rapper named Hepatitis C) but was also able to sit in front of an armed, 400-pound gorilla, make fun of him to his face and live to tell about it. Or maybe he thought it was as funny as Chris did. The rest of us weren't scared of Chris or his goddamn dollar sign, and the grammatical bling was promptly eliminated. Chri$, of course, protested and fed us some bull about his dad spelling his name that way. He said his dad died in Vietnam and that we were defiling his name by not spelling it with a $. So we began printing his name ¢hris. He eventually stopped protesting. And his rap career ended shortly thereafter. I know he'll thank us someday when he grows up.

Chris continued to freelance for us until our little side project, *Jackass*, got bought by MTV in 1999 and half the staff jumped ship to go kick each other in the balls with Johnny Knoxville. This left a few staff positions open. For one, "editor in chief" became available, and for some reason they gave it to me. Now, when I visit my former staff members' homes in the Hollywood Hills, I always have a little laugh at my decision to take that job and remain with *Big Brother*. My consolation prize of "keeping it real" has never been much consolation because today I have a small stack of magazines in my garage to show for my work, while they have large stacks of money in their bank accounts. Still, I've never regretted the decision. Money aside, I've always enjoyed what we did at *Big Brother* far more than anything they ever did on *Jackass*. A lot of that was due to Chris Nieratko, the first person I hired.

Chris became the new managing editor. And like me, he neither managed nor edited. From what I remember, he could barely spell. He moved to LA, and like most people who move to LA, he began complaining about the coffee, the pizza, the fake-ass people and, of course, the traffic. His solution to the latter was a gas-guzzling '72 El Camino that took up two parking spots. A very practical car for Southern California. His solution to the former was to move back home to New Jersey. But that wasn't before he spent a few months living in an apartment four doors down from me on Formosa Street in Hollywood with his estranged girlfriend at the time. She was nice to me. I didn't realize she had ISSUES, though, until I got to witness one of her numerous suicide attempts that you'll be reading about shortly. Have you ever seen anyone try to commit suicide? She was cross-eyed from all the pills, waving a gun around, cops, ambulance drivers, neighbors yelling, tears, lots of tears, it's all very exciting. And apparently she was trying to commit suicide all the time! Just four doors down! I'm kind of bummed that I only got invited to see one. Chris got to watch it all the time. Selfish bastard.

Earl Parker once wrote, "If something bad happens, I'll just write about it." I've always liked that. I think Chris likes it too. Although Chris would probably change it to, "When something bad happens, I'll just write about it," because Chris always enjoys a bad situation. He really likes to get in trouble. He loves, for instance, going to basketball games and wearing the visiting team's jersey, getting drunk and screaming at the home crowd. I've never quite understood that one. But, anyway, when *Jackass* dropped and it was the hottest thing in the world, I'd get all these journalists calling to interview me. They acted like they were very clever interviewing the editor of the magazine that spawned *Jackass*, but I'm pretty sure they called me because Knoxville wouldn't talk to them. They would always ask, "Why?" As in, "Why do you do all these bad things? Why do you make so much trouble for yourselves? I don't get it! WHY? WHY? WHYYYYY?"

The answer was, and still is, "Because it's fucking fun."

Plus we're writers and we need shit to write about.

And that's what this book is all about. Making up shit to write about. All the "reviews" collected here from *Vice* and *Bizarre Magazine* are carefully calculated scenarios that Chris "got himself into" so that he would have something to fill the space where the words are supposed to go in the porn reviews he had been assigned. This material, unfortunately, had no place in *Big Brother*. It's true that we were rather naughty at times and we were indeed owned by Larry Flynt, but we were a skateboard magazine and thus a good portion of our audience was composed of kids. I'm no fuddy-duddy, but I don't think ten-year-olds need to be reading about ass sex. Mouth rape's okay, that's a fact of life, but not butt sex. But Chris (three butts!) had this material lying around, and it needed to go somewhere. What better location than a porno review? Which is pretty much like sticking it up your butt.

I don't know what's worse, someone who writes porno reviews or the dude who reads them. I don't even much care for watching pornos in the first place. It's probably because I always laugh at the fat slob who ducks behind the curtain in the adult section at the video store. "Loser." I understand there are people out there who can get whatever they want but still watch a porn now and then. Some even watch them with their lady, and that's fine, but watching a porno, to me, is like admitting defeat. "Man, I've really hit rock bottom," I think every time I see one. I'll admit, though, that my aversion to the genre may have originated the first (and last) time I was on a porno set, where I watched Jasmine St. Clair blow fire out of her butthole. That was when I decided sex and women were one thing and pornography was something entirely different. Plus I got a porn star for a girlfriend.

The main reason I think I'm not a fan is because pornos are to jacking off what snowboarding is to skateboarding. It's so much work. You need a mountain, snow, gloves, a bunch of gay clothes, a lift ticket, a lift, boots, a snowboard and a shit ton of drinks afterward to help you forget how gay you are for doing it in the first place. Skateboarding, you just walk out the door and hop on your board and you're good. I'm not suggesting that I walk out my front door to jack off, but jacking off requires nothing more than a hand and a penis. Preferably your penis. Simple. Porno equals hand, penis, television,

DVD, DVD player, remote, Kleenex (are you going to cum on your couch?), electricity to run the whole show and a job to pay for the electricity that powers your entertainment center. So the porno review is some 'nother level shit to me. It's like writing about snowboarding. And then to think that there are people out there who actually read about other people watching snowboarding, it just blows me away because we don't even waste our time writing about skateboarding.

Chris, fortunately for his sake, has somehow avoided reviewing the porno. This is one of his many achievements. As I said before, he's just kind of filling the space that would otherwise be filled with the words that make up the review of a pornographic film with other words that he likes better. He's just "spanning time," as Vincent Gallo says. And he gets paid for it. It's like a dream job: You get paid to write whatever you want, knowing that no one is going to read it. You can almost picture Chris as Beckett's Molloy, lying in his own bed writing this trash while Gavin McInnes pays him for it. "There's this man who comes every week . . . He gives me money and takes away the pages. So many pages, so much money." Because I now refuse to believe that there is anyone out there who reads articles about snowboarding or pornographic videos. There's no way. They need to be written, sure, there's that space, but there is no one in their right mind who reads them. So Chris has simply seen the porn review for what it is: a space that needs words, just like a hole that needs to be filled with dirt. And Chris came with his own dirt.

—DAVE CARNIE

Seven years ago *Vice* was just beginning to come into its own in America. The entire staff quickly realized I was the greatest minimalist writer they'd ever come across and began begging me to do something, anything for the magazine. But I am very lazy. And money hungry. So I generally don't get out of bed unless there is money on the breakfast table. Finally *Vice* cofounder Gavin McInnes made me an offer of a regular monthly column. He told me there was a column called "Skinema" that was dead and needed some life blown into its lungs. I was unfamiliar with the column since I did not write it. I have a very strict "If I didn't write it, I won't read it" policy. When I finally did look at it I laughed. Whoever had been writing it before had been reviewing anime, which in itself was a crime since everyone who owns a wristwatch knew that people stopped caring about anime in, like, 1993. To make it worse, I believe it was anime porn that was being reviewed, a genre that is wrong on so many levels. I told Gavin I refused to watch/toss off to/write about cartoons having sex. He told me I was free to review real porn if I liked, with real humans, not animated dick monsters raping drawn girls in schoolgirl outfits.

At the time I had just moved to LA for a job as an editor of the now-defunct legendary skateboard magazine *Big Brother*, which just so happened to be owned by smut peddler and First Amendment pioneer Larry Flynt. Once a month I'd go upstairs to the *Hustler* office and sift through thousands of porn titles until one of them caught my eye. It really didn't matter what the content was or how the girls looked; I generally didn't watch most of the porn anyway. Like everything in my life, my writing has always revolved around me, me, me. Reason being: I am infinitely more interesting than nearly any subject matter I've ever covered.

Needless to say, the first few installments of my column in *Vice* were heralded by scholars and noblemen the world over as being the most important writing ever written on those particular days in history. I was all over the news wire. People were talking about the column from Madagascar to Mozambique. I'm really surprised you didn't hear about it.

The boys across the pond did. One of the editors of the UK fetish/oddity magazine *Bizarre,* Andy Capper, was the first to recognize my genius and immediately asked me to do a similar column for them, but instead of just one review a month, he wanted five. Andy eventually went on to become the editor of the UK version of *Vice.* Funny how things work, huh?

Anyway, that's really the gist of it. Seven years later I've amassed enough self-absorbed rants (disguised as reviews for adult films) that Vice has given me a book. It's not very academic by any means. Hell, I dropped out, flunked out or got kicked out of six colleges in three years, so what do you expect? If ever there were literature made exclusively for sitting on the toilet, you are holding it right now.

I hope you enjoy.

And if you don't, what am I gonna do?

Heart,
Chris Nieratko

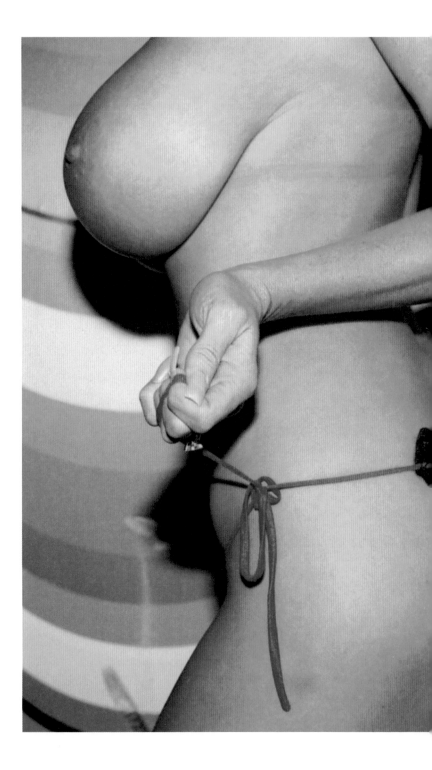

CHAPTER 1

"I Know It's Over
and It Never Really Began"
(The old sex stories)

Roly Poly Gang Bang 7

METROPOLIS ENTERTAINMENT • RATING: 11

I knew this older stoner guy growing up that truly thought he understood life, love and women, and he'd constantly try to pass on his
wisdom to me. Most of his advice was abso-ludicrous absurd bullshit; things like "A pussy is supposed to smell bad. If it doesn't that
means she just took it to the doctor's and there's something wrong
with it," and "Chicks with braces give the best head because they
overcompensate," or "Never tell a girl you love her because once you
do she'll poke a hole in your condoms and make you get her pregnant
without telling you." Most of what he said went in one ear and out
the other. I assumed that he'd done too many drugs in his time, and
disregarded his insight anytime he tried to offer it. I really only hung
out with him because he was old enough to buy beer. But there was
one thing that he said that I think is a very true and helpful guideline
to offer a young man on his way through life, and that is, "Whoever
you end up marrying you'll eventually get tired of fucking, so before
you get married you have to make sure you fuck one of every type of
girl. That way when you close your eyes when you're sticking it to your
wife, you can imagine any woman in the world. Like a mental
Rolodex." Now, when he said one of every type he meant: an older
woman, a virgin, a blonde, a redhead, a JAP, a Jap, a Puerto Rican, a
mom, a married chick, an anorexic chick, a fat chick and so on. For
some reason he never mentioned black women, but whatever. I
thought to myself, This is a great goal to set for myself. I'm going to
have sex with one of every type of woman in the world and then I'll
know I'm ready to settle down. That was when I was 13, and I think
over the past 18 years I've done a fairly good job of crossing off most
nationalities and body types from the list, with the exception of anything remotely Asian (that includes Filipinos and Panamanians). The
reason for their omission is because my father was killed in the
bombing of Pearl Harbor and I have never really forgiven the Asian

people for his death. As for everyone else, I've successfully had a wide variety of women, from midgets to lofty professional basketball players; pristine super models to armless birth-defected mutants; hairy-bushed, unshaved armpit hippies to completely hairless cancer patients. It's safe to say I've had them all and (cue the music) *I did them all myyyyyyy waaaay.* Funny thing is that the kid who started me on my quest so many years back with all his "wisdom" and "understanding" of the opposite sex started his to-do list with a fat chick and never got any further. I think he's married to her to this day. I imagine when he closes his eyes he sees nothing, save for the fires of hell.

Candy Striper Stories 5

JET MULTIMEDIA • DIR: SID DEUCE • RATING: 4

I still remember the smell of the hospital as I sat waiting for the doctor to come out and tell me my first son was dead. It smelled a bit like mothballs and a lot like bleach. I kept rubbing my eyes and fluttering my nose like a bunny rabbit at the toxic odor. Then there were the screams, echoing down the hall begging for God's forgiveness, begging to take her life instead. Heavy complications from a less-than-healthy pregnancy. I wondered if the problems somehow stemmed from an unhealthy relationship, one built on lies, distrust and infidelity. Can an unborn child sense that kind of tension in the womb?

As the morning news warned me of rain I wondered why the doctors had refused me entrance to the emergency room to comfort my then girlfriend through our unsuccessful attempt at a premature birth. When they finally came to tell me the bad news, covered in blood, I silently thanked them for sparing my eyes the horror. I tried to tell them that none of what was happening was real; that it was all a bad dream. A scene from a bad movie. Things like this did not happen to good, law-abiding 18-year-old boys. Such retribution was reserved for murderers and the like. I wanted to tell them that I was too young to carry the burden of death on my shoulders for as long as I shall live. Instead I said nothing.

From time to time, I remember the nurse—the pretty girl, too large in the hips, too small in the chest—who came to me religiously over my nine-hour stay in my baby's morgue, asking if I needed anything. Water. Food. Cigarettes. Anything. She smiled with compassion so real and genuine it scared me. I wanted her to offer me her hand. I wanted her to tell me she knew a place we could be alone, where everything was as it was when I was 10, when life was full of love and laughter. When the blood of an unborn child was a black thought. I wanted her to offer me something, a needle full of anything, nothing, everything that would end the grief I would feel for the rest of my life.

Or maybe I wanted her to tell me it wasn't my fault. I wanted to have her smile for me and tell me God fucked up, not me. I needed to be absolved. Forgiven. I needed the guilt lifted off my shoulders, not a Coca-Cola. But all she had to offer was, "Are you sure you don't want a pillow?" No, dear. I don't want a fucking pillow. I want to die. And ever since, I've hated hospitals. Even if they are the kind where the nurses are the ones that bend over.

Assault That Ass

CLUBREDLIGHT.COM • DIR: DION GIARRUSSO • RATING: 9

Her face must have started turning blue when I ran to get a towel to clean up her vomit. She was choking on her own tongue or vomit or something and to me, she never looked more beautiful.

Seeing her lying in a pool of bile and bad Italian food, tampon string dangling from her pussy and blood coating her inner thighs, I thought to myself, If she lives through this I'm going to marry this girl. Or at least cut off her access to my cocaine. As her skin tone grew darker, I considered doing something. Then I considered not doing anything. She liked the Smiths so much. "To die by your side, is such a heavenly way to die. To die by your side, well the pleasure, the privilege, is mine." Maybe she was doing all this for me, it was her way of showing me how much she loved me. In dying she was giving the ultimate gift of herself, something far greater than the gift of devirginizing her naked body, which I'd unwrapped not 10 minutes before and repackaged in white semen.

I watched as her eyes rolled into the back of her head, laughing at how she'd always roll them and call me a dork after one of my bad Polack jokes. At times even my worst "three guys in a pub" joke would make her laugh until the tears bled from her eyes, and I know she would only do it to humor me. She was a sweetheart in that sense. Actually in most senses of the word. Except on days when work was rough and she'd walk into my apartment and punch me in the nose without warning. I guess that wouldn't fall under the sweet-heart category, so I chose not to think about those times. I wanted to think about long kisses goodnight and dimply smiles from ear to ear.

And when she started to shake in her little puddle, convulsing like a fish out of water, it reminded me of the way she'd dance for me. There was her silly, cutesy dance and then there was her "fuck me" dance. I'll tell you, that "fuck me" dance could make even the most devilish stripper blush. She moved with the grace of angels, the sen-suality of Adonis, and her eyes reinforced the fact that every inch of her was mine.

The needle on the player skipped and hissed at the end of the record and I knelt down beside her, kissed her forehead, reached in and cleared her throat.

I'm Your Slut #3

CLUBREDLIGHT.COM • DIR: MANUEL FERRARA • RATING: 6

The party ended hours ago and I'd just saved her life by cleaning out the vomit lodged in her throat. I stood above her covered in puke, wondering what I would have done if she'd died. Would I have run away or called for help? She tried to stand but her hands slipped in the muck and she smashed her face on the floor. I carried her limp body to the bathtub and began running the water. She had her head rested against the back of the bathtub one moment and the next she leaned forward and cracked her skull open on the faucet. Blood filled the bath, real horror show. I tried my best to stop the bleeding but nothing worked, then again with the gagging. I called out for her roommate but got no response. For an instant I thought to go to her room and wake her friend but didn't for fear of her drowning in the bloody water. I wanted so much to leave her there, bleeding, dying, choking on her own vomit. Couldn't someone else deal with it? Where was her big-time rock & roll boyfriend when she needed him? On tour with the band? Making music in the studio? I considered going through her cell phone until I found his number, calling and saying, "Listen. What I'm about to tell you is probably going to ruin your entire day but I need to say it because I'm in a bit of a bind. So here it is: I was partying with your girlfriend, got her real good and drunk and fucked up on pills and cocaine, then I brought her back to her place and started fucking her in the ass but she got all sick and started puking everywhere. She turned blue for a while but she's white again. Now she's in the tub bleeding out of her head, gagging, and she's probably going to die if she doesn't get some medical help real soon. That's where you come in. I'm too drunk to drive and even if I wasn't I really don't need to be involved in this kind of shit. What I'm saying is I need to get out of here, I've got things to do. And since she's technically your girlfriend, I figure she's your responsibility." I thought if I was able to get all that out without interruption then he might just be the kind of pussy I needed to get out of my jam. I mean this was the same kid who had an emo band and that I'd told to go home when he came knocking at his girl's bedroom window one night. The main problem with that was the same as asking the roommate for help; the phone was in the other room and leaving her alone only ran the risk of her drowning. That's when I realized I was overthinking the entire thing. I shut the water off, wrapped her head in towels, picked her up, walked her down the hall and threw her on her roommate's bed. She instantly started heaving on her friend. Then I grabbed her cell phone and called and hung up on her boyfriend three times, then I threw the cell phone in the bed with the two of them and I left, leaving the front door slightly opened.

I watched the obituaries every day for the next week but I didn't see her name so I'm sure she's fine.

Double or Nothing

REDLIGHTDISTRICTVIDEO.COM • DIR: MANUEL FERRARA • RATING: 5

D id I ever tell you I had AIDS once? Once. For two weeks. God! That was awful. The worst two weeks of my life. I advise anyone out there who is thinking of getting AIDS not to and anyone who has it, get rid of that shit; give it to someone else or do whatever you have to do but don't hold on to that shit.

What happened was I was having stomach issues from excessive drinking. I couldn't stand upright due to a stabbing pain in my gut, I was unable to hold down anything I ate and I was bleeding out my ass every time I sat on the toilet. So I went and saw my doctor. She said she needed to do some blood work to see what the problem was. I had never had blood drawn in my adult life and thus never knew what kind of diseases I might be carrying around. I asked her, "While you're down there, can you check for everything?" She didn't catch my drift. I told her I'd never had an AIDS test and asked if she could sort me out.

A few days later I received a distressed, uneasy voice-mail at my office: "Uh . . . Mr. Nieratko, this is the doctor's office. Could you please give us a call? We got your test results back . . . uh . . . we really need to talk to you . . . one of the tests came back positive," then she left the doctor's office phone number. I dropped the phone, went ghostly white and vomited in the trash can under my desk. "YOUR TEST CAME BACK POSITIVE," I kept hearing it in my head again and again. I decided right then and there that I could not live with such a disease and went to the window, climbed onto the radiator and stuck one leg out the window, then the other. I found myself standing on a narrow ledge on the fifth floor of a six-story building. I tell you in completely sincerity that I would have dived headfirst and ended it all right then and there had my co-worker not said whatever it was that he said to get me to come back in. I wish I could tell you his exact words, that it was some grandiose motivational speech that made me rethink my life, to think that I still had a fighting chance, but I just can't remember. I went blank. As your life is flashing in front of you it's kind of difficult to get much of a grasp on one particular thought other than the obvious underlying theme that it is your time to die. I don't know what it was he said that brought me off that ledge. Maybe I realized that at 22 I wasn't ready to die yet or maybe I just wanted to rethink a more theatrical exit than smearing my skull across some nondescript sidewalk in Cincinnati across from a White Castle. Or maybe it was simply that I wanted to know who had given me AIDS so I could go slash their tires.

Swallow My Pride 35

REDLIGHTDISTRICTVIDEO.COM • DIR: DAVID LUGER • RATING: 6

The first few days after I learned I had AIDS were split between anger toward whoever gave it to me and sorrow about the possible dozens of women I could have passed it onto. Since I'd never been tested before, I had 10 years of partners to sift through and try and figure out the who, when and where's. Needless to say, my mind was a scrambled mess. I had no idea where to begin or how to go about letting people know. Living in a modern age, I figured the quickest, easiest way was to send a mass e-mail to the few girls who I kept in touch with. Impersonal, yes, I know, but I didn't know what else to do. The letter went like this, "To All the Girls I've Loved Before, My Condolences. I write you today with the worst possible news. Yesterday at 1:30 p.m. I was diagnosed positive with HIV. I don't know when I contracted it or with whom, so I urge you all to get tested as soon as possible. I want to apologize to you all but I know that doesn't do much to help you cope with this news. I just pray that none of you were affected and that you are able to live a long, healthy life without fear or concern. Sincerely, Chris Nieratko." Next I began going through my black book, one by one, and calling any number I found, ruining life after life in the process. Some girls were excited to hear from me at first, then after hearing the bad news began to curse me with forked tongues. Some girls were now married with children and not at home when I called, so I was forced to leave a message on their answering machine for them or their husband to hear. Others barely remembered me or my name or I theirs. Many asked if I was certain and all cried. I cried with them. It took me a half hour to compose myself after each call. When I did I promised myself to be tougher for the girls, no more tears—still I wasn't strong enough and wept again and again and again. All this combined with my stomach problems made me barely able to function. At times I threw up mid-conversation; I began to convince myself that in less than 24 hours

I'd gone into full-blown-AIDS mode. I kept remembering Tom Hanks at the end of that movie *Philadelphia* and started to reconsider jumping out my office window. But I still had dozens of ladies to inform before I earned the right to kill myself. Again I picked up the receiver and dialed and started with, "You might not remember me but . . . " Over the course of the following days I received very few callbacks or return e-mails, which was understandable; why would anyone want to talk to the person who completely destroyed their world? I did get a number of calls and messages from my doctor's office urging me to contact them or to come in immediately to begin some sort of treatment. No hope of living, no desire to milk out a subhuman existence, I deleted their every message. Then I booked a flight back to New Jersey to tell my family and to visit some of the girls in person whose numbers I didn't have.

Myne Tease

METROINTERACTIVE.COM • DIR: PAT MYNE • RATING: 8

I went back to New Jersey with ill tidings of having contracted AIDS and received mixed reactions and a broken nose. Some of my friends responded with, "That's what you get for fucking with all those black girls," and some with the exact opposite, "That's what you get for fucking with those white girls." My family didn't stop crying for my entire four-day stay. The nose and the black eye were a result of knocking on the door to one girl's apartment and having her husband answer. Seems she was married when we'd gotten together, unbeknownst to me.

Back in Ohio a number of calls from my physician begging me to contact them waited on my machine. Up until then I was resolved to try and let as many girls as possible know the problem before jumping off the Roebling Bridge into the Ohio River with a cinder block tied to my leg and being done with the whole sordid mess, so how I found myself in front of my doctor crying is still a mystery to me. But there I was, emaciated, tired, confused, an overall emotional wreck. Can you believe that she even had the nerve to ask me what was wrong? I told her to fuck off. She pulled up a chair, sat, put her hand on my knee, urged me to tell her what was bothering me. I told her I didn't want to die. She responded that no one does, but everyone eventually will. I stabbed her with my eyes, wondering how she could be so cold. She looked away, grabbed her file and pen and told me she wanted to put me on medication immediately. I shook my head and told her I didn't want to bother, that it would only prolong the agony and that I was ready to move on. "But it's really powerful stuff," she said. "If you take it three times a day for two weeks you'll be fine." Fine? How is that possible, I asked. "It's a common antibiotic, it only takes two weeks for the infection to pass through your body." I wiped my face dry and tried to make sense of her words, "I-I-I never heard of a pill cure. I didn't know they even discovered a cure yet." "Sure," she told me. "It's really not a big deal anymore, you just need to slow down the excessive drinking." Drinking? What does drinking have to do with anything? "That's what caused the infection," she said. "Wait. What? What the fuck are you talking about? Since when can you catch AIDS from drinking?" "AIDS?" she laughed. "What? What makes you think you have AIDS?" "Two weeks earlier your secretary had left a message at my office that my test had come back positive." She apologized for the confusion, saying the secretary should have just left a message for me to call the office and nothing more. "Yes," she explained, "you are positive. Positive for a stomach infection stemming from drinking. Not for AIDS. Your AIDS test came back negative. Other than the stomach problem you have a clean bill of health."

The Devil Deep Inside

DIR: KOVI • PRIVATE.COM • RATING: 5

I also had herpes recently, for a day. It was more like a week, and that scared the piss out of me too. I woke up a few mornings after shaving my cock and balls to find a slight bulge on the shaft of my dick. Very minor, no bigger than a pimple.

I knew what it was, I'd had them before, always after shaving my parts with a straight razor; I had an ingrown hair. I was 100% certain and dismissed it. But a week later it was still there and I panicked, setting up an emergency doctor's appointment.

My regular physician was overbooked, so I had to see the quack who shared her office, the mutt who handles her overflow. I hate him. I'd seen him once before and he refused to shake my hand. The hand-shake, to me, reveals the person inside. Sweaty palms, limp wrists, dead fish all admit character flaws. The last time I'd ignored his diag-nosis and thrown away his prescription. But this time I was forced to deal with him. My penis, my very existence, the essence of who I am, depended on his knowledge and understanding. Again he refused to shake my hand. He asked what the problem was, with his back to me, from across the room. I told him I had a lump on my penis I was sure was an ingrown hair, I just needed him to confirm it. He told me to pull down my pants and show him. He glanced over his shoulder, from seven feet away, and told me his assessment: "You have herpes. Definitely herpes." The air emptied from my lungs. My legs and spine gave out simultaneously. I fell into a chair, dick still hanging out. My future flashed before me: kids, wife, life, death. Then I began to ques-tion how or from whom I could have gotten it and it dawned on me. "Doctor," I muttered, "it can't be. I've been in a monogamous rela-tionship for three years. There's no way." His head cocked upright and he finally turned to me. "Let me take a closer look," he said, grab-bing my dick and really inspecting it. "It burns and itches, no?" No, I replied. "But it is emitting pus, is it not?" No. "Were there smaller bumps around the larger one?" he asked. "No," I repeated, "just that one red bump. It doesn't itch, hurt, burn or anything. No pus, no pain. Just unsightly."

"Hmmm," he said, biting his lip, "perhaps it's not herpes. Maybe it is just an ingrown hair." He gave me antibiotics and in five days the hair popped through and the bump went away. But for those five days I was miserable, the word "HERPES" in big bold Helvetica letters flashing in my head day and night as I tried to figure out how to tell my girlfriend I had herpes and most likely had given it to her.

Hot Showers #8

HUSTLERVIDEO.COM • DIR: CLIVE MCLEAN • RATING: 5

When I first went to college I was dating a girl who always referred to anal sex as "sodomy." I personally like the word, it makes the act seem much dirtier than it is. But to hear her say "sodomy" gave it a real bad connotation. Imagine an 80-year-old nun saying, "I want your thick cock in my cunt, then I want you to cum on my face." That's how I felt every time she said "sodomy," and that's how I felt every time I tried to perform sodomy on her.

She is the only girl I've ever dated who refused to let me in her ass, except for once, when she was drunk and it didn't last long. I found it surprising that she'd deny me access to her back door since she was known as somewhat of a slut. That is, of course, the reason I started dating her in the first place. Granted, she was a freaky gal in most regards; she liked being choked and spit on and all kinds of fun stuff. Sex in public was her favorite pastime. She said she liked being watched and one night even insisted that we wake my dorm room-mate so he could pleasure himself to us doing it. The only thing I hated was that she liked to mark her territory like a dog. She enjoyed giving hickeys and worse yet she liked to scratch. Fuck. To see me in the shower you'd think I was a failed lion trainer. My neck and back were scarred up beyond belief. It wasn't the kind of scratching that feels good, either, it was completely malicious. She'd start at the top of my back, dig her nails in deep and claw her way down like a cat on a new sofa. The sting of the air hitting my open wounds sent my shoulders forward and my head backwards, eyes rolling in pain. Within minutes my sheets were covered in blood. As if it were some satanic ritual she'd rub her blood-covered hands all over her tits and even use it to lubricate herself. She was a fiendish little thing.

This kind of behavior seemed to happen every time she'd come to visit me. Once my roommate thought there had been a murder. The whole time in college I only showered in the men's communal wash-room once. A fellow saw the claw marks on my back and asked what had happened. I asked why he was checking me out, was he looking for a knobber? He went into macho mode, asking if I was a faggot. I told him he was the one checking out my backside. He stormed out. Pissed off that my clingy girlfriend turned my back into a billboard, I went back to my room where she was passed out drunk. I rolled her onto her stomach and I took it. Like I said, it didn't last long.

The Ladder of Love

PRIVATE.COM • DIR: VARIOUS • RATING: 9

I don't think there is anything wrong with stalking as long as it is nonviolent and doesn't become all-consuming. As soon as you duck out of work to get your stalk on, that's when problems arise.

I used to have a crush on a girl who looked like porn star Michelle Wild. Most of my favorite porn stars resemble girls I once dated, wanted to date or hated in my younger days. This girl, Macy, had a friend who always prevented me from fucking her. It seemed every time I'd try to get close to Macy her friend would ask me into another room and we'd have sex.

One would think it was a good thing—free, unsolicited sex—but

Macy refused to give me the time of day with her friend's stink on my hang-low.

Years later I discovered a porn star named Azlea, star of *Fuck You Ass Whores* 2 and 3, and I fell in love. She looked just like Macy but with big, fake tits. I became obsessed with Azlea. I couldn't stop thinking about her. Finally I got the chance to interview her. But the day before we were going to meet she announced she was quitting the porn business and moving to Las Vegas to open an urban-apparel store. I was devastated. And shocked. Like, do people really aspire to open clothing stores? So what do I do? I go to Vegas. I rent a car and try to find her shop. No luck. So then I call my friend at Metro Video and have him track her down. I told him that I needed a date for Larry Flynt's Christmas party and would he ask her to be my date.

Surprisingly, she was into it as long as I paid for the airfare. I started to freak out. Of course I agreed to airfare, hotel, drugs, booze, whatever she needed. I didn't care. I just wanted her. Then her husband decided he didn't like it. And just like that it was over. My heart was broken. I've stopped watching her movies, and not until seeing this DVD and seeing Michelle Wild have I really thought about either Azlea or Macy. But since Michelle looks better than Azlea and has real tits, like Macy, and loves butt sex, I've been considering buying a ticket to Hungary and seeing if I can track her down and find out where she lives.

Perhaps Private will just make a compilation of all Michelle's scenes so I don't have to spend the money. Or end up in prison for sodomy.

A Cum Sucking Whore Named Kimberly

WWW.ANABOLIC.COM • DIR: VARIOUS • RATING: 6

Sometimes judging a book by its cover is your only option. Look at George Bush. Looks like an asshole, right? Asshole eyes, asshole face, asshole manner of speech. Then he becomes president and proves himself to be just that.

From my writing, people draw the conclusion I'm a dickhead. They're not far off the mark. One female fan from Vermont thought it was all an act and that if we met we'd hit it off. She began e-mailing me but never fulfilled my request for naked photos, so I stopped replying. Then one day she calls my mobile, how she got my number I don't know. She told me she was coming down from Vermont to see me.

"Please don't," I said, but she told me it was too late, she was on her way, that she was going to hitchhike to Manhattan, some six hours away. I laughed. There was no way anyone would hitch that far, no matter what kind of stalker they were. So I told her, "Sure, okay. If you make it here I live on 87th and Central Park West," which I did. I figured it would be safe to divulge such information since there was no chance of her coming.

But I'll be damned if my phone didn't ring again. It was her and she was on the corner of my block. I freaked, hung up. My roommate told me I was obligated at the very least to offer her a glass of water. When she knocked on our door my heart dropped. When I opened the door and saw the child, 18 years of age at the most, my heart fell out my pant leg and rolled away. I was doing a lot of coke and panicked. I thought it was a sting.

I grabbed her by the throat and pinned her to the wall. "Are you working for the cops? Who sent you? How old are you?" She began to cry, with the tears came the answers. She was 17, but she'd emancipated herself from her parents. She was free to do what she wanted including hitchhiking a few hundred miles in exchange for two blowjobs that she freely gave the drivers. I felt the cops closing in. I told her she had to go. She said she had no money, nowhere to go. I told her I didn't care, then handed her $20 and told her to take the subway to the George Washington Bridge, get off the train, walk across the bridge and throw her thumb up and hitch her ass right back where she came from. She begged me to let her stay. I yelled in her young, round face, "I said, 'Good day, madam!'" That was the last time I ever heard from her. I have no idea if she's alive or dead or if she had taken to turning tricks for some pimp in Harlem. But I hope she made it home in one piece. Actually, to tell you the truth, I don't give a shit. I have enough shit to worry about.

Cumback Pussy

WWW.ELEGANTANGEL.COM • DIR: PATRICK COLLINS • RATING: 8

While living in Cincinnati, Ohio, someone gave me a copy of this porno. The title always made me laugh because it reminded me of that episode of *The Simpsons* when Homer loses baby Maggie and he calls the lost-child hotline and they put him on hold and the hold music is that old "Baby Come Back" song by Player.

Ohio came at a weird time in my life; I was finally acknowledging and embracing my drinking problem for the first time and fucking everything that moved. I didn't know anyone, didn't care to make any friends and had a bar right across the street from my apartment. In the nine months I lived there I went from 140 to 215 pounds but didn't eat more than one meal a day, if that. Unless you consider beer and whiskey to be a meal. Yet the girls flocked to me. There's something about midwestern girls that makes them want to suck off anybody who has actually been to New York City. It's a beautiful thing, even if most of them have boyfriends.

I'd been living there about a month before I took to carrying a steak knife with me to the bar. Fortunately, I never had to shank anyone, but I did on occasion have to stick it to someone's throat and explain it was in their best interest to stay clear of me, even if I was sticking it to their girlfriend.

I vaguely recall when I met some wayward punk-rock girl at the bar and convinced her that she should walk across the street to my place for a quick roll in the hay. The details are hazy, but from what I remember the sex wasn't very good. I faintly recall after it was all said and done she asked if she could spend the night. "I don't think it's a good idea," I said. "I snore and grind my teeth and fart excessively." I explained, "It's really best if you left and never came back." She said, "Whatever," or "okay," or something to that effect, or perhaps nothing at all, as she slid her white cotton panties back up her legs, past her knees and over her milky thighs. "Well," she began, or so I think she said, "can I have your microwave?" And in my drunken state it must have seemed a perfectly normal request. I was showing her the door, why shouldn't she be allowed a parting gift? I must have said yes because the next morning my microwave was gone. Normally I wouldn't care if it was some shitty nonworking archaic microwave I only used to cook CDs just to see a spark, but the damn thing was still in the fucking box. It was a birthday gift from my brother I never had gotten around to unpacking and the little slut had stolen it. Who knows? Perhaps that was going to be the day I finally used it.

A few nights later I was back at the bar for free-chicken-wing night when she walked in. Her hair was suddenly pink and her face was lanced with piercings. Had I not studied the curves of her mouth the evening prior I would've failed to recognize her. I called her over and asked if she had taken my microwave. She shook her head yes. I asked her why. Matter-of-factly she answered: "I needed a microwave." It made perfect sense to me, so I bought her a few drinks and took her back to my apartment.

7 The Hardway 2

WWW.REDLIGHTDISTRICTVIDEO.COM • DIR: VINCE VOUYER • RATING: 8

My first time in Las Vegas I planned on getting a prostitute. I figured that's what people do in Las Vegas. That and get soused and gamble away their homes. I wasn't too concerned with the gambling as I'd never been to a casino before; I figured I'd play the slots, get bored and retire to my room and hump a whore.

The friend I was with is a seasoned gambler, which only means he understands the rules, not how to win. His preferred game is craps, so that was the game I learned that night. I watched his every move and asked questions about everything. I was determined to under- stand and win big. My only problem was not only did my friend rarely win, he seemed to always lose big, making me a loser by default. Before I knew it I was $2,000 in the hole and hitting the ATM for more money. I hadn't even noticed I'd been in the casino for nearly 10 hours due to the pure oxygen they were pumping through the vents to keep us junkies awake and the endless supply of free alcohol and coffee. I made it back to only being down $800 before the sun started to rise and my legs started to give. I'd lost my sense of direc- tion, time and reality. I also lost my friend. I chose to quit while I was ahead—well, not ahead, just not so far behind—and got out while still in possession of the keys to my rental car and my kneecaps.

It took a while to find my room but I finally made it and it was just as I'd left it—empty and sterile. I felt like complete scum so I took a shower. Halfway through lathering my balls a knock came at the door. I answered it. A not-so-attractive Asian hooker was at my door expect- ing to come in. "Can I help you?" I asked. She told me I'd called her over and could she come in. I told her I didn't remember calling her and sorry for the inconvenience but I was going to bed and I shut the door in her face. She knocked again, only much louder. I opened the door ready to tell her off, "Listen, lady, I've had a shitty night and I don't want to be bothered," but instead of the hooker, there was a

400-pound bald gorilla, who pushed his way into the room, put his hands around my neck, pressed a 9 mm gun barrel to my head and explained I'd be paying the lady $100 for her troubles. I'm not sure what happened next but, surprisingly, I slept very soundly, well into the next afternoon.

Soloerotica 3

NINNWORX.COM/ PUREPLAYMEDIA.COM •
DIR: MICHAEL NINN • RATING: 5

A tractor trailer had flipped on its side a few miles before our exit for the Meadowlands; the halted traffic did nothing to slow her incessant talking. On and on she went about nothing. Perhaps it was something of grave importance but it meant nothing to me. I'm sure she felt it was worthwhile or she wouldn't have been saying it, but I just wanted to watch the gulls swoop into the murky swamp water for food, to space out on the dickweeds swaying in the wind. I decided to see if I was able to count all the lights along the road.

Somewhere near a hundred I got bored and stopped. I get bored easily. In traffic is when I'm at my worst. The lack of forward movement drives me batty. In the past I have been known to start beeping relentlessly until someone tells me to fuck off, then I get out of my car and force my violent will upon that person. I felt like doing it at that very moment but didn't. She hates it when I reach across her and use the horn while she's driving. Sometimes she thinks it's funny, but I wasn't feeling especially cute. I also didn't feel like being reminded that I didn't have my driver's license and that when I did get my license back I could beep all I wanted. Looking at her lustful lips move around words I refused to hear I decided right then that when I did get my driver's license back I would beep and beep and never stop beeping. I would tape down the horn and possibly have a mechanic remove whatever screw or wire keeps horns from beeping nonstop. All the world will know I am near, long before my arrival, by

the sound of my honk. I laughed at my plan, thinking maybe I was a bit cute. That shut her up.

"What's so funny?" she asked. I shook my head, unsure, and said, "I don't know," and laughed again, for emphasis.

"Oh, you know what?" she asked, but answered her own question and started again. Out the window, past her angelic face, past three lanes of traffic, I saw a silver airplane disappear into the approaching storm clouds. It made me smile just as it did as a child whenever I'd see airplanes. I looked over at her—she was saying something. She could have been telling me she was molested as a child, or that the night before she had shared her body with no less than one dozen men, and I didn't care. I felt awful for it and I wondered how she could love someone so self-absorbed.

Trinity's Desire

PLEASUREPRODUCTIONS.COM • DIR: CASH MARKMAN • RATING: 7

In sixth grade I got in a bit of trouble for attempting to kill my teacher by putting plant fertilizer in her coffee. From the moment we met a hatred sparked between us that could only be quenched by death. In fifth grade, on the other hand, I had a strong childish lust for my teacher, so how I ended up putting her in the hospital is a bit confusing. I'm reminded of the sordid ordeal watching porn starlet Lezley Zen in *Trinity's Desire*; she looks like Gina Gershon and a bit like my grade-5 teacher. I hope I haven't told you this story already. I often forget what I've told you and start repeating myself. I'm like an old WWII veteran reliving horrible battle tales for anyone who'll listen. So please, stop me if you've heard this one before.

My grade-5 instructor had legs all the way to heaven, with hairsprayed high hair. She wore typical '80s garb (colored tights, long sweaters with a belt over it trying to convince the world it was really a skirt) and I loved every inch of her. As did my best friend Dave. So began our rivalry, our passion play for her heart. Candy was bought, cards were made, volunteering to smack clean the chalk erasers happened. But ours was a love scorned. We were 10, she was 30. Yet we were determined to win her over. For Columbus Day we had to write a report on Christopher Columbus. I copied a passage on Columbus word for word from an encyclopedia, 27 pages typed and double-spaced in the hope of showing her my love. Dave handwrote some bullshit about Columbus being a "cool guy" and "that's why we celebrate Thanksgiving," totally off the mark; I figured I was a cinch.

I was not.

She quickly realized that 10-year-olds don't use words like *resiliency* or *attrition*. She asked me the meaning of one multisyllabic word and without thinking I responded, "I don't even know what that word is." She told me the work was not my own, and offered Dave's as an example of how to write an honest paper from the heart. Dave just laughed at me. I told her to go fuck herself.

From that day forth she was my mortal enemy; I did whatever I could to make her life miserable, including pulling a chair out from under her just as she was about to sit on it. She fell hard and fast to the tiled floor, breaking her ass bone and missing weeks of school. Everyone in the class loved her and in turn hated me for what I'd done. But I'd never felt prouder of anything I'd ever done in my life.

Without Limits 2

PRIVATE.COM · DIR: ANTONIO ADAMO · RATING: 10

The cover girl, Sandra Irons, looks much hotter than my ex-girl-friend but they have quite a bit in common. They both have big pierced tits and large tattoos on their backs and love anal sex. My ex had tattoos on both arms and angel wings covering her entire back, which I find great humor in now, after having learned what an evil cunt she truly is. Aside from having me held at gunpoint in my own house and having the police come and arrest me, she broke my fingers once by slamming them in the door and also stole my car. I suppose if you can ignore that and the numerous suicide attempts and lying and cheating she was a very sweet girl.

All in all I'm sure Sandra is a lot more down-to-earth. Then again I'm sure I couldn't persuade Sandra to get my name tattooed on her stomach like my ex did.

One time I was on tour just outside Denver and we met up with some guys who ran a tattoo shop and they offered to give us free tat-toos. They also lined up three girls to come down and put on a little lesbian performance. At the time things weren't good between me and my ex. She had just told me she let some guy from across the street fuck her in the ass because she was tired of playing with her-self while I was out of town on business. What a classy girl. So I opted to get friendly with the lesbians instead of getting a tattoo. The other guys took full advantage of the tattoo offer. One friend got the outline of California on his arm with his name in it while one of the gals rested her tits on his head. It looked about as cool as getting a quarter tattooed behind your ear. By the time it was my friend Justin's turn we were all fairly liquored up, including the tattoo artists. Justin wanted two interlocking wedding bands on his inner arm with his grandparents' initials on each side with the word "Forever" above it and "Together" below it. "Forever together" sounded wrong to me but who am I to tell someone what to get on their body? The artist sketched it up, we all looked it over and approved it and within half an hour it was done. That's when I noticed it. The artist had misspelled the word "together." He wrote it as "Togoither." I felt awful. Being a writer I should have caught the error. My only excuse was that I was wasted with two girls rimming each other on the floor in front of me as a distraction.

I remember taking photos of the typo and fighting to keep myself from laughing. I have a lot of good pictures from that night. There was one of me and one of the girls, the one with the natural 36DDs, where I'm putting a bottle of Budweiser inside her and I'd stuck Budweiser labels to her ass cheeks. I was also wearing a tacky

Budweiser Hawaiian shirt. The whole thing reeked of high fashion.

At some point I thought I should buy some new nipple rings for my girlfriend back home so she would shut the fuck up and stop complaining. She had huge, gaudy ones in up until then so I got her some cute little ones; she loved them. A few weeks later, she called my cell phone fuming after she saw the photos I ran of the lesbian girls in *Big Brother* magazine.

After chastising me for a few minutes she asked when I had taken the photos. Again, trying to fight back the laughter, I said, "Remember that time you let the neighbor fuck you in the ass and I bought you nipple rings?"

Creating Kate

VIVID.COM • DIR: TONI ENGLISH • RATING: 1

My ex-girlfriend's name was Kate and she was more than slightly insane. There were more than a few occasions when I had to rush her to the hospital on suicide attempts. The first was a Saturday and I was working in the office. She was calling every five minutes, threatening me about what would happen if I didn't come home soon. I tried to explain the concept of deadlines to her but she refused to grasp it. She insisted she'd eat all the pills in the apartment if I didn't come home soon. I laughed. "You're a crazy bird," I told her. "I need you to come home right now!" she screamed into the receiver. When pressed for a reason why she had no answer. There was no emergency, no fire, no crisis. It was simply that she was uncomfortable in her own skin and never learned how to face any aspect of life on her own. Something as simple as a relaxing Saturday afternoon curled up with a book and beer for her was sheer torture. I told her I'd be home as soon as I could and said goodbye.

A few hours passed and I finally went home. The front door was wide open and Elvis Costello's "Watching the Detectives" was playing over the low hum of a blue-screened TV. "Kate," I called. No response. I checked the kitchen then the bathroom: both empty.

In the bedroom I found her naked on the bed, pale white, with only the slightest pulse. A number of empty prescription pill bottles lay empty on the floor by her head and for a second I thought she was really gone. "Girlfriend in a coma and I know, I know it's really serious."

I had a brief moment of disillusioned responsibility. I began to cry over her cold face, apologizing for not coming home sooner, promising never to do it again. Then an angel of clarity whispered in my ear, "Are you serious? This bitch is crazy. This is not your fault. Call the paramedics and wash your hands of her."

In a desperate attempt to save her I stuck my fingers down her throat to cause her to vomit up whatever it was she had ingested. I was able to force three mucus-filled heaves out before she finally opened her eyes and said, "What are you doing here, asshole? I thought I saw the last of you." Then she fell back into her pill-induced delirium. I spent that night and the next by her side in the psych ward at Cedars-Sinai Hospital. Soon after I packed her things and sent her home to her mother for closer observation.

So although Taylor Hayes is the star of this film and I really wanted to watch it, I just couldn't. Any mention of the name Kate or Elvis Costello makes me sick to my stomach.

Real Female Orgasms 4

ELEGANTANGEL.COM • DIR: PATRICK COLLINS • RATING: 9

I take great pride in making a woman orgasm nearly a half-dozen times before I allow myself to. I know all you male readers are shouting "Bullshit!" and all you female readers are either looking at your boyfriend watching football like, "Not in a million years," or you're thinking to yourself, "I certainly would like to get my hands on a piece of this Chris Nieratko, whoever he is."

Sadly, the reason for my overzealous need to please is one of defense: I'm not the greatest fuck, I don't last long and if you're lucky enough to get one load out of me, don't expect another because I'm already asleep. I have sexual narcolepsy. As soon as my steaming white poison bursts onto your face I'm rendered powerless and fall into a deep, fairy-tale-like coma. I'm told my penis still functions quite well, perhaps better, with my brains turned off.

If I'm awake I really feel after I slip it in the fun stops for her. I jump in, do my thing, and I'm asleep five minutes later. It's all very pathetic. I'm not bragging about the multiple orgasms. It's a front. I make it seem like I'm putting in work so I can sleep in peace. After a few orgasms it's harder for people to complain about poor performance, snoring or farting in your sleep. Granted, in the past I've woken up alone in the night with notes pinned to me that read, "Thanks for nothing, asshole," but those days are over. My girl's stuck with me and I think her knowing about "my problem" keeps her from getting upset or creeped out when she's taking advantage of my near-corpse.

There was one night we got wasted and nodded out during sex and when I came to a few hours later she was gone. I was like, "Fucking great. Now I've lost her, too. Well, it was only a matter of time," and fell back asleep. When I finally did get out of bed to piss, my head swollen with hangover, I found her asleep, naked, with her head in the toilet. It was kind of sexy. I took fantastic Polaroids. There was vomit everywhere, on the walls, in her hair, between her toes. I wanted to feel bad for her. I wanted to pick her up and carry her to the bathtub and clean her off, shampoo her hair and massage her feet. Instead I stood there smiling, snapping away, just so happy that she hadn't left me in the middle of the night like the others.

2 on 1 #14

DIABOLICVIDEO.COM • DIR: ERIK EVERHARD • RATING: 10

This video reminded me of a story a friend of mine told me of a stripper they hired for a private party. She showed up and was completely spun on crank. He said her smile couldn't hide the fact that she hadn't slept in days. Noticing some cocaine on the table she offered to put on a free show in exchange for drugs. Everyone agreed and the show began. He described it as boring and unimpressive; lap dances and soft touching. Nothing anyone hadn't seen before. But after snorting more coke than the five guys combined, things got exciting. She took one guy into the bathroom and asked to be fucked. The guy had no desire to fuck the whore and his limp coke dick probably wouldn't have let him if he did, so instead he took the rod that held the roll of toilet paper and stuck it in her butt. Seeing that she didn't mind it he brought her back into the room and asked if she'd stick a broom handle up her ass.

And she did.

It earned her a round of applause. And more coke. He said she turned into a trained animal, laying down and rolling over like a dog would for a treat. After each great feat they let her bang back some blow. The next thing that went in her ass was a Heineken bottle, the entire thing. He said only the base of the bottle was left visible.

At that point it became a game, with everyone rallying to find the next thing to stick up her ass. She said she'd had whole feet up her ass before and not to be shy about their suggestions. Someone found a baseball bat. She nodded that she could fit it up her ass but she would need lube. There was no lube. "Do you have any hair gel?" she asked. That they had. She lubed up the thick part of the bat, greased herself up and in one swift thrust slid the bat in. He said she fit it so far that he expected to see it pop out her mouth. Cut that girl some lines. She laid down on the dirty floor and began sliding finger after finger into her ass. After loosening things with the baseball bat her entire fist went in with relative ease.

Next they grabbed a mobile phone, turned it to vibrate, wrapped it in plastic and lubed it up. In terms of size a cell isn't in the same league as a baseball bat but he said it was more exciting because they were able to call the phone while it was in her butt and watch as the vibration caused the phone to go deeper inside her.

He said it got to the point where they weren't doing any more coke themselves. They just laid the mirror on the floor in front of her, like a dog bowl, and threw little bumps down for her after each stunt. Then the sun came up. They still had an eightball but were sick of the girl by this point. They made her an offer she couldn't refuse. If she could think of one last trick to impress them they'd give her the rest of the cocaine to take home. She lubed her vagina up real good, wrapped one of the guys' heads in plastic and greased it up and told him to work his head into her vagina. I saw the photos. It didn't go very far inside her but it went. Just a little bit.

She certainly earned herself that eightball.

Hardcore Innocence 6

ELEGANTANGEL.COM • DIR: PATRICK COLLINS • RATING: 6

I'm sure I went through an age of innocence as a child where the flowery scent of a girl's hair was more than enough to turn me on, I just don't remember it. Many moons have passed and many days have been wasted trying to forget my name and in that time my soul has gone cold. I am bitter and angry and there is near nothing that I can look at without finding fault. My world is an infinitely flawed diamond and I'm reminded of it every time I look out the window, every time I turn on the television. This video, for instance, is full of attractive women who take it in the ass but it's not enough. I watch as they are manhandled and I look at the scars on their tits, the indents of cellulite on their thighs, the rolls of stomach fat that are visible every time they bend over, and I wonder to myself if these women have ever

owned a mirror. If so, why would they put themselves out there to be ridiculed by the likes of me? For most, their flaws are minor—but for me, inexcusable. There's one girl toward the end that just has enormous teeth; horse teeth are smaller. She must know just how big her teeth are. I can't possibly be the only person to notice. Perhaps no one has told her just how big her teeth are, which is a sin. People should be made aware of their shortcomings, over and over again, until they do something to remedy them. This woman, with her tombstone-filled mouth, refused to hide them; instead she flashed them as if they were something to be proud of. Whenever she'd pretend to orgasm she'd clench her teeth together like the Incredible Hulk and her lower lip would roll and unfold downward, only making her teeth appear larger. It was as if she had a billboard in her mouth. It was all quite disturbing. How is anyone expected to concentrate when an ivory flashlight is being shined in your face? What struck me as even more odd was that the blonde at the very end of the movie had teeth nearly as big. Where did the director find such teethy women? To add insult to injury the blonde got fucked on a zebra-print couch while wearing a leopard-print skirt. Aside from the obvious fashion faux pas of clashing species I am diagnosing the woman as clinically insane. She has some kind of chemical imbalance. Any woman I've ever met who wore animal print of any sort has had some screws loose. What does this girl think, she's Jane of the jungle? I'd like to know what the fuck was going through her head when she made such an asinine purchase.

Today at the pizzeria I saw the most amazingly stacked girl, perfect from head to nose. But she had a lazy eye. It repulsed me. I once had a lazy eye yet I felt no pity for her. I seek out perfection, knowing it doesn't exist. It is the hunt that thrills me, not the kill. In high school I dated a girl with a mole on her face. Not a sexy Cindy Crawford mole. This was above her eyebrow and it was as round as my thumb. But I didn't care. She was my girl. I'd kiss the hairy thing as we made love. But that was then. I'm sure she still has the mole. I bet she also has three children and bruises all over her body from her factory-working husband that hates what he sees when he looks in the mirror. If I was him I would too. Perhaps I should start a company and sell mirrors with photos of myself framed in them, so people can see what real beauty is.

 ## Extreme Filth Volume 2

BLACKMIRROR.COM · DIR: JOE GALLANT · RATING: 10

Have you ever gone to the store to buy a new black shirt and returned with a frying pan instead? That's how I felt when I came across this video in my friend's collection.

I went looking for a funny midget video and instead I returned with one of the greatest pornos ever made. The girls aren't hot. The resolution is poor like your father filmed it in 1986 with one of those kids' cameras that tape onto audiocassette. It's recorded onto budget tape and has a xeroxed cover. Yet I cannot implore you enough to find this video and anything else done by Black Mirror. One scene has a girl getting a mop handle rammed up her butt and loving it, a girl urinating on the floor while on the rag, another fingering herself with chocolate-syrup-covered hands, girls peeing on each other's faces, ropes tied around penises until they turn blue with clothespins fastened to the testicles, and a naked girl shooting up then OD'ing that looks quite believable.

It's the type of video you would make if you weren't lazy and knew girls who'd let you use their asses as a storage closet for household goods. Some of Gallant's other videos have girls getting enemas then having their ass corked off until the massive explosion is primed at which point the guy pulls out and a geyser of shit-filled water fills the air. There's also soft drink, paint and piss enemas; public blowjobs; squirting in Times Square; a Russian hooker, right off the boat, getting fucked in a cracked-out hotel; naked women pissing and masturbating in tenement-building hallways; and shit-covered condoms everywhere. These aren't necessarily videos that you toss off to, they're more to have playing during a dinner party, giving everyone something to talk about.

In high school I had a girlfriend who once let me video myself shoving long campfire matches in her ass, sparking them to start a fire of newspaper and lighter fluid. The lighter fluid caught much quicker than I had expected it to and her ass cheeks got singed and her shirt was completely charred. I had told her to take off her shirt in the first place so I don't take any responsibility for that. It was an ugly shirt anyway. I never liked it. I think it had paisleys on it. She said her mother gave it to her before she died, which made her wear it more. It was quite hideous. I felt like I was dating some 1980s drug dealer from Miami who only listened to house music. I wish I had the footage of the fire today, I'd love to send it to Black Mirror, they'd probably eat that shit up. Do you think it would be fucked up if I called her and asked if she still had the tape? I haven't spoken to her in 15 years and the reason we broke up was because she came to my house on New Year's Eve and found me in bed with her best friend, which was my intention, hoping she'd join in. Instead she slashed all four tires of her friend's car with a steak knife.

Can you imagine getting a call like that, after all those years? "Hey, how have you been? How's life? Remember that time I put matches up your butt to start that fire? That was awesome, wasn't it? Do you still have that video? I'd love to watch it. Hello? Hello? Hello?"

She Male Enslaved 2

BIZARRE VIDEO PRODUCTION • RATING: 1

Long before Giuliani became mayor of New York and ruined Times Square by selling it to Disney and MTV, it was a haven of sin and sex and the best place on earth for a 14-year-old boy and his friends to come to terms with their manhood. We'd ditch school, take the train into The City from Jersey, skate all day long, and when night fell and we were good and tired, we'd head to midtown.

Between all the whores, peep shows and sex shops a kid had a rough time stopping himself from creaming in his shorts from the visual stimulation. Generally, we'd sit on a stoop, befriending and heckling the streetwalkers for a free flash of ass or titty. They all got a kick out of us kids and always obliged. I think it was there inside some semen-scented hot box in some peep-show parlor that I first felt the inside of a woman. Back then for a dollar you could see her naked, for two you could touch her breasts and for five she'd bend over in front of the open window and you could slip your fingers inside her. It's an innocent part of childhood that future generations will never be allowed to experience.

One time one of the streetwalking girls was really teasing us, refusing to show us her pussy. It only made us scream and holler louder, begging her for just a glimpse. Finally, after sending us into a full-blown frenzy, she agreed. She slowly slid up her miniskirt. Inch by inch our hearts pounded louder with anticipation. We'd seen dozens of pussies by that point but had never been teased in such a way. First, we saw a few strands of pubic hairs and someone called out, "Here it comes." Just as we couldn't wait another second she yanked her skirt up all the way only to reveal a dick. She laughed at the disgust on our faces. We were too young to understand. The math didn't add up. She had tits and a dick? We'd never heard of such a thing and the sight of it fried our circuits. We ran and hit the peep shows to get the image out of our heads. Two decades later the sight of it is still burned into my subconscious.

A year after we all went off to college we had a little, unofficial reunion at some football player's bachelor party. By three in the morning everyone except myself was blacked out, puke-drunk in the limo. Since I was the most coherent I was nominated to go pick out a hooker to give the groom a blowjob on that special night before his wedding. As I surveyed my options I came up with a little joke I've never told anyone about before. I started talking to the hookers, not to negotiate prices but rather to find one who was a transvestite. I eventually came across an extremely tall Asian lass with bad skin and big hands.

I explained it was my friend's bachelor party and would she please take good care of him. She gave me a wink and climbed in the limousine. We all waited outside while she took care of business; all the while I was laughing to myself. On the ride home the groom said it was the best blowjob he'd ever gotten and he would be picturing that "girl" every time his wife went down on him for the rest of his life. That only seemed to make me laugh more.

Liquid Gold #2

JERKOFFZONE.COM • DIR: JIM POWERS • RATING: 4

My family gets a real kick out of embarrassing each other in front of guests. My mom, for instance, could single-handedly save my town from flooding if ever the occasion arose. She once worked at the United States' largest producer of maxi pads and tampons and before being laid off stockpiled truckloads of the stuff at a discounted price. The next six generations of girls in my family will never have to worry about purchasing feminine-hygiene products. One might think this is the type of thing I'd use against my mother. Instead, she uses it against me. Every girl I've ever brought home has been greeted in this manner:

Me: "Mom, I'd like you to meet (enter name here)."

Mom: "Nice to meet you. Let me ask you, do you use maxi pads or tampons?"

Dead serious. She's that blunt. The conversation then goes one of two ways. The girl either clams up or she has a sense of humor about it. The latter is the most lucrative, since whichever napkin they prefer my mom will force me to carry out case after case to fill their car with. For me it is quite disturbing. I don't want the first conversation with my mom and a love interest to be about what they use to stop up their bloody leak. I don't even like that women have menstrual cycles. I think that a ban should be placed on that entire week of bleeding. It's completely unfair to deprive men of sex for such a lengthy amount of time. Shit. One week a month, 12 weeks a year. That works out to three months annually that blood puts the kibosh on any hump action. It seems like there are enough men in government that we could do something to stop the red tide.

Another one my mom loves is "Have you noticed the scar Chris has above his penis?" Now if that isn't a loaded question, what is? "He had a hernia when he was 5. One of his balls ruptured and was nearly dragging on the ground. Before the surgery my other son told Chris the doctors were going to cut his balls off and he'd always talk like a little girl. Chris would cry and cry. We thought it was the funniest thing. Chris, do you remember in the hospital when the nurse came to get a urine sample and you were so afraid she was going to cut your balls off you pissed all over her dress and face? Remember she screamed when it went in her mouth? God, that was funny."

Yup. Nothing but good times at the Nieratko house.

Rich Bitch

PRIVATE.COM • DIR: FRANK THRING • RATING: 5

As a kid, I was a greaser; holes in my jeans, dirty sneakers, unwanted by all the high-class, crosstown girls in my school. "When you grow up things will change," my brother told me. "Keep doing what you're doing, fighting and getting in trouble. As long as you're a bad seed, good girls will want to be around you. You're exactly the type their parents warned them about."

It was advice I didn't think about until I found myself in the bed of a councilman's daughter. I asked her what she was doing with a dirt-bag like me. She replied, "You're trouble and I like trouble."

When I entered high school I began getting arrested more and generally wreaking havoc any way I could. I found myself being woken up in nearly every class to receive a note from some rich bitch who wanted to meet me between class to suck me off.

My brother's words were proving true and I began to test the theory. I stopped showering. Still they came. I didn't bother to change my clothes. This served only to make me more attractive in their eyes. I read an interview with Mötley Crüe's Nikki Sixx in which he said he'd gone four months without showering, having daily unprotected sex with random girls. Sounded like a good idea, so I tried it. I could see their disgust for the putrid taste of my balls written across their faces, yet they kept coming back.

I've modeled most of my adult life in the same fashion. I'm level-ling the playing field between the wealthy and those not quite so lucky. Just before I left New Jersey I was seeing a wealthy, older New York City real estate agent who was trying to clean me up so she could show me off to her high-society friends, sort of like Tom Cruise in *Cocktail*.

She handed me five grand in cash one day and told me to get some new clothes and a nice watch and meet her at so-and-so's restaurant. Forty-eight hours later I was halfway to California, home of the dumbest, wealthiest women in America. And I haven't changed my pants since.

Briana Banks
a.k.a. Filthy Whore

X-TRAORDINARY PICTURES • RATING: 10

Briana reminds me of this girl I used to fuck in college, Shirley. Shirley was friends with this snobby bitch I was seeing and mesmerized me with her first glance. As the three of us sat watching some awful comedy I felt Shirley's "fuck me" eyes calling. I looked over. She licked her lips and winked at me.

The girl I was dating was so tuned in to Adam Sandler that she was oblivious to our flirting. Shirley slid her hands across her thighs and reached between her legs. I was counting the moments until the girl between us had to go take a piss so I could pull my dick out and stick it in her mouth. But the bitch had a strong bladder or she sensed what we were up to and refused to leave the room the entire night. Immediately after the picture my Shirley took off for the night without consummating our lust.

As me and my girl lay naked she asked if I thought her friend was attractive. I said yes and asked why. She said all the boys felt that way but there was no way she'd be attracted to me, that she was too good for me. "Well," I asked, "is there any way you can persuade her to join us one night?" The idea of her pretentious self sharing with another woman made her furious. She got up to leave.

I rolled my eyes and told her not to let the door hit her in the ass on the way out. I forget what she threw at me. "Hold up," I thought, "if she leaves I'll never get to fuck her friend. I don't even know her last name or where she lives." I ran into the street without caring that I was stark naked and made a half-assed attempt to apologize.

She must have thought my running out nude was proof I was sincere and came back inside. I had to put in four hours of uninspired sex while begging for her not to go home before she finally passed out. I stroked her hair as she dreamt, then reached across her body and grabbed her purse off the nightstand. From it I pulled a pen, a piece of paper and her phonebook, which I quickly turned to the page marked "S."

Lesbian Awakenings

BOBSVIDEO.COM • DIR: BOB ALEXANDER • RATING: 6

There's a cute little Bettie Page–looking piece of ass in this lesbian romance named Mary Jane who reminds me of high school when I was fucking the daughter of one of the heads of the local anti-drug task force. He was a strapping man who could have knocked all my teeth out in one punch and he looked like a cop. Cop eyes. Cop hair. Cop shoes and cop glasses. I don't know who the hell he was trying to fool; only a blind junkie could be tricked into buying drugs from or selling to that guy.

One good thing about him was he was so wrapped up in the problems of the drug world that he couldn't see his daughter was no angel. She was a coke whore, to put it bluntly. Before I started hanging out with her I'd see her at parties giving blowjobs to be cut in on someone's eightball. You're probably thinking, "Tell me this asshole tried to get her to change her ways." Fuck that. I didn't want her to change at all. I had coke. I had friends who had coke. Me and my friends had coke and liked to fuck and she was cheaper than taking a girl to the movies with no guarantee of action. Her mother was dead, which explained a lot. Their house was modest but paid in full. But I wasn't after cash. I had this notion that since her dad was surrounded by drugs daily he probably had back-doored some really good dope.

I started spending more and more time with her at her house. I'd hump her a few times until she passed out or I'd send her to the market to fetch me cigarettes, then I'd start combing the house. Three days I searched, always coming up short. The fourth day I found it. Under the father's bed was a safe in the floor, covered by carpet. In minutes I'd gone to the garage and returned with bolt cutters, a mini-blowtorch, crowbar and hammer.

It's funny how adrenaline can make you deaf because I never heard her dad come into the room. But I can tell you, sure as shit, I heard him cock the hammer on his pistol and ask me what the fuck I thought I was doing.

Forbidden Tales

DIGITALPLAYGROUND.COM • DIR: JOONE • RATING: 7

There used to be a chick at one of the other magazines in my office building who had the hots for me. She was a Filipina with a Puerto Rican's ass and looked just like Tera Patrick, the star of *Forbidden Tales*, except with smaller tits. You can understand how a boy would be attracted to her, despite the fact she moonlighted as a stripper and pro-fessional gold digger. Not to say all strippers are gold diggers, but many are, and the many always ruin it for the few, don't they? Many strippers are just sweet young ladies with bills to pay or a desire for higher education and those girls should not be judged because of a few bad apples. But let me tell you, this girl in particular had it down pat. She had one regular who paid her rent directly to the landlord, and another who owned a Mercedes dealership who kept her in a new car every other month. At times I was jealous of her vagina and her breasts because there I was working my ass off 10 hours a day for 10 years and I didn't even have a car and was barely making rent each month.

For as manipulative as she was, one good thing about this chick was she believed in fair trade. One day she was in my office and saw the new Jay-Z and was all like, "Oh, shit! The new Jay-Z. Let me get it." Since I can't stand Jay-Z I didn't really care, but hoping for a cheap feel I said, "Well, what are you going to do for it?" As matter-of-factly as can be, she said, "I'll suck your dick for it," sounding nothing like Chris Tucker at all. And she did. And she was quite good at it for someone who'd never done it before. So began a relationship between us. Once or twice a week she'd call me and ask if I'd gotten any new CDs and then hurry down to earn her hip-hop under my desk. We never spoke other than her asking about the CDs and me saying, "Yes, come on down."

This went on for nine months until she decided to quit and dance full-time. And although I can't remember her name, if I ever knew it at all, not a day goes by I don't wish she still worked in my building. I still keep a pile of crappy rap CDs under my desk just in case she ever comes back.

Wild Cherries

METROINTERACTIVE.NET • DIR: PAT MYNE • RATING: 8

I've just heard of this procedure that enables doctors to resew a woman's hymen to create the illusion of being a virgin. What gold digger thought up that idea? You know it wasn't a man. Sure, men want all their women to be virgins, but we are smart enough to realize none of them are. I don't care if they're 16 or 60, chances are by the time you or I get to them they've already been fucked and had everything from Barbie-doll heads to live lobsters crammed up their butts. That's the sad reality of life. None of us are saints and no one gets to wash away their sins regardless of what the priest tells you in that confessional. I don't think whores deserve a chance to rip off their scarlet letters for any fee, just to marry a rich motherfucker who couldn't tell if the odometer had been turned back.

I remember this one girl who gave the most marvelous blowjobs. She was 19, with the talent of a woman twice her age. Rarely did I want to fuck her, her blowjobs were so good. But one day I found myself in the mood and I bent her over my bathroom sink. She told me, "I'm a virgin, so take it easy." I smiled and winked at her. No virgin could shine a trophy like she did. So I plowed into her like a bus into a cyclist. She screamed. Then she moaned. Then she came. At least I thought she came. I proceeded to pump away until I was ready myself and told her to turn around. As she twisted into position my life flashed before my eyes. My penis was covered in blood. I wondered if I had somehow missed her, secretly slicing my dick in two with a razor. It looked like a snuff film. Yet I felt no pain. Then I noticed blood all over my new bathroom carpet. I completely forgot about my severed penis. My new carpet took center stage. "What the fuck did you do?" I asked. "Are you on the rag or something? Why the fuck didn't you tell me?" She smiled a coy little grin. "I told you I was a virgin." Liar! I told her to leave. Hours later she called. "You are an asshole. I wanted my first time to be special and you ruined it."

"I'm sorry," I said. "I didn't believe you. I thought virgins were extinct. Come back over here, clean up my carpet and we'll give it another go and pretend like you never fucked up my carpet, okay?" The line went dead. Bad connection, I suppose. But she never called back. The problem must have been on her end.

Wicked Ways

WICKEDPICTURES.COM • DIR: JONATHAN MORGAN/ALEX SANDERS •
RATING: 10

I'm very specific about what I need from a woman. When it comes to sex: a bald pussy and a receptive hole. I don't think that's asking much. I don't need to choke someone until they pass out or kick a girl in her stomach or even shit on their face to have a good time. I'm also quite keen on butt sex (but who isn't?). That's why I love porn stars; they all love it in the ass.

One of my earliest memories of registering what a porn star was is when I saw this video years ago. See the hot blonde on the cover? That's JR Carrington and boy, does she love it in the ass! To this day,

I believe her to be the hottest porn star ever. That may simply be because she was the first I'd ever seen or it may be because she's the only one I've ever gotten to fulfill my fantasies with. Well, sort of.

See, when I watch porn I create these little scenarios in my head of what it would be like to hang out with the girl for a day, aside from the sexy stuff; this includes food shopping and taking out the garbage and other domestic tasks, chores that most would find uninteresting or mundane. A few years ago I got to find out, to some degree, what it really was like when I found a website where you could rent time with your favorite porn star, and JR just happened to be one of the girls.

One of the perks of working for Larry Flynt was if you wanted to have sex with a porn star you could ask the company for $1,500 to cover the tab and in return get paid for writing a story about it. So, one cold November evening, I met up with JR in an NYC hotel room. When she asked me what I wanted to do, I told her, "Let's watch MTV, drink some wine, I'll spill some on you, then you'll get out of your clothes, we'll fuck, then we'll shower, then you throw the sheets away and take out the garbage." I think she was taken aback. "Have you been thinking about this for a while?" she asked. I smiled sheepishly and uncorked the cheap chardonnay I'd picked up at the bodega around the corner. And we sat down to watch *TRL*. Sadly, we both got drunk and passed out before anything got hot and steamy. On the next few pages you'll read the piece I wrote for *Hustler*. Needless to say, it is slightly embellished. They asked me to change the lady's name and the heavy-handed pervy language was all added by the editors who obviously know what their readers want.

This is the actual story as printed in the Hustler *July 2001 issue. HUSTLERworld.com.*

Porn Sluts for Rent
by James Edgeboro

(The etymology of my pseudonym: James is my middle name and Edgeboro
is the name of the landfill near my home in Sayreville, NJ.)

Ever want to fuck a porn star who comes equipped with tits twice the size of you head? Find yourself imagining that your girlfriend is as slutty as the surgically enhanced Barbie dolls that spread their legs in porn videos? Well, I do, every day of my life, with every chick I've ever been with. Sometimes, when I'm stuck in the standard missionary position, banging the faint pulse beneath me, I close my eyes and imagine a pouty, cock-hungry porn bitch begging me to fuck her in the ass. XXX fantasies help me escape the blasé reality of sex with ordinary girls, but I recently found myself in the position to make my wet dreams come true.

I was flipping through AVN Online, a trade magazine for Internet sex sites, when I came across an ad for www.exotica-2000.com, an all porn star escort service. "This is your opportunity to meet a real adult film star one-on-one" was written across the tits of none other than my all-time favorite XXX fuck toy, Anita Rodman.

I've never hired a woman for sex, because I can usually compel someone with a hole and a heartbeat to spread her legs in the path of my oncoming meat missile. During the occasional dry spell between sex partners, though, I've been tempted to purchase the services of a street skank, but fear of catching a disease always dissuaded me.

Something about the fact that Anita was a porn star made her pussy seem likely to be free of the clap. In some dark corner of my mind, I think I understood that the woman I was hoping to buy time with probably had unprotected sex with as many men as the average whore, but the thought that I could literally, physically plunder the vagina that belongs to the very woman I've whacked off to hundreds of times overwhelmed me.

This of course was the star of such steamy films as *Booty Queen*, *Rebel Cheerleader*, *Gangbusters*, *Anal Sweetheart*, we're talking about. Perhaps one of the most beautiful women to open her ass for the camera ever. Just thinking about her in my office reminds me of Anita in her little cheerleader outfit, smoking a cigarette, smiling at me on the box of *Rebel Cheerleader*. That image alone sends hot tremors throughout my body. I remember the very first time I saw her face in *Anal Sweetheart*, getting fucked every which way by two disgusting longhaired dudes, she smiled and laughed through that entire scene, loving every minute of it. It was that scene that made me truly fall in love with her. It was when the green anal lube slid out of her ass onto her pussy while she was getting fucked in the back door and she slid her hand down by her lips, wiped it off, smelled her hand then started laughing out loud, that's when I knew that without a doubt Anita Rodman was the girl for me. That may sound odd but the mix of her elegant looks and childish attitude toward sex made her seem quite special to me. Looking at her just gave off this warm, safe feeling.

My dream fuck would never give me the burn; she was too classy.

Anita was advertised alongside some of the most familiar faces in the sleaze biz in a clickable gallery on www.exotica-2000.com. Houston, the busty blond gang-bang queen, and Mila Shegal, the Russian moxie who paints abstract art with her asshole, were both available. But for what? Sex, I most fervently hoped, but doubt crept into my mind when I perused the website more closely. One passage from the ad made me wonder if the site was a scam:

"Now you can dine with Kasorn Swan, spend a night on the town with Alexandria Quinn, or sip cocoa in front of the fire with Houston."

What the hell do I want to sip cocoa in front of a fire for with a sex toy like Houston unless I'm drinking it out of her asshole? I had strong reservations, but if there was any possibility at all of turning my VCR-based fantasy into flesh-and-blood reality, I felt a duty, as a devoted monkey spanker, to pursue that fat chance.

My first hurdle was geographic. Exotica-2000.com is based in New York City, and I live in Los Angeles. Fortunately, I had plans to return to New York for my tenth annual family reunion, so I already had a plane ticket taken care of for the end of December.

The next challenge was checking the schedules of the Web sluts, which are posted on Exotica-2000. It just so happened that the only girl in town at that time was my dream girl.

My heart raced as I dialed the Exotica-2000 phone number. A bouncy-voiced girl took my call.

"Hello," she chirped. "We have Summer Hayes available this evening, and her rate is $1,200. Is there someone in particular I can help you with? Hello?"

I froze up. I couldn't speak. My stomach jumped up into my throat, and the words just wouldn't budge. I hung up.

The truth is, I'd never hired a woman to fuck me before. The only time I'd ever been close to paying a woman to do anything other than my laundry was when I was a teenager, at Mardi Gras in New Orleans. Drunk off my ass, I spotted a lady of the night standing under a streetlight in the French Quarter, chomping gum like a horse and wearing next to nothing, aside from six-inch "fuck me" pumps.

"How much for a blowjob?" I asked. The broad backhanded me one across the chops.

"I'm a goddamn bartender, not a whore, you asshole!" she yelled. With the telephone in front of me, and Exotica-2000's phone number staring me in the face, I harkened back to that humiliating moment. I couldn't handle an ordeal like that again, especially from a woman whose body of work I admired so much.

I poured myself a stiff drink and made the call, hoping the alcohol would nullify my inhibitions. I assumed the most authoritative voice I could muster and told the girl on the other end of the line that I'd sort of hoped to maybe make an appointment with Ms. Rodman for Monday evening.

"Well, she might be leaving town that afternoon; but I'm sure we can find a girl that's perfect for you," the operator replied. Did this moron know how to listen? I had already found the perfect girl for me, and her name was Anita Rodman. "Well I'm only interested in Anita . . . ," I said, sticking to my guns.

"I'll see what I can do and call you back," the girl said. The phone clicked. I kept the receiver pressed to my ear, then finally hung up. Thoughts of sodomizing Anita Rodman faded from my mind. Maybe butt-fucking my dream girl was asking for too much, I thought. Perhaps I should settle for gang-bang queen Houston—she had recently hired a surgeon to trim back her pussy lips, which had apparently been stretched out by a long career in the fuck vids; so shtupping Houston would be almost like deflowering a virgin.

The clang of the telephone interrupted my musings. Exotica-2000 called back to inform me that my dream fuck had agreed to stay through the night on Monday and was looking forward to meeting me. An hour of her company would cost me $1,500 cash or $1,600 on a credit card; $3,600 would buy me the pleasure of her company for the entire evening.

"What can I expect for my hard-earned $1,500?" I asked. As though she was reading straight from a piece of paper, the operator told me I would enjoy "private and personal quality time with the entertainer of your choice in a comfortable and quiet environment."

"Does that mean I can fuck her?" I asked.

"I can't provide that information over the phone," she said—which didn't exactly sound anything like a yes. I booked an hour anyway. I was told to call Exotica-2000 when I reached my hotel in

Manhattan to let them know I was ready.

The Edgeboro Family Reunion seemed like it would never end. My foot was shaking under the table so much at dinner that the plates and glasses were vibrating. All I could think of was living out an anal sex scene with Anita.

I've had this reoccurring fantasy about her nearly every day since I first saw her getting tag-teamed. It always starts and ends the same way, with us jumping up and down on a bed wearing scuba-diving goggles and snorkles. I'm not sure where the scuba gear comes from; I don't even go in the ocean. I always envision myself jumping higher and higher on the bed as Anita gets on her knees, her face into the sheets, spreading her ass open, then with the agility of a master gymnast I flip in the air, landing, with loving ease, balls deep in her ass. As if fucking like that needs a cherry on top, Anita always rolls me onto my back and, still bouncing on my cock, begins to pummel her pussy with her snorkel, all while smoking a cigarette. Thinking about how good that snorkel must taste seemed to make my Aunt Sally's meat loaf go down a lot easier.

The next day, I woke up bright and early and took a train to Manhattan to find a hotel room. Since I was going to be dropping $1,500, I didn't much feel like spending a penny more than I had to on accommodations. The Best Western on 32nd Street in Koreatown was a relative bargain at $75 a night.

I had about 10 hours to kill, so I bought a ticket to a cineplex downtown and watched about five movies, the entire time contemplating if I should stop and pick up a snorkel or not.

When night mercifully fell, I checked in to my room. I assumed that a Best Western would, at the very least, not have hypodermic needles sticking out of the pillows, which turned out to be the case, but not much else can be said for my room. The door hit the bed upon entering, forcing me to slide inside and step on the bed to get inside. By stretching my arms out, I was almost able to touch the two farthest walls with my fingertips. The television was the size of a Palm Pilot and received three channels: sports, MTV, and snow.

The place was disgusting, but luxury was not a concern of mine: I just needed a horizontal platform for fucking, four walls for privacy and a door; I had at least that. I unpacked my luggage—a six-pack of beer and a bottle of wine—and waited for the ten o'clock hour.

I cracked open a cold one and chugged it down. I put the wine on ice—real classy—for when Anita showed up. I was nervous, and fearful that since sex was not guaranteed, I might be flushing my hard-earned cash down the toilet. I don't mind spending $1,500 on an evening that would make me happy for the rest of my days, but burning three months of rent on pleasant conversation and a kiss on the cheek would break me. My mission was to do everything I'd seen in film to this slut; anything short would be a failure.

After a few beers, I rubbed out a load in the bathroom to an imaginary layout of my girl taking my johnson up the poop shoot. After I finished spanking my monkey, I took a cold shower and tried to relax; but my fantasy-turned-reality was just 20 minutes away. I broke out into sweat in horny anticipation. I unzipped my pants and shot off another round; I had passed the point of worrying if I was going to have the opportunity to fuck Anita Rodman; my anxiety had shifted to worry over how long I would last. If I came too soon, would Anita just leave?

A knock came at the door at 10 p.m. sharp. Through the peephole, I spied my girl. Sure enough, it was her, along with a guy who could have passed for an undercover cop. Fear overcame me. What if I was arrested for soliciting? What if I was sent up the river to end up on the wrong end of a wild anal fantasy? Who would say grace at the next Edgeboro Family Reunion? I wasn't sure if I should pretend to not be in the room or not. I took another look out the peephole, and caught Anita licking her lips. I cracked open the door slowly; the couple burst into the room, pushing the bed back.

The goon peeked into the closet, which was empty, and then the bathroom. I was shitting my pants.

"Is your friend a cop?" I asked.

Anita laughed. I asked him. He said no, after which she apologized. She then called in to the Exotica office to let them know she made it and then turned to me and asked for the money, which she handed over to her bodyguard. He said he'd be back in an hour and left, with my cash in his breast pocket. She took off her full-length mink coat assuring me that she wouldn't stick me for the money and that her display of nerves was a simple misunderstanding.

I vaguely remember her telling me she was in the middle of an ugly divorce, and was trying to retain custody of her child and didn't know what her husband might do to undermine her.

Truth is, I wasn't paying much attention to what she had to say, I was lost in her 36DD tits. She wore a tight black, sheer long-sleeve shirt. The outlines of her pussy were visible through her black spandex pants. She may as well have told me that in five minutes, she was going to cut out my intestines with a rusty bobby pin and sell them on the black market. I could've cared less. I was beholding one of God's greatest creations—that is, if God were a plastic surgeon. The woman standing in front of me, droning on about her ugly divorce proceedings. This was everything I'd prayed for, and she was all mine—for the next 60 minutes. Time, I realized, was of the essence. Nonetheless, I stood there, dumbfounded. I had no idea how to proceed.

She saw the nervousness in my eyes

"Lie down, have some wine and relax," she told me, then went into the bathroom. I felt pretty ridiculous. I had a willing and paid-for fuck doll two feet away, in the bathroom, and I was worried about how to make conversation with her? What if she didn't let me stick my dick in her—what then? What the hell was I supposed to talk to her about? Were we going to spend the evening watching sports highlights on the 10-inch TV?

Fortunately, Anita Rodman was a pro; I never had to say a word. She came out of the bathroom in a see-through bra and a G-string, both of which were off and on the floor within seconds. My anxiety over how to talk to my idol, and about being scammed, were gone with the wind as she pulled my half hard-on out of my pants. She tugged my dork gently and rubbed it against her tits, and blood gorged my manhood until I thought it would burst.

"What if I come too quick?" I asked. "Are you going to leave?"

"You bought me for an hour, baby," she whispered in my ear. "Come as many times as you like."

I was starting to gather my wits about me. I finally thought of a way to make conversation.

"Can I lick your pussy?" I asked.

Anita slid onto her back and spread her legs. I ran my tongue across her clit. This is the pussy from TV, was all I could think. The snatch was absolutely perfect—completely bald and fresh-tasting. A little tattoo of a sun or a flower or something completely generic adorned her lower belly. I guided my tongue down the velvety trench of her pussy lips to her asshole. A pubic hair snagged in my teeth, which puzzled me, since her beaver was shaved clean. When I tasted her asshole, I went into a lapping-and-probing frenzy. I was rimming "The Anal Sweetheart," the woman who starred in countless anal features and infected me with a backdoor bloodlust when I was in college. When I rammed my tongue deeper into her browneye, she moaned my name. "James," she said. "Oh, James."

My name! Anita Rodman was calling my name, running her hands through my hair, while I ate her ass. At that point, $1,500 seemed like a bargain. While I was prepping her turd-winker for a session of bodacious backdoor love, my mind raced with the possibilities: Once I was done plowing her poop chute, Anita would go into a wild frenzy and insist on staying all night, free of charge. She'd tell me that no one ever touched her the way I did. She'd tell me of her wild fantasies, all the same as my own. She'd ask me why I didn't bring a snorkel. Tomorrow we would take a romantic carriage ride in Central Park together, then travel to a sunny beach in the Pacific, where clothing was optional and we could fuck like rabbits from dust 'til dawn.

All of these fantasies were predicated on the possibility that Anita would let me in her ass, which she did not. My index finger was in her shit spot up to the first knuckle when Anita clenched her cheeks and pulled my hand away.

"That stuff only happens in the movies, honey," she said. "Sorry."

I must have looked crestfallen, because she brought me back to life with an offer I couldn't refuse.

"You can fuck me from behind while I finger my ass, if you like."

Anita slid a condom down my shaft, climbed on all fours, and I banged her from behind. She reached around her back and plunged a finger in her ass; I could feel her finger through her vaginal wall. I rolled her onto her back so I could watch her saline balloons bounce, which nearly made me nut right then and there. After a good 25 minutes of hot and heavy pounding, I was ready for my very own, real-life money shot. I imagined spurting jets of cum all over her hooters. I made a strategic error at that point that has plagued me ever since that night.

"Can I come on your tits?" I asked. Stupid.

"No, that's what condoms are for," Anita said. I should have just built up to ejaculatory inevitability, whipped off my rubber and sprayed her down with come. Instead, I pumped a few times, let my chowder fly in the spermcatcher and rolled over onto my back. Anita beelined to the bathroom to wash up.

One hot shower later, Anita snuggled up next to me in bed; we watched big-assed Jennifer Lopez count down the top 100 videos of all time on MTV. Anita laughed at Lopez's black-girl hair.

"She's so ugly," Anita said. I agreed with her, even though I would pay plenty more than $1,500 to gain access to the greatest ass in the world. Well, second-greatest. We were naked together in bed, watching TV, and I was telling her whatever she wanted to hear. I started to feel as though I was on a real date—except I was paying through the nose for it.

Feeling as comfortable as I ever had with a girl, I turned to her and asked her if she wouldn't mind if I took a photo of her and I together, so that I could remember the night forever. She seemed a bit uncomfortable with the idea, telling me that it could be used as evidence of prostitution. The sound of my heart breaking could be heard over Jennifer Lopez's voice as she explained herself. That Anita would think I would ever do anything to hurt her, or jeopardize what we had, really hurt and I made sure she knew that. I told her that I only wanted a romantic photo of the two of us that I could frame and put on my desk, to prove to myself that our night together wasn't another wild sexcapade thought up in my head. That put her mind at ease. "We have to put our shirts on, then," Anita told me. I was happy to oblige. She put on her top and snuggled next to me, while I outstretched my arm as far as I could to try and get every inch of her into the frame. She laid her head on my shoulders and blew a kiss at the camera. We held each other like lovers do.

Anita told me about being a full-time stripper.

"I haven't done a video in years but I'm considering going back."

I had my arm around her, we were establishing a rapport. Feeling loose and comfortable, I remembered the pube that caught in my teeth when I was eating her out and asked how she could have missed such a long hair when she was shaving. Anita's answer revolted me.

"You're the fifth appointment I've had tonight," she said. "I shower between every one, but I could very well have missed a spot where the last guy was."

A wave of nausea passed though my gut. Reality hit. I had just fucked and, worse, eaten out a very used and unwashed woman. I had shoved my tongue deep up inside this woman's vagina and anus, as if she were a virgin bride. I took the two steps to the bathroom and threw up my dinner in the sink. After heaving my guts out, I washed my face and returned to bed. I was both relieved and disturbed to find that Anita was still naked in bed, waiting for me. She ran her fingers through my hair and pulled my face onto her bosom.

"All the others were creepy married men, not young and sexy like you," she said.

Her lies comforted me and even more so when she told me that she was flying back to California the next morning and was never going to do a job for Exotica again. I would be her last out-call client. As if that would matter at that point. I laid back on the bed, and suddenly accepting the fact that I had just had another man's crotch hair in my mouth wasn't an issue. All that I could think was, I did it. I changed Anita Rodman. She was giving up her whoring for me. Just then Anita did what any professional would do to keep up customer satisfaction: She jerked me off. The handjob worked like a charm—and the pube was completely forgotten. I came again, this time without a condom, straight into the air like a geyser and all over the bed.

After washing me down, getting dressed and kissing me good night she turned to the door, opened it and then stopped suddenly. She turned to me and said, "I'm serious, this really is my last time doing this. And I had a lot of fun." She blew me a kiss, told me I was sweet and walked into the night, slowly shutting the door behind her.

I couldn't help but feel I'd made a real connection with her. Paid sex aside, it was rather romantic, like a high school date making out, fucking, watching some TV and fucking some more. In subsequent days and weeks, I found myself imagining that I'd see her around, at the grocery store or the mall, and maybe we'd have a second date. A real date. Maybe by then, this whoring around would really be behind her and she'd be onto some new and wonderful occupation like hair-styling. She'd tell me how I changed her life and that everything she was now was all thanks to me, and most importantly she'd confess that she hasn't been able to be with another man since our night in the big city. That's when she'd hand me the small gift she'd bought me from the scuba-diving store, Sinatra would start to play in the distance and we'd lock lips and never let go. Before long, "Strangers in the Night" faded and wedding bells were heard throughout the land. Truth is, in my heart I felt that it was all possible.

That was two months ago.

I haven't seen her in the produce aisle once and it's not for lack of trying. I find myself buying broccoli at 4 a.m. on a Wednesday. I began to doubt I'd ever see her again and if she ever really cared. I went back to Exotica-2000.com to get those thoughts out of my head. To prove to my heart that what we had was special and she'd given up carrying boxes of condoms for curlers and a blow-dryer. But all I wound up proving was that I'm just another sucker. Another john, on a long list of johns pulling other johns' pubic hairs out of their teeth. Because there she was, her photo still on the website, looking at me with those loving, lying eyes.

I still didn't want to believe it, but when I called the office to see if and when Anita would be back in Manhattan, the office girl assured me she'd be back after the New Year and once a month thereafter.

I suppose when getting paid to fuck is in your blood, it's a hard addiction to kick. But for a long New York minute I saw something in her eyes that told me this girl was special, not a high-priced hotel-whore, but a wholesome girl with a somewhat different way of making ends meet.

Looking back on that night, at the photo of the two of us wrapped in each other's arms, the only two people on earth at that moment, I can't help but wonder if one day the photo will disappear off my desk and I'll wake up from this surreal fantasy. Although I have the picture and bank receipt to prove it, I still have my doubts about the events that took place that night. If it was all just a dream I can live with that, and I'll cherish it as the greatest dream I've ever had, but if any part of that night was real, then why hasn't she called?

Rocco's Initiations 4

ELEGANTANGEL.COM • DIR: ROCCO SIFFREDI • RATING: 8

The first scene has three sexy blondes and two guys and I'm pretty sure one of the blondes has some kind of STD. I'm no doctor but when they first showed the girl's pussy it was covered with small pus-filled pimples and I can tell you they weren't any type of razor burn. I'm talking about noticeable-sized lumps that could be genital warts or some other kind of pass-along gift. It's sad to see things like that. The girl looked so young and clean and delicious. It only goes to reinforce the old adage "Don't judge a book by its cover." The only clean girl in the world is your baby daughter and trust me, that's not going to last too long. I knew this foxy brunette back home who was a poster girl for clean living. When I saw her I'd imagine it was probably safe to lick her butt after she shitted.

It was around 1998 that I saw her at a local bar, drunk, giving me "fuck me" eyes. One thing led to another and she went to the bathroom to fix her lipstick so I could smear it off back at her house. As I waited for her to doll herself up, her best friend approached me and asked if I was leaving with her friend. When I said yes and asked if she wanted to join us she bit her lip and looked away, trying to find the words to tell me something I didn't want to hear. "What?" I asked. "Listen," she said, "if you're going to fuck her make sure you wear a condom. She has genital herpes." She paused. "And they're bad."

"Oh, come on. What? Are you jealous? There's no reason to be catty." She said nothing but her eyes told me she wasn't bullshitting me.

I'm sure someone else got a lifelong gift from the girl that night, but not me. And that, kids, is just one of many times that Uncle Chris ducked a herpes punch.

Seymore Butts Does Europe Part 2

SEYMOREBUTTS.COM · DIR: SEYMORE BUTTS · RATING: 10

Okay, what the fuck? This video was shot in Amsterdam. Is that even in Europe? If so, since when? I went to Amsterdam once. Once. It didn't feel like Europe to me; it felt like Woodstock Supersized. I hated every minute of it, as I knew I would, because I hate hippies and people who smoke weed. Especially people my own age. It's like, "Hey, asshole. You got your driver's license 15 years ago, grow the fuck up already. You're balding and the stupid-stoner thing stopped being hot or cool the day after prom." I mean, it's not like I didn't know what I was getting myself into. It's Amsterdam, for fuck's sake. Why does anyone go there? To hide in an attic and pretend to be Anne Frank? Tourists flock there for either the weed or the whores in the red-light district. For me it was the whores, but you can't have one without stepping in the other, and so I was plagued by red-and-glassy-eyed zombies staring at the clouds, getting in my way as I was trying to window-shop for prostitutes. Not that I wanted to necessarily have sex with a hooker, I was just trying to be a fine ambassador of our great nation while abroad, thus doing my part to boost the local economy of the region I was visiting. I wouldn't actually stick my

dick in them, I just wanted to stick an eggplant or a zucchini up a foreign ass. But despite everything you've heard about the loose women
of Amsterdam, they do have their limits, and the line is drawn at
inserting produce into their privates. I tried offering twice the amount
they would charge for sex, yet I found no takers. Even with me paying
in US currency. And this is when the US dollar was worth something!
One moralistic rental started yelling at me, "What if I stuck that zucchini up your ass? How would you like it?" Later I thought I had a
taker in one of the older, more road-weary, less desirable whores, but
then she floundered and offered me an alternative: "Why don't you
just shit on my chest or fist my pussy?" Whoa, lady. She was being
for real. She preferred to be shat on than have a vegetable up her
butt. I tried to explain to her that most doctors would agree that vegetables are far more sanitary than feces, not to mention good for you.
We couldn't reach an agreement, and I was left holding the bag. Of
vegetables. In this video Alisha Klass fists herself with one of those
fake flesh-colored hands. Have you ever seen one of those things? So
creepy. I'd say even more creepy than a fake pussy. It's like a severed
arm. Yet despite it being far bigger than the eggplant I was trying to
administer, I'm sure any one of those prostitutes would've gladly
taken the fake hand over my vegetables. That doesn't even make
sense. The only explanation I can offer is that like everyone else in
Amsterdam all the hookers were stoned out of their minds. How else
can you make sense out of wanting to be shitted on instead of probed
by a plant? I just don't get it.

1001 Ways to Eat My Jizz, Vol. 1

ARMAGEDDON ENTERTAINMENT • DIR: AUGUST ARKHAM • RATING: 6

I hate cooking shows. I can't see how anyone other than the hired
help of a wealthy glutton could get anything from those types of
programs. Do the producers of all cooking shows believe that all

viewers happen to have kitchens with three ovens and eight burners? Do they think I just happen to keep every Indian and Ethiopian spice known to man in my cupboard? Don't they realize most people own standard pots and pans and typical utensils, not 50-gallon drums and ladles shaped like pythons? You want to know what I cook—and this is when I'm feeling really ambitious? A cheeseburger. On my Foreman grill. And you want to know my secret spices and herbs that I add to it to give it that oh-so-succulent flavor? Ketchup. Granted, I can cook very well. I can also take out your car's transmission and replace it for you, but that doesn't mean I'm in the fucking mood to do it. Does it mean I have a spare transmission up my ass just waiting for you to ask me to install it? No. I'm busy. I watch porn. I have to brush my teeth. There are bars out there that don't close and they need me to pay their electric bills. There are women lusting for a man like me, a man that is at least one-eighth the man they'd always dreamt of. I don't have time to cook. I don't have time to write this damn review, but if I don't I'll have no money for beer, and I'd hate to be held personally responsible for putting even one bartender out of work and onto the streets. And so it is for them I suffer. But who are the women in this video suffering for, I wonder? Their pimp? Their dealer? Their fathers? I just can't figure out what would possess a girl to eat a can of tuna covered in semen, or a bowl of dog food mixed with man juice. But there are a lot of things I don't understand. I lived with a girl once who insisted when I had to piss that I piss in her mouth. My entire wad of piss she'd slurp down in one clean gulp. Don't get me wrong, I didn't mind at all. My water bill had never been lower. But I just failed to see the joy that could be had by swallowing urine directly from the tap. I also failed to see that she had stolen my car and moved halfway across the country, never to be seen or heard from again. I suppose you could say that if I wasn't at the bar all day and night I might have noticed our relationship deteriorating, but I could respond by saying had I cared I would have tried to stop her, but caring requires conversations, long drawn-out talks that go round and round and really don't get you anywhere. Talks that directly detract from my main focus of around-the-clock drinking. You tell me who really has time for those kinds of talks?

Vouyer Vision

REDLIGHTDISTRICTVIDEO.COM • DIR: VINCE VOUYER • RATING: 7

When I was at the peak of my obesity I became so self-conscious of my weight that I resorted to lying to a blind girl about my appearance to lure her into bed. Isn't that sad?

It wasn't as if she didn't have any hands or any sense of touch where she wouldn't notice the disgusting rolls of my stomach smacking against her ribby little frame. She called me on my bullshit immediately after running her hands down from my chest. "Did you say you were a bodybuilder?" I said I had because that was the lie I'd told her. "You don't feel very muscular at all." Well, I'm not, I told her, I'm completely covered in flab. When I moved to this town, I said, I was a mere 140 pounds, and over the past eight months I've built my body up to a whopping 215. In that regard I am a bodybuilder. She laughed, I

assumed, because it was the most retarded thing she'd ever heard because who has to lie to impress a blind girl other than me? She than asked me what she looked like, to describe her every detail to her. I asked her how old she was. 25. How long have you been blind? Since birth, she said. "Now, after 25 years you want to know what you look like so you can develop a complex and become as insecure as the rest of us?" Should I be insecure, she asked, am I horrid? "Does it matter?" I asked. Suddenly, she said, it does. "Well, my dear, the truth is I am a chubby chaser and you are 400 pounds of grade-A meat. Run your hand down your side, feel all those ribs and bones pushing against your taut skin? That is what fat people feel like." She pressed her hand to her side; her face remained expressionless. "I'm kidding. I'm fucking kidding," I told her. "You're a beautiful girl. It's a shame you have no eyes to see just how pretty you are." Well, I have eyes, she said, they just don't work. "Whatever," I said. "It's all semantics. You might as well not have them at all if they don't work. You're kind of like my mother. She loves to save junk. We have 20-year-old washers and refrigerators in the basement that don't work. I don't see why she doesn't just throw them away. Do you want me to throw away your eyes for you?" She giggled and asked how I would do it. "With a knife, of course." With that I went into the next room to the drawer where I kept the steak knives and rattled them about, then I removed one and took it to the sharpening stone and began to sharpen it for heightened effect. She found it all quite laughable. "You're quite brave, I'll admit. If I was blind as a bat and someone started sharpening knives and claiming to cut my eyes out I'd run for my goddamn life. If I could find the front door." I know you won't hurt me, she told me, you have too gentle of a soul. "Is that right? You've known me three hours. You shouldn't provoke me. You don't even want to know where I have the last girl buried that provoked me." She feigned fear. "That does it!" I yelled at the top of my lungs. I climbed onto the couch, stood above her, unzipped my pants and poked her in her useless left eye with my semi-hard penis. "Take that, you blind bitch!"

The Ass Watcher

FUSXION.COM, METROINTERACTIVE.COM • DIR: PAT MYNE • RATING: 9

I wish this movie was called *Ass Washer*. Pat Myne could have had all the girls in bathtubs, washing out their asses with soap and sponges and plungers and whatnot. Not that there's anything wrong with this movie as it stands, but I just think that the ass-cleansing-fetish community has been sorely overlooked in porn and someone should do something about it.

From the time I was 18 to 25 there was a strip club just outside of Philadelphia called Fantasy Show Bar that would do a fantastic job of catering to ass-washing enthusiasts. For the most part it was typical strip club fanfare but in one corner of the room there was a shower and for five dollars you could pay to give a girl a sponge bath. In my younger days I didn't really understand the concept or the extent of things. I was shy, nervous, awkward. I held the sponge loosely with my thumb and my index finger. I patted the stripper's ass cheeks with it. It was the poorest display of sexuality ever performed in a strip club. She said to me, "You know, you're allowed to clean me better than that." I took the remark as an order to scrub harder, so I made wider, rounder circles on her buttocks, trying to stay as far away from touching her private parts as possible. After one song she got annoyed and told me to go sit down. I made Fantasy Show Bar a weekly event and quickly learned exactly what the girl had meant. I'd watch men of all shapes, sizes and races give girls "sponge baths," which were just five minutes of finger-banging a stripper's vagina or asshole or both if they were so inclined. Did I mention it only cost five dollars? Those were good times. I'd spend the majority of each and every paycheck on pretending to wash the dirty off of strippers. It almost became a second job. I'd walk into the club, see Bambi or Tiffany, say hello and let them know I'd be over to clean them up in a minute. After a drink I'd go over, sit on my ass-shine stool, dip my sponge in the bucket of soapy water and proceed to insert my fingers one by one until I had three in. Three was the limit, by the club's unwritten policy, but I'm pretty sure most of the girls wanted a fourth or even a fifth. Once inside them we'd strike up a conversation. "How have you been, Chris?" Not so bad, Bambi. Same shit really. How's things with you and your boyfriend? "Oh, he's an asshole. He needs to get a fucking job. Lazy fuck . . . but I love him. How about you? You're a nice guy, how come you don't have a girlfriend?" "You know," I started as I removed my fingers, dunked the sponge back in the bucket and went back in for more, "I don't have time for a girlfriend. I work all week, I just want to relax and have a beer. This here, finger-ing your ass, that's enough for me." That made her blush, then she told me I was sweet. I asked if I could get another five minutes.

Anal Mermaids

PRIVATE.COM • DIR: KOVI • RATING: 6

How can mermaids have anal sex if they don't have buttholes? Is there something I missed while sleeping at the back of the room during my undersea-studies class? A mermaid just has that tail thing going on down there, right? Unless we're talking about Darryl Hannah in *Splash* with Tom Hanks, in which case I would like to think she does take it in the ass. Perhaps even from me someday. To date, though, I can't ever say I've fucked a mermaid in the ass, aside from Crissie, an ex-mermaid, but I have stretched the asses of many women who have drank like fish. Does that count? There was a time where I picked up girls exclusively from AA meetings. Many years ago, when I was made to attend Alcoholics Anonymous for my first DUI, I realized the most loose and easy women to bed were recovering addicts. They all needed a crutch and if that crutch only happened to be seven inches long so be it. See, for me I wasn't trying to quit drinking, it was either AA or 30 days in jail, so the answer was easy. When I'd take these dependent young things back to my apartment I'd immediately crack open a beer and, like any good host, I'd offer them one. "I can't," they'd say. "I haven't had a drop in (enter duration of time from one week to five years)." Suit yourself, I'd say. But by my fifth one the temptation became too much and they broke down. Before long all inhibitions were out the window and we were playing hide the beer bottle. Remember, I wasn't using the alcohol to get laid, simply to not be a rude host. I don't think that I should be held responsible for anyone's relapse or possible graduation to crack cocaine or possibly suicide as a result of depression, which spawned from a relapse that led to them selling their body for bar money. There's no way any of that is my fault. I am allowed to drink in my own home, aren't I? No one forced anyone to drink. Certainly not me because I didn't really want to share in the first place. Yet somehow the word got out at Tuesday-night meetings that I was only in AA for

the courts and that I was still a heavy drinker and that girls should beware that I'd lure them into bed with booze. I was forced to transfer to Thursday nights across town, which was fine because it was the punk-rock AA meeting and the girls were more my type, not at all like the Tuesday meeting that was strictly waif models and wannabe actresses who desperately needed to eat something other than a dick. Thursdays were good to me for a while, met a lot of good people and really connected with a few of the prettier ones, but it didn't take long before one of the Tuesday girls happened upon my Thursday meeting and blew it for me. That's when I found myself a great Friday night in the rich community of Bel Air where no one knew my name. I figured Friday was a good night because that's the biggest drinking night of the week and where else would a rich and beautiful woman who was trying so desperately to abstain be on a Friday night? Bel Air was amazing simply because for as wealthy as those women were they were too cheap to buy cigarettes. Buy two packs of cigarettes and hit an AA meeting in Bel Air on a Friday night and you can pretty much guarantee you're going to get some ass.

Girls of the Ivy Leagues

VIDEOTEAM.COM • DIR: JONATHAN MORGAN & ALEX SANDERS •
RATING: 5

I skipped my senior year of high school. Not because I was brilliant by any means, rather that I'd had enough. I'd told my counselor I planned on dropping out of school and moving to California to lolly-gag about for a few years. He urged me to stick it out and found me a loophole that allowed me to skip my last year by attending summer classes for 20 days. When I first started college I was a good year or two younger than everyone else. I was never exposed to sophisticatos prior to college. I'd never read a book unless it detailed how to hot-wire an automobile. I was a partier. I didn't attend class for the first month because I was too high, too drunk or a combination of the two. It was my first real exposure to beautiful women, to women that fell outside of the realm of the typical high-haired, low-expectations Jersey Girls. No, the women in university wore their glasses with pride, they wore cardigans and business suits. Mmmm, business suits. I was deathly afraid of them. I felt inferior with a snowball's chance in hell of surviving a conversation with one of them, let alone ending up naked, rolling in the hay. I was a waste; born addicted to the bottle and having since graduated onto anything that was smok-able, snortable, or ingestible. I remember one girl that I had the world's largest crush on. Check the Guinness record book; I still hold the record for largest schoolboy crush in history. Her skin was porce-lain, hair stained of ox blood and lips of pornographic pink with never a hint of makeup. She hid sea green eyes behind Elvis Costello glasses and she couldn't stand me. She thought I was an ogre, a sloppy drunken mess who was attending college just to be able to move out of Mommy's basement. She was spot-on. I was told she was a les-bian, that I shouldn't bother, but I refused to believe it. I thought that the others were just trying to thwart my efforts to increase their chances. At the time I didn't know there existed women who absolutely hated men with all their being. I'd never met one so I had no point of reference. The only lesbians I'd ever come across were in porno films and generally they had a penis to share between them. I basically thought being a lesbian meant that the girl simply preferred to be with a woman and a man at the same time. And if that was the case, I thought, I would like to get between this girl and her girlfriend. I pursued her relentlessly, trying to change my spots, forcing myself into long bouts of sobriety, actually attending and excelling in class. I began to write poetry, bloody awful poetry. I traded my contact lenses in for dork glasses and dusted off my Sundays, Smiths, and Pixies records. Nothing worked. Finally I asked why she wasn't attracted to me. She told me she was a lesbian. I told her I could work around that. She laughed, thought I was joking and offered me a cup of tea. "What do you want to do later? Do you want to go to the poetry jam?" she asked. "No," I said. "I want to fuck your face." She told me she thought I should leave and so I left. That wasn't the first time I was rejected, but that time was very special to me. It taught me that above anything else I really love the taste of beer.

How to Fuck a Stripper
And Still Have Money in Your Pocket

M ost people think the way to a stripper's pussy is with money, buying lap dance after lap dance, throwing stacks of singles on stage as they dance and surprising them with expensive gifts. Those people are idiots. "Marks," as the girls call them. Someone to be siphoned until not one drop of cash is left. There is only one sure-fire way to pull a stripper and it has nothing to with personality or money (although those things don't hurt). The secret is DRUGS. Contrary to what many pro-stripper films and documentaries tell you, 9 out of 10 strippers are on drugs of some sort.* Be it coke, dust,

(*All research conducted and collected solely by Nieratko and proven to be 100% accurate.)

weed, pills, booze; if a girl's job is to climb up on stage and spread her gash for a bunch of sweaty, drunk, overweight mutts in ill-fitting work clothes you'd better believe it takes a certain type of courage that can only be had from illegal substances. Knowing that, the key to making a needy young sex kitten your slave for the night (or the week) is to always be holding. But you have to make sure you're carrying the right stuff for the type of stripper you're trying to bang. It just so happens that this whole thing can be broken down racially. Along with the genetic yarns that make a woman a certain color go these little strands that decide their drug proclivities. Don't freak out—I didn't write the rules here. God did. I just follow them.

WHITE STRIPPERS (BLONDE): White chicks love coke. It's as simple as that. Any stripper worth sticking your dick in is between the ages of 18 and 28, meaning they were born between 1978 and 1986, which makes their moms either '70s disco coke whores or '80s yuppie coke sluts. Either way, the "coke slut gene" has been inherited by their daughter. When she asks if you'd like a lap dance, respond: "No, I want to get out of here and do some blow. What time are you done

tonight?" That's usually enough to get you in, but for added emphasis it helps to pull her to the side, dump some powder on your fist and give it to her to prove you're for real. (Don't buy beat shit. Strippers who love coke know coke. You're not getting anywhere with shit that's been stepped on 10 times.)

WHITE STRIPPERS (TATTOOED AND/OR WITH PUNK HAIRCUTS): This is a somewhat trickier bunch to read because they like pills and saying someone "likes pills" is like saying someone "likes music." You've got to either roll the dice on a narrow spectrum of possibilities (uppers, downers, psyche or pain) or you can be smart and invest in a smorgasbord of pharmaceuticals and have all your bases covered. There's nothing worse than sparking a girl's interest only to learn she likes Xanax and you've got a pocket full of Ritalin. Pretend that you're going fishing and you've got an empty tackle box. You're going to need a little of everything: lures, bobbers, hooks, etc. Pills are inexpensive ($5–$8 a pop), so see if you can work out a deal with your man on a variety bottle. At that price you shouldn't think twice about pissing them away. Offer a blue to the first girl you see. If she takes it, she'll go and tell the other girls. Give 10 mg to each and every girl in the club. 10 strippers = 10 pills = 50 bucks. No big deal. If you have enough to get each girl high on the job, one of those girls is going to have enough brains to realize you've probably got more. She'll be the one to ask you, "What are you doing later?"

BLACK STRIPPERS: The black stripper is difficult to snare, especially for a white male. Their drug of choice, weed, is the cheapest drug on the market and easiest to obtain. This makes them the most affordable fuck, but you're white and you have to compensate. That's where things get expensive. Don't freak out, it's still completely doable. First, start by tipping. Don't go crazy. Just a dollar or two here and there to let her know you're interested. This will automatically put you ahead of most black patrons in the club because it is well documented that many black males do not tip at strip clubs. Sorry to hurt anyone's feelings, but that's what all the girls are saying.* Your next move is to have better-than-average weed. Like flowers, girls like weed that smells nice. It helps to tell them that it's from your boy's crop and has been featured on the cover of *High Times* three times and it's Redman and Snoop's favorite weed when they come to town. It's important that this lie and the two following lies be convincing: "Yeah, I know Snoop," and "Next time he's in town, I'll introduce you." That should take care of it. For added effect I like to lie and say I make beats and ask them if they want to go over to my studio after they get off work. This helps to both sell the con and save money on hotel rooms. Be sure to know where a local recording studio is. A cheap one is between $75 and $150 an hour, which is cheaper than taking her to a nice hotel. Be sure to bring the new Usher CD and when her favorite song comes on tell her you made the beat but "Jermaine pulled some shit and I didn't see a dime." Then turn one of the knobs on that big mixing board thing in front of you. Ungh, ungh. I thought I told you we won't stop.

OTHER STRIPPERS: That is correct, I am going to lump together all Asian, Latin, Paki and Euro strippers, along with anything else that might have just come off the boat, including amputees. This category

is really your best bet, especially Euro girls, because all they want is to be loved and taken care of and what drug emits more love than Ecstasy? The reality is you could give them mescaline and they'd take it without caring.* A key with foreigners is to make them feel welcome in America. This is accomplished by telling them you don't detect an accent, that they speak great English and that you basically understand and agree with whatever they are saying regardless of the fact that you can only make out every fourth word. To do this convincingly, you must practice. Go to your stereo and put on some rap music that you can't understand the lyrics to (most any Trick Daddy will work), turn up the volume just slightly, then go into your bathroom and shut the door. You should not be able to easily hear more than reverb and bass. Stare dead in the mirror, strain your ears and try to decipher the lyrics without looking unsure, without creasing your forehead and pursing your eyes. If you can convince your mind that you know every lyric to that Ghostface song using only your eyes and facial expressions, you'll be able to win any foreigner over, completely negating their self-consciousness. Using drugs as bait, of course.

Before you go running to your phone to cop there are a few more things you need to be aware of when trying to run this kind of game. First, and most important, is that you don't ever do the drugs. If you're an addict don't even bother because you'll always take the drugs over the girl and might even get arrested for beating a girl for touching your shit without asking. You can get high all you want when she's gone but while you're with her you have to pretend to inhale, go take a piss when your turn to bang a rail comes around, throw the pill over your shoulder and pretend to pop it. Sounds lame but you need to have full control over the situation. I'm telling you from experience, strippers are cunning, any sign of weakness and you'll wake up without your pants, your wallet, and your drugs.

Secondly, realize you only get one shot of pulling them out of the club. If it doesn't happen that night, it doesn't happen. Don't play yourself by giving your number and don't take a number. Consider it a failed attempt and go home and get high. Lastly, and I can't stress this enough, don't let them know where you live. If you can, take them to a hotel (or the studio). If you've blown all your money on the drugs and are forced to take them back to your place, take the most ridiculously fucked-up route ever to get there. Then after you're done with them, give them some more drugs to fry their brain a little more and put them right in a cab and send them on their way (instructing the driver to use an alternate, more confusing route). As a child you had a great many dreams of things you wanted in your lifetime, and I'm pretty sure that a drug-hungry whore knocking on your door at four in the morning begging to come in was not one of them.

Super Freaks 10

ELEGANTANGEL.COM • DIR: DALE JORDAN • RATING: 10

When I was in high school I wanted nothing more in this world than to be black. I did just about everything I could to make that dream come true. I'd talk gangster, wear my pants far past my ass, memorize X Clan lyrics, bad-mouth white people and grab my dick when I talked, regardless of who I was talking to. I even swore off pork and dating white devils. There was a time for a few years that I would only date black chicks. I remember this one girlfriend; an elegant Nubian princess with an ass that jutted out like a coffee table. She was to be my wife, I knew it from the moment I met her. "Birthday, gave her two 50-cent coins." Her and I would help break down the color barrier for our generation. Is there even a color barrier anymore? Does anyone still use that term? I don't think I've ever used it until now. It sounds like a good term to advertise color-safe detergent. "No stain will penetrate the COLOR BARRIER of new Tide!"

The only downside to dating my little chocolate thunder was that her brother and father hated me and resented the fact that she was dating a white boy. Is *white boy* one word or two? I tried time and again to explain that I was no whiter than they were, and that in actuality I was just "light-skinned." But they weren't buying it and they forbade the girl from seeing me anymore. It was on some Romeo and Juliet shit. Real epic proportions. I was ready to take the poison and everything until she dumped me and started dating the point guard of our basketball team.

I wish I knew how to get ahold of her now because she is way hotter than any of the brutes that are in this video. From what I heard she has two kids now, so you know she needs money. Baby, if you're reading this, holler at your boy. Let me get you a job. Let me kiss you on your betty-boo bump. Let me take care of you. Remember when you'd smell my boxers? We can have that again.

CHAPTER 2

"Sometimes I Look Up at the
Stars and Analyze the Sky"
(Drug-induced rants and paranoia)

Miss Strap On

SMASHPICTURES.COM • DIR: DANIEL DAKOTA • RATING: 10

I receive, on a slow month, at least 200 porno DVDs in the mail. I watch less then one-tenth of the films that show up at my door. When I first started this column some seven years ago, I was so overwhelmed with the sheer volume of discs showing up on my door that I had no clue what to do with them all. I have since adopted a system and there is now order in my life and in my office; no more box covers strewn across my hardwood floors all willy-nilly. What I do now upon opening a box is determine which of three designated stacks the film goes into. The first stack is always the largest and that is the outgoing stack. I look at a box cover and if it has no redeeming qualities (hot girls, strange sex acts, funny title, typo in the name), it goes into the outgoing pile. Once a month that pile is carted over to my friendly neighborhood Arab at the liquor store who trades me copious amounts of beer and wine in exchange for the smut. The last of the three stacks is often the smallest. It is compiled of the very few titles that automatically make this column without having to be watched. It is very rare that such a movie comes along. It has to be quite unique. The title must make me giggle out loud after repeatedly reading and rereading it. There must be some unnatural sex act that I've never seen or known was possible. There must be some circus sideshow creature somewhere in the film (be it a 350-pound woman, a hermaphrodite, a gal with T. Rex arms). Since the aforementioned are so rare, it is the second and middle pile that most of the titles you read about come from. That is where all the maybes land. The ones with the semi-clever names. The DVDs with one or two attractive girls. Or a box cover that promises "something you've never seen before!" I hate the second pile because I'm forced to actually watch each film in it, one by one, hoping that something in the film is noteworthy enough or sparks some funny anecdote to make me want to write about it. Generally, it's a big waste of my time and the movie is as formulaic as I suspected it was before I put it in the player. This film, this little movie called *Miss Strap On*, is my *Million Dollar Baby*. It defied all the odds. It has done something that no film has done in the past half decade: It rose from the dead. Upon first glance, it was thrown into the Outgoing stack. First, I hate POV (point-of-view) shots of any sort and secondly I can't stand orgy films because there is too much action to take in in one shot, forcing the director to jump-cut like crazy to try and cover it all, leaving no room for character development. That said, *Miss Strap On* was on its way to the Arab. Then something happened. Maybe I was just in the mood to see some lesbian action since I don't get any at home, I don't know, but somehow this disc was suddenly sitting in the "Maybe" pile. Then I took the time to actually read the back cover where it says, "The 6' 2" Emilianna sports six strap-ons all over her body." Uh, wait. What? Immediately the disc was thrown in the machine and sure enough this woman had dildos strapped to each of her feet, both of her thighs and her two wrists. She also wore a strap-on around her waist, as is customary, bringing the total to seven dildos in all. She looked like a strange dildo monster from an extremely cheap B horror movie and I loved her as she sat, covered with women bouncing about her, alone in the last pile.

Irregular Practice 2: Open Leg Surgery

RELISHXXX.COM • DIR: HAZZA B'GUNNE • RATING: 8

I was addicted to prescription painkillers for three years. You name it, I either ingested it or snorted it. At first I was making runs to Tijuana to score Valium, Somas, Oxys and Vicodin; that was before I learned drug dealers actually made house calls. There's no denying the bargain prices down in ole Mexico but the risk of Mexican jail was never very appealing. Once, my stuff was wrapped in aluminum foil and I was made to walk through a metal detector crossing back into

America. I thought my life was over. The metal detector went off and I simultaneously pointed at my big cowboy belt buckle and shoved my US passport into the border guard's face and said, "It's my belt buckle, I'm an American." I think it was too much for him to process at once and he just waved me through. After that, I stopped making TJ runs. Luckily, it was around the same time I was run over by a taxi crossing the road, which required three shoulder surgeries over the course of two years. For those two years I was prescribed no less than 100 of the highest-grade Vicodin every other week. You know Vicodin makes you constipated, right? I was such a bloated pile of shit then.

I'm glad to say I haven't touched any drugs for one year and I'm back to my slender, handsome self. There is not one day that goes by I don't want to eat a handful of pills and relax, though. I still have drawers full of them. I keep them lying on my nightstand as temptation. I figure if I can wake up every morning and look them dead in the eye and still say no, then I've got a handle on the problem. So far, so good. As much of a waste as I was at the height of my addiction I can't help but appreciate how on my toes I was around my doctor. Leading up to my second surgery he had given me a prescription for 100 Dilaudid. Do you know what that is? They call it Drugstore Heroin. It's what killed Heather Graham in *Drugstore Cowboy*. It's a really brilliant drug if you like being numb for eight hours and drooling on yourself.

So here's the kicker: They anesthetized me and put me out for my surgery. Afterwards, when I came to, I was groggy, confused and uncertain of my whereabouts. My doctor came to check on me and asked me if he'd prescribed anything for the pain and somehow I still had the wherewithal to lie and say, "No, doc. You didn't." He proceeded to write me a scrip for another 100.

Innocent & Blindfolded

CHERRYBOXXX.COM · DIR: RICK DAVIS · RATING: 7

I'm on a flight bound for Los Angeles and a rather plain woman in uniform just tried to sell me headsets so that I could watch *Seabiscuit*. I've been drinking for hours leading up to departure and I'm feeling a bit uneasy; maybe "rambunctious" is a better word. I've nearly gnawed my fingernails to the nub and oh! What's this I see? Do I know you? Yes. Yes, I do. Across the aisle from me sits a girl that some 10 years ago I was wildly, passionately in love with. For an entire week. What we had was such pure poetry that being in the same room with us would have made Shakespeare jealous and of course the physical side of things would have made Larry Flynt blush. The things I did to that tender young girl should be outlawed if not for moral reasons, then at least sanitary ones. What I remember most were the length of her nipples, long beyond long. My friend, after having shared her, took to calling her "eraser nips." I would love to see those eraser nipples again. I wonder if you had them shaved down

since then? Is that even something that a doctor can do? I would hope so, because I'm sure by now they are hanging down like an 80-year-old's limp dick, but I won't judge you. My love is undying. Do you still have that gag-reflex problem? Does too much cock in your mouth still make snot shoot out your nose? You know I loved when you did that? I still think back to using that snot as lube. Oh yes, yes, the fun we had and now, nothing. Do you not recognize me? It's your Christopher, your love, for seven glorious days you were ready to ride off into eternity with me. Can't you see it is I? Sure, time has changed me. I've gotten wider, rounder, the man spread has begun, but behind these tinted lenses I am still the one who made you call your police officer father at work and ask him to borrow his car whilst I rammed celery stalks in your butt. Say you don't remember and I'll leave you be. I'm lying. I must persist. I know it is what you want. You need not say a word, nor offer a sideways glance in my direction. I know I am all you think about. That man beside you, on whose shoulder you now rest your head, who is he? No one to me. I'd say you feel the same way, for contempt bleeds from your eyes each time you lock your gaze upon him. And what manner of man is he? Neither black nor Hispanic, Indian or mulatto? Has he duped you into believing he is light-skinned? My dear, my dear, still so naive. I fear that gentleman is no gentleman at all but rather Taliban. Perhaps I should scream it at the top of my lungs, "TALIBAN! TALIBAN! TALIBAN!" Then the stewardesses will come and we will be forced to make an emergency landing and I'll make my move. I'll rescue you from that lech. Or perhaps I'll just wait until we land in LA, at the baggage carousel. Of course, brilliant, I'll take one of these pillow sacks from the plane and throw it over your head and rush you off into a taxicab. You'll try and fight me but once I remove the mask you will see my eyes and know what I do I do for love. So go ahead and rest your eyes, my dear, soon we will be landing and you'll need all your strength to fight off a love as strong as mine.

My Ass Is Trippin'

ACIDRAINVIDEO.COM • DIR: BOBBY DAMONE • RATING: 7

I like to poke my girl's ass. Well poke, smack, punch, whatever. I'm constantly touching her butt. I'd been drinking wine for hours the other night and she was brushing her teeth and I started to pretend I was trying to hitchhike a ride from her butt, you know, punching into her ass crack but with my thumb up. Then my thumb got stuck in her butthole and when I tried to pull it out it actually sucked me in, like my entire body, right into her butt. Pretty fucked up, huh? Stranger yet was everything inside her was made of candy. Mmmm, chocolate. There was a colony of Swedish gummy fish that put me on their backs and said, "Hey, we're heading up to the stomach for a party, wanna come?" Of course I did. I've never been to a stomach party. I wondered who'd be there. No meats, of course, she doesn't party with meats. Only vegetables and fish. Oh, God! There's a bunch of potatoes on bicycles! "What're you doing, guys?" "Going to pick up some wine, then head over to the party." "Me too. Should I pick up

beer or something?" I asked the fish. "No, it's cool. There'll be plenty for everyone." We passed by a large yellow lake. Every few minutes it would spout like a geyser. "What's that?" I asked. "Oh, that's Pee Pee Pond. After the party, when we're all good and shitty, we'll stop back and go swimming. That geyser is strong enough to shoot you in the air," the one fish with the mustache told me. There was a line at the stomach to get in the party. A big asparagus was turning people away at the door. I saw Chicken and Beef get sent packing. The fish knew the bouncer so we went straight to the front but the asparagus was kind of a dick to me. He was all, "Who's this? Can't go in there, Meat."

Luckily, the fish told him, "Listen, he's not from around here." And I totally got in and inside it was crazy, like shit floating around everywhere and lettuce and cucumbers cutting a rug like it was their last night before going to jail. And everybody was wasted. I must have drank 100 gallons of pinot and didn't have to piss once. I grabbed one of the fish I came with and said, "This is the greatest party of all time. And I haven't peed once since I got here." He pursed his lips and gave me a pitying look, then motioned toward my pants. They were soaked through and through. I'd been pissing myself all night and hadn't even felt it.

She-Male Domination Nation

EVILANGEL.COM • DIR: NACHO VIDAL • RATING: 2

My friend Chris is nuts for this porn star named Belladonna. I don't know why. She's got gappy teeth and she has a stupid tattoo where her left tit is supposed to be, like a breast-cancer victim. If you're going to get a tattoo on your tit, which is just the most hideous place for a chick to get a tattoo, at least get something good. I've seen hundreds of her movies and I still don't have a clue what her tattoo is meant to be. If that weren't bad enough she recently

shaved her black, shoulder-length hair off and dyed it blonde to look like a full-on bull dyke. Not that there's anything wrong with that.

One of my ex-girlfriends worked at a fancy Beverly Hills hair salon. She had luxurious reddish brown hair. One day she came home from work with similar short, spiky hair dyed blonde. Let me tell you how long our relationship lasted after that. About as long as it took for her to pack her shit and get the fuck out. So, not being one to hold on to any porno for more than a few days before passing it on to a friend, I mailed my buddy Chris my copy of *She-Male Domination Nation.* Filling out the address label I felt bad about tainting his perception of his favorite pro slut (in case you can't guess, she gets double penetrated by a guy and a she-male) but not bad enough not to send it, just bad enough to write the word "SORRY" under his address. A week later my phone rang; a voice on the other end told me I was a sonofabitch. Chris kept saying things like, "She's gross. So disgusting. You ruined her forever. She's beyond mutant." Yet he admitted that the whole thing gave him a hard-on. He went into great detail about how the tranny was making Belladonna choke on its cock. He finally admitted he nutted to the tranny getting a hummer. He began to question what that said about him as a person, reassuring me that he wasn't gay. So I posed the question: "Would you act on it? If you could fuck Belladonna but you had to share her with a tranny, would you do it?" "Yeah, of course." he said, "As long as I don't have to touch the tranny. Like if our nuts rub during the double penetration that's okay. I mean, what are you gonna do? It happens in those kinds of positions, you can't help it. It's almost hetero at that point." Then he threw it back at me: "Would you do it if you had the chance?" My answer: "Hell, no. People who do that shit are fucked up."

World Sex Tour 27

ANABOLICVIDEO.COM • DIR: CHRISTOPHER ALEXANDER • RATING: 9

My previous day job as a mild-mannered editor of *Big Brother*, the greatest skateboard magazine ever, allowed me to travel the globe on someone else's dime getting drunk and hanging out with the best skaters in the world. Mind you, my trips aren't full of anal sex like this DVD but they were fun and always full of adventure. One of the best thing that's happened was in Salt Lake City, Utah. A bunch of us were at a bar drinking watered-down drinks until the early morning. Come time to leave we couldn't find our friend Damian.

We later learned he wandered off into the darkness and met some Polish or Swiss chick who he went home with. Back at her place she started making him all kinds of food and desserts and coffee. From the way he told it, it sounded more like she was trying to fatten him up to eat him rather than fuck him. He said he must have had two pots of coffee, which didn't mix well in his beer-filled stomach. They were necking while he finger-banged her when he let out the loudest fart. They both stopped for a moment but she jumped right back to action. He was feeling embarrassed and could feel the contents of his gut bubbling and brewing inside. He tried to continue kissing her but

another, even louder fart erupted. He stopped everything, withdrew his hand from her meat purse and stood up and said, "I'm sorry. I'm not feeling well. I need to get going. Maybe we can try again tomorrow night."

They kissed goodnight and he let himself out. Just as he closed the front door behind him another fart came but this one was half fart, half diarrhea. He knew he couldn't make it even one step further. So right there, on her front step, not a foot out of her house he dropped his pants and shat everywhere. He said the spray was so massive that it covered his pants, her three steps and her front door. I asked him if he'd taken his shirt off and wiped his ass with it. He said he'd wanted to get out of there so badly that he just hiked up his pants and ran away, with shit running down his legs. Then he looked down and pointed at his jeans saying, "These are the pants." This was two days after the fact. I like to imagine the girl's reaction watching the whole sordid ordeal through the peephole. It probably only helped to reinforce the global opinion of Americans.

Sluts with Nuts

ELEGANTANGEL.COM · DIR: PATRICK COLLINS · RATING: 2

I just got back from Rio de Janeiro, where the local economy depends almost entirely on its most abundant natural resource: young, gorgeous women. In the time I spent down there I was approached by the most healthy, sexy, exotic girls in every place from liquor stores to pharmacies to bakeries to the beaches of Ipanema, all trying to offer me their body for the low discount price of $100 US for four hours; as if I know what to do with a woman for four hours. I tried negotiating $6.25 for 15 minutes but they weren't really interested. I told them I'd pay in US currency and still no takers.

One nightclub called Help was actually a meat rack of whores, I'd learned shortly after having my nuts fondled and nipples bitten by seven girls in the first 10 minutes of being there. I said to my local tour guide, "Man, these are some friendly girls down here. They really like Americans." "They're all whores, dipshit" was his response. And they don't take kindly to nonpaying customers. I was cursed at, snarled at and even called a fag for refusing to fuck any of the girls. I tried to explain that I was already drunk and staying drunk was more important to me than getting laid, but I think something was lost in the translation.

On the way home that night, as we drove along the beach, I saw a tall, slender girl with her shirt off, flaring her large fake tits in all directions, occasionally kneading them and trying to flag down someone to take her home. From where I sat she looked pretty good. In some strange fit of horniness I decided to ask the driver to let me out of the car. The drunk side of my brain was in control and it was ready to give in and shell out the money for four hours of unbridled, unsafe sex. It was a magnet planted in the silicone tits of these topless women of the night that made me want to risk the possibility of catching AIDS. As the car came to a halt and the seabirds squawked high in the night sky I asked my tour guide if it was common for street hookers to stand on the corners topless. He said, "No, only the men do it. Get close enough and you'll realize there are only transvestites working the streets, that's why everyone goes to the clubs."

Not everyone. Later that night the fellow I was sharing my hotel room with came in with an ear-to-ear smile. He told me he'd paid a street hooker to give him a blowjob on the beach and it was, without a doubt, the best blowjob he'd ever had. I didn't have the heart to break the bad news to him. At least not without an audience. I waited until all 13 of us were gathered on the beach the next morning, drinking beers and ogling women before telling him the truth about his experience.

He went green in the gills, threw his beer down and walked off. That was the last time any of us saw him. He took a cab to the airport and took the next flight Stateside.

 ## Female Ejaculation: A Complete Guide

TEAMTUSHY.COM/SEYMOREBUTTS.COM/PUREPLAYMEDIA.COM •
DIR: SEYMORE BUTTS • RATING: 10

At the porn convention in Las Vegas I asked the director, Seymore Butts, if it were normal for a girl to not squirt on the first attempt. He told me all girls react differently and some positions work better for different women. Still, I face two problems in allowing my girl to achieve a soaking-wet ejaculation. First, it takes time to get your girl ready to squirt; it requires a lot of oral and digital stimulation. Expect to put in 30 minutes of finger-banging before seeing results. I've been going to the gym a lot lately trying to strengthen my fingers because without stamina it's damn near impossible. Couple that with the fact that after 20 minutes of eating box lunch and playing with her both me and my girl are ready to have sex. I don't think either of us has the self-control to wait it out.

The other issue I face is my nail-biting. It is beyond obsessive. I barely notice I'm even doing it anymore. I'm actually typing this with one hand as I gnaw away on my left hand's thumb. All my fingers are fucked, gnarled, unsightly. My lady refuses to let me put my fingers in her parts anymore because she says the rough edges of my nails irritate her innards. My fingers haven't been inside her in years. I almost forget how awesome it is to make finger puppets inside her.

I made a New Year's resolution to stop biting my nails, which hasn't been very effective. I'm biting them less but I haven't stopped entirely. Then again it's only March. Rome didn't burn in a day and I'm not one of those people who expect instant results. I'm a work in progress and eventually I'll stop eating my cuticles but in the meantime I'm depriving myself of squirting practice and there's no one I can blame but myself.

My girl wants to be able to do it nearly as much as I want her to. I don't think she realizes how often she's going to have to wash our sheets. I don't know how to do laundry and I'm too old to learn. I've always been of the opinion that if you don't bother to learn how to do something, then no one will ever expect you to do it. That's how I've avoided doing laundry for 31 years.

Blankets should be made of sponge, to absorb floods, anyway, don't you think? Or perhaps a more comfortable, less grippy rubber sheet.

You know what's fucked up? When I saw Seymore Butts I thought, "I'd let him have a go at making my girl squirt," and I didn't look at it as another man touching my woman. I saw it more like a doctor. Is that weird?

M.I.L.F. Money

SKINTIGHTPICTURES.COM • DIR: CRAM & GRIP JOHNSON • RATING: 7

I'm writing this review on a plane bound for Tampa, Florida. I'm sure you could give two shits and in most cases I wouldn't ask you to but for now bear with me. Minutes ago I was writing the review for

Ass Obsessed, typing about my arms being up to the elbows in the asses of two women, when out of the corner of my eye a movement caught my attention. It was nothing more than eyelids tensing to squint but I caught it. I shot a look back over my shoulder. It was a woman, mid-30s. I could tell she was a mother by the way the skin on her face hung. And by the child sleeping in her lap. She was reading what I was typing. Now, I'm not certain, as I use a radically small typeface to try and strengthen my worsening eyes, but I was pretty sure. At first I was somewhat embarrassed by the filthy words she'd seen, but that emotion was fleeting, and I quickly enlarged my type-face to something a bit easier for her to read, and I began to write just for her: "Have you read everything I've been typing? I wonder. Do you think I'm insane? Do you think I am handsome and dashing? What are you thinking? Are you laughing inside? Have you been fantasizing about having my arm up your ass? I'm sure I could fit my entire head in your vagina. Would you like that? Is that your husband beside you? What say you and I meet in the restroom in five minutes? You go first. I need to get the lube and the gloves out of my backpack. While you're waiting, wipe your ass down with a wet cloth and try not to think about your children or husband. It'll tense up your ass. I need you to relax and think about daisies and spring days. If this arm is

going to get in deep you're going to have to take it easy. You seem like a dirty little woman. Probably not the first arm you've had up inside you, huh? Maybe you're just the type of girl I've been looking for, the type that will take my arm right up to the shoulder. How does that sound? Yes, yes. I hope that little monster in your lap doesn't cry when it's awoken, I'd hate to let anything delay our rendezvous. Do you have chloroform? If not, let me know. I have some. We can use it to make sure he doesn't wake up. Be careful not to use too much, it's quite potent."

With that, I snapped my head back in her direction. We locked eyes. She looked at me in horror, clutching her child close to her bosom. I smiled the devil's smile and she began to cry.

Real Female Masturbation 15

DIR: RANDY WEST • RANDY WEST PRODUCTIONS • RATING: 5

I don't bring porno mags with me anymore when I travel. I bring digi-tapes. As of recently I've been filming my girlfriend playing with herself and her girlfriends quite a bit, so instead of wasting my time trying to get it up to still imagery, I just take out my handheld digi-cam and sort it out like that. My girlfriend is much hotter than any of the girls in this video and much dirtier. These girls barely slip one finger in, and if they do, it's for two seconds. What am I supposed to do with that? Pause it? Maybe play it on super-slow-mo? Am I 12 again? Am I supposed to be able to nut in eight seconds? Grow up. What's great is my girlfriend is really into being filmed. Some nights, I'll be dead asleep, and she'll wake me up. "Hey, I was going to play with myself, do you want to record it?" She's considerate like that. So I've got like 15 tapes that I cart around with me wherever I go. I just flew to Tokyo last week and that shit is like 13 hours from LAX and despite snorting a bunch of Xanax, popping two reds and three blues, there was still a good hour where I didn't know what to do with

myself and I sure as fuck wasn't about to watch *Minority Report*. Does Tom Cruise even read the scripts he takes anymore? Redo *Cocktail*, already. That shit was awesome. Yeah, so this fat-faced two-year-old bitch wouldn't stop crying and its parents were looking at it like, "What the fuck? Is it broken?" So I reached into the overhead and grabbed my video camera and my electric shaver and headed to the bathroom. People were probably bugging, wondering what the fuck I was doing. Good thing I didn't grab my ninja mask, they would have thought I was hijacking the plane. I bet they thought I was a film student. Filming oneself shaving in an airplane shitter seems like an artsy, film-school kind of thing to do. I hate film-school kids. They think they're so smart, all false bravado and ungrounded ego. Next thing they're working as a grip on *The Bernie Mac Show*.

I'm really into having a clean-shaven ball sac when I toss off; I'm on some porn shit. I think I read somewhere that it visually adds two inches to your pecker. So I prop my camera on the sink and open the LCD screen to watch my girl slide the purple dildo inside her (she really likes the purple one) and I plug in my razor and start cutting. My razor is kind of shitty. It's more of a beard trimmer but I can't grow a beard, so it's strictly for my nuts, but it's dangerous. If I don't take my time, sometimes it catches skin and slices me open, which doesn't hurt as much as it looks unsettling. As I'm thinking, "I hope I don't cut myself again, I hope I don't cut myself," we hit a patch of turbulence and my cock skin gets snagged and torn. Blood everywhere. I wanted to scream but it was the part of the tape where she winks at me and the pills took most of the bite off the wound, so I was like, "Fuck it. Let it bleed." I start kneading my shaft, using the blood as a kind of lube, and then I caught myself in the mirror, hand and dick covered in blood with homemade porn playing and a big booger that someone wiped in the middle of the mirror, with a toilet-paper-clogged toilet in the background, and I thought, "I wish I had another video camera, this would make a great bit." Does that make me an artfag?

Private Tropical 18: Puerto Rican Affairs

PRIVATE.COM • DIR: ALESSANDRO DEL MAR • RATING: 6

There is a book by Hunter S. Thompson called *The Curse of Lono* where he goes to Hawaii to cover a foot race with good friend Ralph Steadham, Steadham's wife and their child at the height of monsoon season. Needless to say, high jinks ensue, the rain sets in and before long they are waist deep in water in their rented living room, fighting to stay alive. I haven't thought about that book in many years and the only reason it crossed my mind on the flight to Puerto Rico was that we were scheduled to arrive in San Juan at the very same time as Hurricane Emily. I was already making funeral arrangements before I left for Newark airport. Do you think it was any kind of sign that the in-flight movie was *The Perfect Storm*, where the New England fishing boat is destroyed in the biggest hurricane in Northeastern history? I've never had much desire to go to Puerto Rico. Truthfully, I've never had much desire to go anywhere. I'm just

as content in my small town of Sayreville, New Jersey, as I am in Tokyo or Denmark. I suppose I'm simple in that way. Of all the places on the globe my finger could have stopped on, Puerto Rico would probably be the last I'd hope for. Perhaps it's because New York is overrun with Puerto Ricans and if I wanted to feel the warmth of their customs and culture I need only hop a train and head to the Bronx; a three-hour flight seems excessive, especially when it could end up costing me my life. I could have stayed home, rented *Carlito's Way*, instead I'm risking life and limb, and for what? I'm not about to win a Pulitzer. Stewardess. Two more. Do I want it in the can? No, I'll drink it right here.

Turned out all my fears were for naught; Emily was actually more afraid of me than I was of her. She pissed down rain for the first 24 hours on the island and I simply ignored her. The next day we sized each other up on the beach of San Juan, me covered in suntan lotion, her trying to run me off the beach with a weak display of lightning and thunder. I laughed in her stupid hurricane face and ordered another mai tai. I told her I was on vacation and that she could kiss my grits because I wasn't going anywhere. It was going to take an army of hurricanes to send me packing and with that I took a rather large gulp of my drink, which Emily instantly replaced with rain. After a minute or so my glass was completely filled with water. I raised my glass to the sky and yelled, "Fill my glass a hundred times! I don't care. I'm not leaving," then I dumped the glass over my head and laughed in her stupid face again. With that display she got the point and left, heading due west and laying waste to major parts of Cancún, where I assume she faced no opposition from the likes of me. It didn't rain again the rest of my stay. Granted, the weatherman on the television in his Hawaiian shirt and all-too-thick mustache warned of approaching storm fronts but I paid them no mind. Puerto Rican storms know better than to mess with me.

Sexy Luscious Liquids

DIGITALPLAYGROUND.COM • DIR: LARRY UNGER • RATING: 8

I'm on a plane from Seattle to Los Angeles and I've been drinking for 12 hours already. The stewardess comes by with the drink cart. I order three vodka and cranberries, easy on the cran. I've been on a health kick of late, despite the heavy drug and alcohol use, that's why I'm on sissy drinks.

A mid-30s Japanese student sits to my right. He orders a soda but watches inquisitively as I pour and slam each of my drinks in less than a minute.

"What that?" he asks in his broken English, pointing to my vodka mix. His question throws me off.

"It's vodka and cranberry juice," I tell him matter-of-factly.

"What does it do?" he asks. I let out a little laugh. I was unsure if he was being serious or not. I waited for him to flinch but he didn't. Now there I was, a drunk at 30,000 feet with a virgin drinker by my side. What to do? What to do?

"It's a health drink," I tell him. "You mix the two together and swallow it down in one gulp. It's really good for you." He nodded, taking it all in. I pointed to his soft drink. "Soda is bad for you. That shit will kill you. You shouldn't be drinking that garbage." He kept on nodding. The next time the drink cart came by he ordered three vodka and cranberries and, like I instructed, swallowed the first one down in one fell swoop. He made an awful face of disgust. I wanted to laugh but restrained myself.

"No good," he said.

I explained, "Nothing good for you ever is." The reasoning made sense to him and he proceeded to pound his other two drinks. I watched as he picked up his physics textbook and tried to read.

It looked as if he was driving the book like an automobile, fighting to hold it in an upright position. Three drinks and he was wasted. Once again the drink cart came by. I got myself three more drinks and bought three more for the drunken Chinaman. I also handed him a Xanax and told him it was a vitamin.

By the time we landed he couldn't walk. Making my way out of the baggage area I watched as three Japanese businessmen in suits greeted him, then quickly began yelling at him for being drunk. Sometimes I wish my eyes were cameras.

Bangin in Da Hood Vol. 5

WWW.LEGENDDIRECT.COM • DIR: MARK WOOD • RATING: 4

Have you ever seen that movie *Boyz n the Hood*? It's all about the Bloods and Crips in South Central. That whole movie was filmed in the neighborhood I used to live in. If you watch the film closely you can see my little green ghetto house with a white porch.

The block was all Crips and I was woken up on a daily basis by 9 mm alarm clocks at 6 a.m. One morning, walking out to my car with my laundry basket, I caught hard glares from some of the thugs on my block. I asked them, "What's your problem?" Not in a threatening way, more like a friend would out of concern.

I had no problem with anyone on my block (my roommates were

scared shitless) because I'd laid my cards on the table the day I'd moved in. First I saw some of the younger kids on skateboards and in a sign of peace I offered them free skateboard products that I had in my car. Secondly, as a sign of strength, I went in my house, took off my shirt, loaded up my 9 mm, put on my shoulder holster, then loaded up a shotgun and a .357, which I stuck in my belt. I grabbed a 12-pack of beer and some cigarettes and sat on my front steps, to let everyone know that I was equipped and prepared to blow anyone's head off who tried to threaten me or my home.

There I sat for three hours, drinking and smoking, having a Mexican standoff with no one at all until word spread: "The crazy white boys (as they referred to us, since we were the only whites for a good 30 blocks) are not to be fucked with." And we never were.

Except that one morning carrying my laundry. I'd forgotten I was wearing a red shirt, the color of the rival gang, the Bloods. They asked me, tugging on their shirts, "What's up with the shirt?" At first I didn't understand, then I made the connection. And I laughed. I looked at the leader and said, "You know I don't give a fuck about your gang shit. And you know the only color I ever wear is black. So why are you getting bent out of shape? You see me with my laundry. This red shirt is the only clean shirt I have." They shrugged it off, half saying, "You better be telling the truth," half "Oh. Sorry. My bad."

That night, two people were killed in a drive-by around the corner as they waited to order hamburgers.

Russian Bra Busters

SCORELAND.COM • DIR: JOHN GRAHAM • RATING: 7

I never really grasped what they meant when doctors said people who lose a limb often feel a pain where their arm or leg once was. It didn't make any sense to me. How is that possible? I always thought it was some sort of cry for attention, like, "Ouch, it hurts

where my arm was," or "Ow! I've got a charley horse in my invisible leg." It's like, "Hey, pal. I may wear glasses but I'm not fucking blind. I can see you have no arm. You reinforced the fact by shaking my hand with your left hand like some kind of palsy victim. You don't need to whine about your 'phantom pain.' I get it. You don't have an arm. You made your point." I'm dead broke. I don't have a pot to piss in. I used to have a little bit of money but I drank it all away. You don't hear me crying that I have a phantom pain in my wallet where my money once was.

That was my attitude before, but that has all changed since I spent four days in Costa Rica without my cell phone. Now I understand what those poor people go through. Everything makes sense. I can relate to their "phantom pain." It was as if every five minutes I'd feel the vibration of my phone going off in my front left pocket but there was nothing there. My phone was back in America because I don't get service in third-world countries. And yet somehow I felt it, as if I too had lost a part of me. Repeatedly I reached for my phone, swearing it was buzzing. Once I even had a panic attack feeling the "phantom phone" go off and then not being able to locate it. I turned over couch cushions and mattresses trying to find the source of my "pain." I wonder if that happens to people without legs or arms. Do they feel the "phantom pain," then realize their arm isn't where it's supposed to be, freak out and start tearing the house apart like, "Where the hell is my arm? What the hell did I do with that thing?" And you know their wives always ask, "Well, where did you see it last?" Wives are stupid like that sometimes. If I knew where I left it last it wouldn't be lost. I guess that's two ways I can relate to the dismembered. Despite this wave of self-realization and my newfound respect for the no-handed I can't help but feel a little bad for all those times I made fun of the armless by trying to give them invisible high fives or the legless by asking them if they wanted to play kickball. Now that I understand their pain I want to take it all back. Maybe not all of it. But some of it. I'd like to take some of the mean things I've said back but therein lies the problem. I have said some pretty funny things about the limb-lacking and I'm not talking Def Leppard or

"How do you get a one-armed Polack out of tree?" jokes. I'm talking real genius comedy. It seems impossible for me to sift through and decide which jokes I want to retract and which I don't. See, this is why I hate growing as a person. It's way too complicated.

Hey, Grandma Is a Whore 8

METROPOLIS ENTERTAINMENT • DIR: ANDRE MADNESS • RATING: 1

I plan to kill myself at 55 so I don't end up looking like a withered Mr. Burns. The thought of becoming a human paperweight gets me so depressed that I start biting my lip until it bleeds and looking for something sharp. Shouting in people's faces without concern is probably the only appealing thing to being elderly. That and pissing my pants whenever I feel like it, of course, but the rest of it is all so brutal. I wake up these days to cold floors and an empty bed and wish God had taken me in my sleep. How is that lovely outlook on life going to change in 60 years, especially when my mind officially shuts off and I can't remember my name? The only difference between being old and being dead is more people come to visit you in the cemetery, if only to make sure you are dead.

Last year, while my partner and I were directing a Tanqueray commercial with Doug E. Fresh and Biz Markie, I met an elderly woman who made me realize there is one other privilege to being at death's door: farting. This little old thing screamed at everyone. From the makeup girl to the guy holding the boom mic to my partner and me. She was cranky, smelled of mothballs and, when her mouth opened, 80-year-old stale air steamed out with vulgarities that would make pirates blush. I alone loved her. And 100 times more so when she began farting at levels so high and long it was the only thing audible on the sound feed. People looked around the room to figure out who did it but it seemed quite obvious. The little old lady was paying it no mind. I'm not even sure she knew. I called for a 10-minute break, thinking perhaps she had to take a shit. Instead, she walked down the hall for a smoke, blasting loud gaseous bombs as she limped along. Remember how booming and unconvincing the lengthy sounds of a whoopee cushion were? Her farts were more unbelievable. I tried to capture them with a handheld camera but they were like vampire farts and didn't show up on film. All I know is she must have been having the greatest laugh at our expense. It was like teaching a class of juvenile delinquents. Every command we made would be punctuated with a blast from her ass. It almost made me reconsider not jumping off a cliff for my family to collect my life insurance. Almost.

Interviewing Jenna
PEACHDVD.COM • DIR: JIM MONROE • RATING: 4

My small little town is home to no less than six strip bars, ranging from total shite to the ultimate (butt-naked and bring your own beer). Recently one beloved staple, On the Rocks, the only place I've ever come across that seemed to exclusively hire C-sectioned strippers, was taken over by new management. The name changed to Sweethearts and all the scarred mommies were sent packing, replaced by younger, less-weathered slabs of flesh; but the place remains a dive. The pool cues are cracked, the beer tastes like soap, the bathroom has no door and the girls are at that transitional point in their lives when baby fat becomes lady fat; I love the place if for nothing more than sheer comedic value.

Last week there was a torrential downpour and flood warnings, so we took refuge in Sweethearts. Not halfway through my first beer and all the power went out. No lights, no music, no dancing. I tried singing but the other patrons asked me to stop. Without missing a beat, the bar owner propped open the front door, went outside, pulled his car around and beamed his headlights into the club. Then there was light. Another patron tried the same trick with his radio; he insisted, "My shit really bumps." It didn't. Barely audible, his distorted treble was washed out by tired old men exhaling their cigarettes, hoping to see a glimpse of a fresh piece of ass before heading home to the women they hated. The dancer, fed up, waddled over to us and struck up a conversation. "So. Haven't seen youse guys in here before. From around here?" I took a deep drag of my smoke, looked her up and down then blew it in her pudgy face and said, "Listen, honey. I didn't come here to talk to you. I've got a woman at home who's been begging me to talk to her for three years. So either start dancing or get me another beer."

With that her thighs started to sway to the sweet sound of awkward silence. I gave her a dollar and off she went. When I got home I found my lady watching *Interviewing Jenna*. "Have you watched this?" Before I could answer, she saved me the trouble. "It doesn't make sense. There's no fucking, just a tour through Jenna's house and some naked girls. They don't even touch their pussies. It's just a bunch of talking. Who the hell wants that?"

North Pole #30

PETERNORTH.COM • DIR: PETER NORTH • RATING: 7

There was like two weeks there when I was all about porn girl Holly Halston. Just looking at her gave me a hard-on. I was so obsessive that I scanned in *North Pole #30*'s box cover, printed it out on a color laser printer, glued and mounted it to sturdy cardboard and cut her naked image out and pinned it to my left sleeve. I took her everywhere: to the bank, to the supermarket, to the bar, to the bathroom. (I covered her eyes. Sometimes I had to cover her nose, too.) We were inseparable. When I was feeling down I'd look over and she'd cheer me up, when I was bored she'd strike up a conversation, when I was pissed at my Mac for freezing up on me in the middle of deadline she'd kiss my neck and tell me everything was going to be fine. I was falling for her and I think she knew it. But we were from different worlds and we could never be. She tried to spare my feelings by sending me an e-mail with an interview that revealed that not only was she married but had children and worse yet, she only fucked her husband. On film. At home. Or otherwise. Basically, breaking my heart and telling me whatever I was feeling was never to be recipro- cated. I took her picture off my arm and put it in my desk drawer. For days I refused to look at it. Then it began to hurt. I couldn't get her out of my head, I needed to see her, to talk to her, to let her know that I understood and that what we had was special and if it meant being only friends then I could live with that so long as it meant I'd have her in my life. It was around 1:30 p.m. when I put *North Pole #30* in the disc player. I remember because my breath smelled of egg salad and my hands were clean and smelling like blueberries and my hands only get washed with blueberry soap after I get back from lunch. Try as I did to have some private time with Holly, her husband kept get- ting in the way, sticking his dick in the frame and ultimately in Holly's mouth. I wanted to yell, "Do you mind?" but it was his wife, I had no place. Each passing thrust infuriated me more, I was getting worked into a jealous rage. Then I began to question myself, wondering what he had that I didn't have, aside from Holly. Sure, he was better-looking and in better shape but, uh, I bet I own more CDs than him.

I felt stupid and little. I wanted to find a flaw of any sorts to try and even the playing field but there were none. Just as I was ready to con- cede defeat I saw his hand and I reeled in ecstasy. I don't know if it's just this particular DVD or if he's gotten it fixed since, but on Holly's husband's right hand there is a goiter the size of a baseball. It's dis- gusting and unsightly and I loved it. I couldn't look away from it. It was as if his hand had been burnt in some awful fire and the burns swelled up into foul, bulbous pus-filled mounds and the entire area was discolored from a skin graft. It was then that I disrobed and stood in front of my full-length mirror naked, looking over my fat, bloated body and knowing I still had a chance.

Nothing to Hide 3: Justine's Daughter

CALVISTAPICTURES.COM • DIR: JAMES AVALON • RATING: 6

I received this letter in the mail recently:
"I had a dream about you. You killed my mother. You took too much crystal meth and broke her neck. My dad and I walked in right as her eyes were bugging and she was clawing at your forearm. You were so cracked up, you were sweating and laughing and saying she asked for it and she wanted it. My dad became enraged when you finally dropped her limp body on the floor. I went over to look at her and was so sad I couldn't feel anything. I kept trying to pick up her arm that was usually so light because she's petite but it felt like a ton of bricks. I couldn't cry because I didn't and couldn't believe she was dead. My dad punched you so hard he broke your jaw with his first blow. You were still laughing. You had this crooked smile the whole time. So he punched you again and your head snapped back and hit the wall and you passed out. Then he dragged you outside where he ground your face into the pavement until he got to the bone. The whole time he didn't say a word. I passed him a shotgun and we agreed to shoot you in your shin so when you ran it'd exaggerate the futility of it all. Then I woke up to my clock radio and the sound of Led Zeppelin playing something horrid."

It wasn't signed. I could tell it was a female who wrote it, I assumed one a bit older from the lack of bubbly or loose curves in the script. Yet it was completely unfamiliar—strange, given that I tend to remember sophisticated penmanship. So I was confused and intrigued. Was it some kind of morbid love note or should I consider it a threat or was it just a friendly "Hey, had a dream you killed my mom" note?

Nearly a week has passed since the letter found me; since then I've had my fingers broken in a door, sprained my ankle in a hole and vomited blood from too much drinking. Are my streak of bad luck and the note somehow connected? Well, don't spend too much time thinking about it. I'm not. What if I hadn't mentioned those freak accidents and instead said, "In the past week I've eaten steak five times, chicken once and had four cases of Guinness and three gallons of ice cream with fudge," you'd probably think to yourself, "My! Sounds like Chris is putting on weight again."

Best of Wendi Knight

CALVISTAPICTURES.COM • DIR: VARIOUS • RATING: 9

The first time I laid eyes on Wendi Knight she was having sex with three men, her mouth was full and she had no clue I even existed. That was the best of Wendi Knight. This is a collection of her tamer scenes but you still have to appreciate her gorgeous cosmetically altered frame. She has this Carmen Electra look that I can't get over. I became so infatuated with Wendi that I set up an interview/date with her, if only to smell her hair and get to know her a little better. Although I didn't get to sleep with her or even get a handjob, I felt like it was a very successful first date. She really opened up to me on many levels, discussing how she married the first guy she ever slept with when she was 19, and that she was homeschooled and came from a very strict Southern Baptist family and that her husband at the time had suggested she get into porn.

When porn girls tell me that I'm always taken aback. What kind of prick tries to sell his wife off to the porn industry for adoption? I guess he didn't care because her first scene was with two guys, a double penetration that lasted two hours for a Seymore Butts video called *Behind the Sphinc Door*. I found it shocking that she'd only been with one man all her life and then suddenly had a dick in both her front and backside. But I didn't judge her, I wanted her to know I was a comforting shoulder for her to nuzzle up to and tell all her dirty secrets. If she wanted to cry, I was there for her, to hold her and tell her everything was going to be okay, and if by chance she looked into my sad brown eyes and saw my loving tenderness and felt compelled to kiss me then that was fine too. Whatever you need, Wendi, I'm here for you. But she hid her feelings for me. She changed the subject to something a bit more lighthearted, saying she wouldn't mind having her pussy eaten out by a dog. Not for pleasure but as a funny performance for friends. "It'd be funny, I think, to put peanut butter on my pussy in front of all my friends and let a dog lick it off," she said. "I'm sure it would feel good but it'd also be hysterical, don't you think?" Yes, I thought so, but I didn't answer. I was lost in her eyes, searching for some deeper meaning to her words.

Feeding Frenzy 2

EVILANGEL.COM • DIR: JULES JORDAN • RATING: 2

For as deranged as some might think I am, I consider myself rather tame in terms of sexual deviance. I don't like pooping on girls, I'm not into girls pissing in my mouth and I find bondage and the whole S&M thing very uninteresting. Make no mistake, I am no missionary-position, steak-and-potatoes animal. I have my carnal vices but like I said, there will always be someone more perverse than me out there. A friend was recently telling me about one of her ex-boyfriends and the one time she was sucking him off and didn't feel like swallowing or getting nut in her hair. I know it sounds lazy on her part, but these things happen. So in the heat of the moment he offers to cum in his own cupped palm. I stopped her, mid-story, and told her I'd done that many times, mostly when a passenger in a car, with my girl driving. It's very unsafe for her to try and duck down and catch my nut in her mouth. The one time she tried we almost went off the rode and hit a tree. So what I do is cum in my hand, it's much cleaner then trying to get on my knees and stick my prick out the window and shoot on a car behind us. But this story was not one of cleanliness or compassion. Instead, her ex-boyfriend shot in his hand and pro-

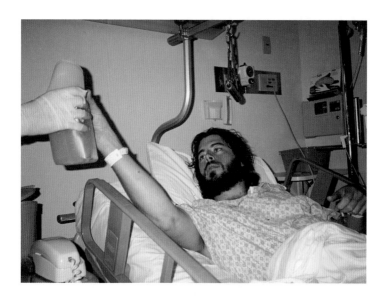

ceeded to lap it up himself. Slurping up every last drop and loving every bit of it. Now I'm not one to judge but—wait. That's not true. I love to pass judgment and that story sickens me. I don't know if it's the taboo of a man ever tasting his own spew or the fact that the dictionary defines a man who likes the taste of man as a homosexual but her story made me sick to my stomach. I've had girlfriends who have asked me to do a snowball (when you cum in a girl's mouth and she in turn spits it in your mouth) and they quickly became ex-girlfriends. To me it's a power thing. It is not intended for a man's lips (unless those lips are gay), had it been, then man would be able to shoot it into their own mouth. The same goes for red wings—eating a girl out on her period. The point is for the man to take it all in, not to slide up and rub blood all over the girl's face. My girlfriend knows to not even try and kiss me on the lips after oral sex. If she plans on getting any lip service she knows to go and brush her teeth. The girl has since broken up with the guy. I prodded her to find out if it was anyone I knew but she assured me I didn't. I'm glad. I'd hate to find out something like that about one of my friends. I could never look him in the eyes again and take him serious, I'd always be thinking, "That guy probably wants to drink my piss right now. Look at how he's looking at me! He wants my piss." It would be so embedded in my head that I'd most likely get drunk and accuse him of it. There are some things you can apologize for but it'd be hard to explain away an outburst like that at a friendly dinner party.

Casting 19
PRIVATE.COM • DIR: PIERRE WOODMAN • RATING: 5

R ecently I was asked to do a story on the reality dating show craze that has been taking America by storm. Not exactly sure what they wanted, I began applying to be on the television shows, albeit halfheartedly. I am not one for being on television. I don't feel comfortable in front of the camera and I don't like being recognized in public. I was on TV once for all of two minutes and for nearly six months afterwards I couldn't leave my house without someone asking me to puke for them. When filling out the applications I'd make up despicable lies that I was certain would keep me from getting any callbacks, things like I've spent years in prison, I'm a heavy user of acid and PCP, I like to bite girls' faces, I like to be whipped by black women (well, that one isn't a lie). The list went on and on. I also had a head shot taken to seem semiprofessional, sporting a Hitler mustache and a silly, menacing scowl. I felt certain that none of the dozen or so shows would call me back and I was right. Except for one, a new show, with even less scruples than any of the other bottom-feeding programs. As I took down the address and time for my casting interview I started to panic. I did not want to be on television. Shit. Shit. Shit. How does one sabotage a casting call? In the name of journalism I couldn't just cancel outright, but I couldn't be myself. I'm much too charismatic; I'd somehow dazzle them with my uncontrollable charm and end up on next week's episode. Or worse. They'd love me so much that they'd ask me to be the new host. I decided I'd go into the 10 a.m. Tuesday interview drunk as a skunk, and to make sure I was ready in time I'd commence drinking Sunday night. By the time I arrived at the casting agency I was blind drunk, failing to hit any buttons in the elevator on my first seven attempts. Some kind old lady asked where I was going and what floor I needed. I told her to mind her own ass and then asked, "Do I smell like piss?" She left me alone to figure out the buttons on my own and took the stairs. The one thing I neglected to consider when opting to get shit-house drunk was the old Hollywood casting couch. Stories be told that Hollywood big shots like to get attractive people to audition in hopes of getting in their pants. And there I was, sexy as they come and fully susceptible to any forward advances, and the broad who interviewed me knew it. She was nearly 50 and I imagine her pussy had about 10 years of built-up cobwebs and dust. You could hang your coat on her nose and clean up an oil spill with her fried, dyed, frizzy hair; the bags under her eyes were big enough to hold a sandwich. To look at her was to induce vomit, so I tried to count squares on the carpet but never could remember what number I was on and which number came after eight. "Why don't you take off your coat and make yourself comfortable?" she said. I am comfortable, I thought, yet there I was, taking off my jacket. Then a plane flew by the window in the distance. A big, silver one. I'd like to own a plane. As I tried to count the windows on the jet I realized she was beside me. "Aren't you hot? Let's unbutton that shirt of yours," she said, already working on the third button. I think her hands were made of kryptonite because I was unable to move, frozen, unsure if I was still breathing or if I'd shit myself. After undoing my pants, she went over to her filing cabinet and pulled out a strap-on dildo and—hey, there's another airplane! A gold one this time.

Rave Sexxx

EXTREMEASSOCIATES.COM • DIR: TOM BYRON • RATING: 9

I always hated ravers. The mere mention of the word *rave* gets me to thinking about overaged fashion victims in oversize pants sucking on pacifiers and waving glowsticks in the mid-90s. And that gag-inducing music was just awful: techno, trance, electronica, whatever people call that garbage that Internet nerds created using Pro Tools on their Macs. It's not music. It's programming.

My hatred for ravers led me to my most lucrative college job. Thirteen years ago Ecstasy was $25 a hit in New York City and it looked like many over-the-counter diet pills at the pharmacy my buddy worked at; diet pills that cost $4 for a bottle of 100. You can see where I'm going with this, can't you? One of those bottles of "diet Ecstasy" over a few hours would earn me $2,500. That was my main source of income for years: paying 20 bucks to get into a party, selling 50 to 100 fake hits and then leaving an hour later. Sometimes I'd find myself at Grateful Dead concert parking lots doing the same,

since I despise hippies nearly as much as I hate ravers. I remember one time at a Dead show I traded 20 "diet Ecstasy" for a huge ball of opium and got twisted out of my mind. As I made my way through the parking lot selling my pills, I started to forget where I was. Then some guy who I sold shit to grabbed my shoulder and spun me around. "What the fuck?" I yelled as I pulled a knife from my back pocket. I don't like being touched and I swear to you, in my drugged state I was ready to slice his throat. "You sold me beat shit, man. I want my money back," he yelled. The anger washed off my face and a big smile took its place. I put away my knife. "No, man," I said. I never say "man" unless I'm talking to a hippie and want to get that Cheech and Chong effect in my voice. "You got it all wrong, man. Look at me. I'm wasted." He took a good hard look at me and true enough I was wasted—just from the opium not the diet pills. I reached in my pocket, pulled out another "diet Ecstasy," handed it to him and said, "Here, man. No hard feelings." He thanked me, apologized, popped the pill and ran off to see the band "jam out."

That's why I think I like hippies a little more than ravers, they just seem a little stupider.

Millionaire

PRIVATE.COM • DIR: ALESSANDRO DEL MAR • RATING: 7

At the height of my pill addiction and alcohol abuse I was able to persuade my physician to prescribe me Viagra for my performance problem that stemmed from my lack of consciousness. It's difficult for anyone to fuck with a wet noodle, harder yet when your brain shut off three hours prior. Since pills were able to provide me everything else I needed in my life like sleep, energy, serenity, I figured I might as well get some that did the fucking for me as well. But it didn't help at all. The blue pill might help an 80-year-old geezer who hasn't felt a hard-on since he stormed Omaha Beach but it can't do shit against a kid of 25 years with a case of beer, a fifth of whiskey, a dozen or so Vicodin and a few Valiums in the tank. I don't think my heart rate even sped up, if I had a pulse at all at that point. And Viagra is fucking expensive. I could have thrown a pill party and gotten everyone wasted for what I spent on two bottles of Viagra. I think they worked out to be in the neighborhood of $30 a pill and that's with medical insurance. Had it done anything in the way of stimulating me it would have been well worth it but I was so far gone I could've started a fire with $100 bills and saved myself a trip to the pharmacy.

The funny thing was that although they had no real effect on me I continued to refill my prescription week after week. I figured that eventually, if taken in the proper dosage, they were bound to work. And I was right. Granted they never seemed to kick in while in the company of a girl. Generally what would happen was I'd take four or five of the little fuckers while completely blacked out, then the next morning I'd wake up alone in some state of undress usually missing my wallet, pants, TV, stereo or all of the above with a massive stiff one between my legs. It made it impossible to get a pair of jeans on. I'd try bending it, folding it, and tucking it any which way with no luck. I'd call in to my boss, explain that I wasn't feeling well and that I'd be in as soon as possible. The next several hours were spent in a 10-frame bowling match between me and my cock. It'd set them up, I'd rub one out and knock them down and instantly my dick would jump back to attention like one of those inflatable punching bags. After throwing my shoulder out and wearing my foreskin and palms raw I was forced to yell at the erection like a dog: "If you don't lay down I'm going to kick your ass until you bleed." Still the prick stood tall, mocking me. I wanted so much to punch that son of a bitch with all my might but I refused to let him get the better of me. So I found a pair of sweatpants and pulled them up over my raging hard-on and that's how I went into work. "You think I won't walk around with a boner all day," I'd tell him, "you got another thing coming."

Hot Rats

SMASHPICTURES.COM • DIR: NARCIS BOSCH • RATING: 9

I just burnt the head of my penis by dunking it into my girl's boiling hot cup of coffee. Why on earth would I stick my dick into hot coffee? The answer is simple; I thought it was only lukewarm. She came into my office to see how I was doing, mentioning her coffee didn't taste right. I told her I could remedy that by dipping my cock in it. In a strange game of chicken she brought the mug beside my desk and held it level with my pants. "Think I won't do it?" I asked. She shot me an unwavering poker face, pushing the mug further in my direction. I stood up, unzipped and took her up on the dare. It all happened in slow motion; I dipped, she screamed "NO," I yelled out in pain, she pulled the cup away and I fell to my knees nursing my burnt bell-end. I had been drinking coffee all morning and just assumed that her mug was full of tepid, four-hour-old coffee. She neglected to mention she'd just brewed a fresh pot and it was piping hot. My eyes welled up with tears and she felt awful, on one hand, but wasn't entirely certain if I was hurt or just trying to trick her into giving me a blowjob as I am prone to do on a semi-regular basis with lies such as "Help! Help! I got my dick stuck in the trash compacter!" or "Ow! I slammed my dick in the car door again!" So she stood there watching me writhe in pain, unsure of her next course of action. "This better not be a trick," she said. "If I go down there you better be burnt for real or else I'm going to be pissed." I couldn't do much but moan so she was kind enough to assist in my speedy recovery. After a few minutes I began to laugh because that's what I do after I've successfully tricked her, or anyone for that matter. I suppose that's why I've never won a hand of cards in my life. Granted it hurt like a son of a bitch when I first put my cock into the mug but it all happened so quickly that there wasn't much real damage done and after 30 seconds or so I was fine. For my efforts I felt I deserved some kind of reward. I mean, she said I wouldn't, I did, so I won. That's how I saw it. Why shouldn't she bow before me and give praises? She saw it somewhat differently and began swearing at me, telling me she'd never touch my penis again for as long as she lived, then stormed out of the room. I shook my head, shrugged off the whole ordeal and went back to responding to an e-mail from a fan who wanted to know about my writing process. "Not much of a process," I wrote. "Like a machine I churn out the words with no real emphasis on the final product. Once finished I never read it again." I hit Send and reached for the cup of coffee she'd left behind. As if she had surveillance cameras in my office, the instant the stuff hit my lips she screamed from the other end of the house, "Hope you like the taste of your own dick because you're going to be sucking yourself off for a long time, asshole."

Private Penthouse Six-Pack

PRIVATEBIZARRE.COM • DIR: ANTONIO ADAMO • RATING: 8

I remember I was on a country kick for a while. I even considered buying a ten-gallon hat when I bought the 12-disc boxed set of Hank Williams. Have you heard of the country artist Wayne Hancock? He's brilliant. He's nothing like that Dixie Chicks pollution. The best part about Wayne "The Train" is that he once checked himself into rehab for marijuana. He told me that he felt he was getting too high and needed a break from the weed and checked himself into a drug center. For those two weeks he was completely sober and looked on that as a major accomplishment at the time.

I haven't smoked weed in 10 years. I look at it as a drug reserved for hippies and can't believe I ever was dependent on it. To smoke

weed now would cause my brain to shut down. I get very introverted from it, unable to communicate even the simplest thoughts. I become a complete retard. Back when I was at the height of my weed use, I could function on it rather well. Anything I did, I did it high. School, work, sex—all completely fried. I think I probably sounded a lot like Tommy Chong, equally as bright.

Now I'm into pills. I am able to keep my wits about me and yet have zero motor skills. The other day, going through security at the airport, I reached in my pocket to grab my cell phone and other metal objects to run through the X-ray machine, completely forgetting I had an assortment of pills in there. Sure enough all the pills fell on the floor. I tried my best to catch them but missed them all. There I was, holding up the line, searching the ground for my drugs, picking them up one by one while trying my best to act cool. One pill nearly went under a woman's shoe. On my knees I crawled over to her and grabbed it. She wore a black skirt and I saw she had on a pink G-string underneath. She was older and didn't seem to mind that I was looking up her skirt. She actually seemed amused by me. Her legs were fit and I wanted to stare at her pink knickers for a hundred years but began to worry that security was going to arrest me for the pills. Drug users are overly paranoid. Stupid drug users who allow their drugs to fall on the floor in front of airport security are just plain terrified.

Luckily for me we are at war at the moment, otherwise I'd certainly be incarcerated right now. All anyone cares about are bombs and shit. I'd like to say thank you to Iraq for allowing us to attack you without just cause, otherwise I might be in jail, somebody's bitch. Instead, Iraq, you're our bitch and I'm good and high, laughing at you for being such an innocent target.

Dead Men Don't
Wear Rubbers

NEWSENSATIONS.COM • DIR: JACE ROCKER • RATING: 4

The other day I was thinking of really retarded porn titles I'd like for someone to use. Here are a few: *A Bird in Hand Is Worth Two in the Ass, Don't Look a Gift Whore in the Mouth, How Many Times Do I Have to Say I Love You . . . Before You Let Me Fuck You in the Ass, Those Aren't Pillows, My Other Car Is Your Ass, Penny for Your Thoughts (Nickel to Rent Your Mouth), One Time in Band Camp . . . , It's Like Having Three Mouths!, Boy-Band Ass,* and *One Finger Isn't Gay.* Then I got *Dead Men Don't Wear Rubbers* and I was like, "That title sucks awesome! Why didn't I think of that?" I considered e-mailing New Sensations some of my ideas but opted not to. I have a certain artistic vision of what these films should look like and I wouldn't trust just anyone to achieve the feel that I would want from something as cleverly titled as *My Other Car Is Your Ass.* You know? I'd have to make the film myself. I'd probably try to cast only sluts with a lot of tattoos because that's an entirely untapped market. Every one of you fags

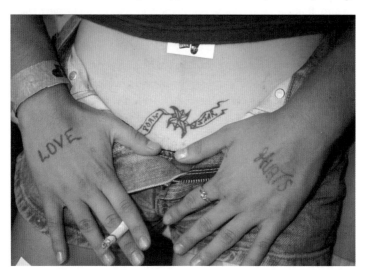

reading this book wishes you could hump a girl with a lot of tattoos, and it's understandable, because we all know that tattoos on a girl is basically a neon sign that says, I LOVE ASS SEX. Do you think I'd make a good porn director? I directed a pilot for a black dating show for BET called *Singles Match*. (I'm being serious, you jerk. Stop laughing.) Hopefully it will get picked up and you'll all be like, "Holy shit! Nieratko can direct." Or not. But BET is not porn. Porn requires a strong will. I think I'd wind up just wanting to fuck all the girls and never get any work done. It's kind of the same reason I never wanted to become a bartender. Plus, most porn directors are ugly and greasy and I'm hot as shit, so you'd have to assume that the girls would be wanting to be with me the entire time they were getting humped and not really turn in a convincing performance. If it were ever to happen I can assure you no one would wear condoms. I don't care if their penis was one big open wound with the words "Don't Do It! I Have AIDS!" tattooed above it; there would be no rubbers. They're just not aesthetically pleasing (unless they're green, then that's just funny-looking). And I don't believe in them. I've never used them and never will. I think wearing a condom is cheating, like using loaded dice, or having an ace up your sleeve. Life is supposed to be risky. There are no sure things. If you choose to roll the dice, you should have to face the consequences. Got a girl pregnant? Shouldn't have stuck your dick in her. Got crabs? Shouldn't have stuck your dick in her. Got AIDS? Shouldn't have stuck your dick in her. Fucked three girls in one day without showering and the doctor still gave you a clean bill of health? Well, shit! You're in the zone. Meet me in Atlantic City. Grab those dice and let them fly. You can't possibly lose.

Natural Bush 16

HOMEGROWNVIDEO.COM • RATING: 2

I hate hair. On men, on women, on dogs, on cats; it all disgusts me. I'm usually not that neurotic but hair just creeps me the fuck out. Like hippie chicks with hairy armpits and beavers just don't make any sense to me. Don't they know that hair traps odor? They're just making themselves smell so squalid that any hopeful lover would be forced to vomit on them.

I can recall many occasions where I've pulled a girl's pants down only to discover a tuft of hair as thick as a lion's and as matted as a Rastafarian's. I gave them the option: Leave or go to the bathroom and shave. Return bald or don't return. Those are the house rules. If you think you're getting any love from me your pussy better have fresh razor burns on it, otherwise pick up some batteries on the way home from the pub. I can't help you. From the women I've been with, they feel the same way. It's hard enough for a girl to give a blowjob without worrying about choking on a hairball. So I cut it all off. I've

got no pubic hairs, no ass hairs, no chest hairs, no stomach hairs and no armpit hairs. The only thing I don't shave are my legs because shaving your legs is gay. I have hair on top of my head but I'm sure that in a few years that'll all be gone, just not by choice.

The first time a pubic hair sprouted between my legs was just days after I saw *Dracula vs. The Werewolf*. I thought I was becoming the famous monster, and began to cry. I believed my days were numbered. Soon, the hair would spread to cover my entire body and I'd begin to go insane. I'd kill the neighbor's chickens, then the rabbits, then the dogs. Eventually I'd be forced to eat humans. I'd have to go into hiding, living in the woods, only to gaze on my family from afar, never able to eat my mother's meat loaf again. One day I'd screw up, leave a trail of blood back to my cave and the townsfolk would come for me. My own brother would call for my head, never knowing that under the mask of hair was his own kin desperately wanting to come home, to be normal again, to be loved. So I decided that day, in front of the standing mirror, at the tender age of 12, with my pants around my ankles, that I'd do all I could to prevent such a catastrophe. I'd try and stop the hair from taking over and if that didn't work I'd take my own life.

Planting Seeds

SMASHPICTURES.COM • DIR: JORDAN HEART • RATING: 8

I like the term "planting seeds" for impregnating women. I also like the term "saving the children" for when you are away from your woman for days on end and make it a point to not masturbate to allow a sperm buildup, thus saving the children to be deposited in your lady's vagina. I, of course, have never been able to "save the children" because I am a chronic masturbator, unable to go longer than 24 hours without a release. But I have "killed the children" a few times. There's no way to count how many women I've shot my load

into but I can tell you that as a safety measure against getting them pregnant, I make it a point to always punch them full force in the stomach before leaving their company. I'm not really sure if this old method works but I like to think it does because it's really a lot of fun. If it doesn't, I fear I may have a number of four-eyed, big-nosed, gap-toothed spawn running around the globe, which is a very scary thought.

Then again . . . an army of soldiers that looked like me would be kind of cool. We'd get together and plot to take over the world, forcing ourselves on women everywhere in an attempt to impregnate any and all and create an entire civilization in my likeness. Oh my God! Do you think this is how Hitler got started? Just looking in the mirror admiring what he saw and thinking, "Man, this mustache is awesome. Why doesn't everyone have a mustache like mine? Maybe I'll take over the world and make everyone get a mustache just like mine!" Maybe that's how it happened. Maybe historians have it all wrong and WWII was a result of facial-hair Fascism. Not that the cause of the war makes a bit of difference; shit, it actually makes things even more grim. To think that millions were killed over a mustache style is absolutely sickening.

I'm a fan of the Hitler mustache, though, so I'd have survived the war because it would be a nonissue to grow one. But even if I hated that mustache with every fiber of my being, I think I'd have to throw my hands up in defeat and say, "Fine. You want me to grow the damn mustache? I'll grow the damn mustache. It's not worth losing my life over a mustache." It's not like Hitler was trying to get everybody to grow Puerto Rican sideburns and gay Village People handlebar mustaches. If that was the case maybe I could see the point of resistance.

Nasty Nymphos 1

WWW.ANABOLIC.COM • DIR: BIFF MALIBUR • RATING: 6

The name of the girl on the cover is Sierra. She's not very attractive. She has a hairy crotch and a pig nose. Yet when I was 15 I saw a porno that had a preview showing Sierra in a confessional booth, telling a priest all her naughty sins, which then cut to her sucking off the priest. It turned me on a lot.

Did I ever tell you about the time the priest died in my brother's arms? He was an altar boy and at the end of the mass as he and the priest genuflected in front of the altar, the pastor froze. Everyone thought he was just praying his ass off. But after about a minute, people began to stir. They wanted to go home, already. Then he just dropped into my brother's young arms, dead as a doornail.

I was going to tell you how I joined the choir so that I could gain access to the church after hours and how I eventually did see something that I think was the ghost of the priest. Then I was going to tell you about this girl in the choir I had a crush on and how one night I jumped off the roof, landed on her back and hit her in the head with nunchucks and then proceeded to choke her with them.

But I can't be bothered. I'm in Hawaii at the moment and haven't slept in days and last night, as I made a wholehearted attempt at rest, my friend Alan, with whom I'm sharing my hotel room, brought back a 20-year-old hooker with a set of lungs like Roberta Flack and proceeded to fuck her until she was hoarse. There's actually a party going on in my room as I'm typing and someone just tried to throw the microwave into the pool, some 37 floors below us. Mind you, the pool sits about 50 yards to our left and even the best arm in baseball wouldn't be able to clear the distance. It's only a matter of time before we are kicked out.

Alan assures me he has the home address of the prostitute from last night and that we can stay with her if need be. But that's not my concern. It's the drugs that I'm worried about. They're everywhere and if the police come to my door, I'm fucked. So pardon me if I'm not in the mood to tell you the details of my little supernatural encounter. I've got some things to deal with at the moment.

Fantastic. There's a knock at the door.

Art School Sluts

VCAPICTURES.COM • DIR: EON MCKAI • RATING: 6

What do you call an artist who can't paint or draw? A photographer. That's what I studied at art school simply because I have no idea how to sharpen a pencil or which hand to hold a paintbrush with. In school I spent as much time mastering the art of critiquing others' work (i.e., bashing it) and elevating my own as I did learning technique. We'd have group reviews where everyone showed off their stuff.

Artists are a fragile, spineless lot (read: pussies), so these reviews were one big strokefest until I took the stand. One girl's photos were of her diary, mixed with photos of ex-lovers and her hand in the foreground, covered in fake blood as a result of a staged wrist-slitting. She was a meek little mousy thing with buggy eyes, at least six years my elder. I looked up and asked, "How old are you?" She said she was

26. I was 19 at the time. I shook my head in disapproval. "Threatening suicide because you broke up with your boyfriend? Give me a break. It's time for you to fucking grow up."

Her jaw hit the floor, her eyes welled up with tears and she started bawling and ran out of the room. The rest of the class was in shock. One kid tried to defend her. "What's so great about your photos?" he asked. "It's a guy with one leg hopping down the street without crutches, you asshole."

I explained: "It captures a moment, unlike your out-of-focus pictures of your *Star Wars* collection, loser. You need to go get laid." Everyone hated me and I loved it. My teacher told me I had a bad attitude, and when the class finished he kept me behind. I expected a lecture. Instead he told me I was 100 percent correct. "All these kids' photos are shit," he agreed.

 # Zodiac

PRIVATE.COM • DIR: PIERRE WOODMAN • RATING: 6

I don't have a home, thus no television, which serves as a good excuse as to why I'm in the bar in the middle of the day, alone; I'm watching a basketball game. I try to give the world the impression that I am unapproachable. I never remove my sunglasses, I generally wear a scowl on my face and I've taken to sporting a Hitler mustache.

If I were someone else in a bar full of people I would be the last person I tried to strike up a conversation with. But I live in Los Angeles and people here have their heads up their asses. They can't seem to grasp the sanctity of a man—a salty, angry man—enjoying a game by his lonesome. They think that since they can't survive without human interaction that the entire world is the same way.

Last Thursday I had enough. I was watching the Nets vs. Pacers game when a guy took the seat next to me. He hadn't ordered his drink yet, hadn't even shimmied his ass about in the leather stool to

make it more comfortable when he turned to me and asked, "So what do you do?" I looked him in the eyes and said, "I watch basketball games alone, in silence." The words stunned him. He thought it over, then turned to his left where he found a Hispanic male, mid-30s, well-dressed, slick hair, to whom he asked, "So what do you do?"

Luckily the Spaniard wanted to tell him all about what he did. From somewhere on the floor he produced three, count 'em, three portfolios of his photography. Now tell me, who the hell goes to the pub with their portfolios? Once, I forgot to wear pants to the bar (luckily I had on boxer shorts so they let me stay)—how does one remember their portfolio? When my brain tells me it's time to go to the bar, all thoughts turn to alcohol. Who packs a bag? But at least it got the curious one off my back. Then I felt him.

"Who's winning the game?" he asked. I got so close to his face he might have thought I was going to kiss him. I said, "If I had only one wish, I'd wish that you would fall down dead right fucking now. Leave me alone." This shocked him and he apologized, not even knowing what he was apologizing for. My team made a winning run and 10 minutes later the asshole had the balls to ask me, "So, how long have you lived in LA?"

Houston's
Big Boob Brigade

METROINTERACTIVE.COM • RATING: 7

You should know Houston once held the record for banging 620 dudes in a day. You'd have to assume that a woman who could handle that many men at once would have to know what she was doing. Just as I noticed her on the box cover looking all glossy and mutated I began to wonder what it would be like if Houston had a kid and what if when that kid turned 14 one of his friends found her gangbang video and showed it to him. Now, I imagine that to learn that your mother was in a porno at all would be a shocking thing, but to be told Mommy got porked by 620 guys over the course of an afternoon would really fuck a kid's head up. As I was beginning to theorize about the direction that that child's life would take from that moment of discovery a friend of mine from *Hustler* came into my office; I presented him my concern about a child and he told me that he believed that Houston did indeed have a kid. A daughter, as a matter of fact. Can you imagine? That poor girl is destined to either have a very glamorous life as a porn starlet, perhaps doing 1,240 men in

one weekend to outdo her mother's legacy, or she is headed for one long life of ridicule, torture and rape by men who assume she is as promiscuous as her mother. Either way it's a sad life and it raises questions about the illegality of porn stars procreating. Not to say all girls who have sex on film should be ineligible by law to have children, but perhaps we should instate some sort of code of decency for potential porn mothers. For instance, Jenna Jameson and her ilk should be clear for parenthood. While they are still having sex for the camera, their sex is rather meat and potatoes—no anal, no quadruple penetrations—therefore it should be made acceptable. The ban should apply strictly to those women who perform sex acts that separate the individual from the rest of humanity, things such as multiple penises in the ass or vagina, more than a dozen partners at once, bestiality or excrement play, and anything else that could shatter a child's psyche upon viewing. I began to draft up the specifics of my Mutant Sex Mother Law when I noticed one of the other busty blondes on the corner of the box cover lying down with her enormous fake tits defying gravity and I was like, "Holy shit! I hung out with that chick in Philadelphia once! She gave me a blowjob in her hotel room!" I'd tell you all about it but it's kind of an uninteresting story so I'm not going to go into it.

Scale Bustin' Bimbos 3

VISUAL IMAGES • DIR: RODNEY MOORE • RATING: 1

The box notes that this is "a chubby chaser's dream come true!" But for the rest of us who are sickened by not only imagining fat people naked but the mere thought of fat people in general, this is nothing shy of a nightmare.

Listen, I'm not the slimmest man. I know this. I have a beer gut that can only be reduced with a steady diet of cocaine, which I gave up for New Year's. There was a time, not long ago, when I was anorexic. I weighed 135 pounds at age 23. Then I ballooned to 215 pounds. Moving to Ohio had a lot to do with it. I somehow turned into everything I hated: a fat pile of shit who sat on his couch drinking, smoking and watching porn. Not a good look for one of America's sexiest bachelors.

And yet, even though I once had four chins and man tits I'll tell you what . . . I can't tolerate fat people. If a person gets to a certain weight where they're too disgusting to look at, they should be quarantined, killed and used to feed whales or dogs. Whales would be funny. Dust to dust. Whale to whale. Don't you agree?

Have you ever sat in a restaurant trying your damnedest to ensure that whoever you are with will spread their legs for you later that night only to catch sight of a 300-pound sloth of a man vacuuming up what appears to be 24-ounce T-bone steak? It's as if they don't chew. Everything is instantly swallowed so that their stomach can process it over the years like the Sarlacc pit in *Return of the Jedi*. Is my date still talking to me? I can't hear her. I'm fixated on this man whose body could feed an Alaskan village through a harsh winter. This man who hasn't seen his testicles in decades, if ever.

"Are you even listening to me?" she asks, snapping me back to

attention. "Look at that fat man," I say. "Would you be here with me tonight, contemplating whether to have sex with me, if I was that fat?" She takes another look. "Be honest," I tell her. She looks at my pained face, trying to decide what is the right answer. Again she looks at the fat slob, her eyes lock on mine and I know her words are true when she says, "If you were that fat I would probably spit on you." That's when I tell her I love her.

Meet the Motherfuckers

METROXXX. COM • DIR: ROMAN PORNASNSKI • RATING: 4

Yes, it is truly awful for a young woman to star in a porno while pregnant. We are all in agreement that there is something inherently wrong with a woman taking a stranger's cock inside her while a fetus is doing the doggie paddle in her guts. There is no argument there, but I don't think it's fair for us to cast stones. Until we walk a mile in these women's slippers we have no right to judge. We have no idea what their home life might be like; perhaps they have a very high mortgage and their day job of pumping gasoline is not cutting it and they need a few extra dollars to make ends meet. Maybe these women are actually model mothers and they are just doing porn so that they can invest the money they make off sucking cock in some lucrative stocks and bonds so that their unborn child can attend Oxford. We don't know. And does it really matter? Not to me, because when I look at the box cover of *Meet the Motherfuckers* I see an atrocity far worse than a pregnant woman making porn; what the fuck is the story with that hideous tattoo on cover girl Charlie Marie's stomach? I don't even know where to begin. First, I'd like to know what the hell it is. Is it an octopus? A tribal sun? King Diamond's drummer's corpse paint design? Whatever it is, it was a bad idea. Secondly, when it comes to tattoos, especially on women, you need to have some foresight when you're choosing the spot on your body to get permanently altered. It's important to choose body parts that won't get as stretched out and mangled over the years as tits, stomachs or asses. I've never understood why women are so drawn to tattooing those areas. It's one thing if you're completely covered in tattoos and have run out of room. At that point, it doesn't matter what you get tattooed; go ahead and let them tattoo your kidneys. But look at this dumbass on the cover. She has one tattoo, and where does she stick it? On the worst part of your body you can pick if you're considering getting pregnant. Now tell me what that thing is going to look like after the kid comes out. When her tummy is dangling over her belt, all flabby and gross. We can't tell what the hell it is now. I bet when it's all said and done that that thing looks like varicose veins on her gut. Now, that's a real popular tattoo for females. I'm sure tons of women walk into tattoo parlors all over the world and say, "Yeah, could you put some varicose veins on my thighs and ass?" It's not as if she's going to be fit after the childbirth. She's making porn while she's pregnant, for fuck's sake, do you really see this girl going to the gym? I think that as soon as her child is strong enough to hold a handgun he should put a bullet in his mother's head and get rid of that blemish upon humanity permanently.

Assturbators 2

TAYLORWANE.COM • DIR: TAYLOR WANE • RATING: 10

I've decided that either porn stars should not be allowed to have friends outside of the sex industry or they should be put into containment camps like we did with the Japs in World War II. It's porn entrepreneur Taylor Wane's fault that I feel this way. Recently I was in Los Angeles to interview a metal band called Nile. I didn't know anything about the band aside from their name, which led me to believe they were from Egypt, so I decided to have some fun with them. Being from Egypt I thought they'd enjoy it if I dressed up as a pharaoh. Then I thought, "Everyone loves T & A, I should get a sexy lady to come with me dressed as Cleopatra." I decided to call Taylor because she's a good sport and has a great sense of humor. She loved the idea. The next day we went to a costume shop and picked out our outfits and I bought a rubber chicken. Afterwards we returned to her place and had crazy circus sex that involved every one of her orifices. That's a lie. She just gave us a tour of her home, showing us where all the magic happens on her own personal porn set equipped with bed, whipping post, sex swing and anything else one might need to film a dirty movie. As we were leaving and saying our goodbyes she gave me, my photographer and my filmer a bagful of DVDs each. Inside were a variety of movies from Taylor's catalog, with her bent, folded and opened up in every possible manner. We kindly thanked her and returned to our hotel. That night, in our separate rooms, we lay awake in our beds each having simulated sex with Taylor for hours on end. The next day at breakfast no one spoke. We looked long into our eggs with shame. I finally asked the others, "So. Did youse guys watch any of Taylor's movies last night?" Like Peter in regards to Jesus of Nazareth, they each denied me three times, yet their faces told the truth. I told them it was okay, that I had in fact watched Taylor in compromising positions including this film where she masturbates using her ass (as the title indicates). One lad began to cry. He

admitted he watched all the DVDs and got no sleep at all. He then confessed that he didn't think he could shoot Nile that afternoon out of fear that he would be thinking filthy thoughts about Taylor the entire time and most likely would not be able to keep his camera still. We all felt the same way. There was no one to blame but Taylor herself. She was far too nice to us. Even her husband welcomed us into their house and made us feel comfortable. In our few hours together we cultivated a friendship and she had to go and throw her goddamn vagina into the mix, in typical porn fashion, and screw everything up. I mean, at one point she was letting us hold a mold of her ass (available on her website) and telling us to put our finger in the hole, while saying, "That's really what my ass feels like." Now you tell me how the hell a man is supposed to have a normal, platonic relationship with a beautiful, big-breasted woman and discuss politics and wedding planning after he's had his digit in her fake ass? It's just not right, I tell you. Those people are sick and they need to be caged up.

Whores Don't Wear Panties

HUSTLERVIDEO.COM • DIR: ANDRE MADNESS • RATING: 8

I suppose it's true, you do learn something new every day, because I was unaware that whores didn't wear panties. If nothing else I can take comfort in knowing that none of the women I've ever bedded down with were whores since they all, at one point or another, wore panties, even if they were on their heads. Strange as it may be, whores may not wear panties but they do have MySpace accounts. Perhaps it is the high cost of high-speed Internet that cuts into money allocated toward buying panties; I don't know. I am certain that since giving in to the addiction that is MySpace I have unearthed every stripper's, porn star's, amateur whore's and neighborhood slut's MySpace page. I know I'm about two years too late in discovering MySpace but that's just how I am. If everyone else gets into something I must, by nature, hate it on principle until everyone else is over it, then and only then will I allow myself to indulge and pretend as if I single-handedly am resurrecting the dead. Like Tarantino with Travolta. I can't explain it. It's just my thing. And so I hated on MySpace for years. Until recently. Then in less than an hour I became so engulfed by its might that I stayed logged on for one week straight. I sought out people I hadn't seen in years, kids I went to grammar school with, drunks I met once in a bar in Albuquerque. I would type in names like Peter or Dave, because I've known some people named Peter and Dave, and 7,000 pages would come up and I'd go through each and every page to see if I knew any of them (which I did not). Mind you, my purpose on MySpace is strictly voyeurism. I do not initiate contact. I do not collect friends like one would collect comic books. I just like to watch, to see what has become of those who have crossed my path over the years. And I have learned a lot in my weeks glued to the computer. I learned a friend of mine moved to St. Louis and another married the girl I introduced him to six years ago and moved to Minnesota. One girl I once knew is now dating one of the guys in Nine Inch Nails and another works for the NCAA. I have since stopped reading the newspaper. I no longer care about current events. All I care about is MySpace and filling in the blanks in my mind left vacant by years of alcohol and drug abuse. Yesterday morning I tried to log on and the machine said MySpace was down due to some technical difficulties. My heart palpitated. I felt dizzy and uneasy. I went flush and my hands began to shake worse than Muhammad Ali's. I didn't know what to do. I had lost my only source of contact with the outside world. It was like September 11th all over again. Only worse. Were my friends trapped in the computer? Would they burn alive in there? Would they be forced to jump out of my Windows 95 to their death? I smacked the side of my hard drive because that is the extent of my knowledge when it comes to computer repair. Nothing. I went to my front window only to see the last leaf fall from the tree. I knew then that life as I know it would never be the same. I put on my coat with the fuzzy hood and went out to the flagpole and lowered the stars and stripes to half-mast. I have not logged on since. It hurts too much.

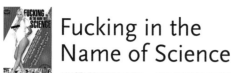

Fucking in the Name of Science

HUSTLERVIDEO.COM • DIR: CAESAR BONOBA • RATING: 7

You don't need to be Sherlock Holmes to realize I'm not a brilliant man. Each passing year of schooling for me was a more difficult struggle than the previous. I was a borderline failure in every class I've ever taken, from penmanship to Spanish. I'm certain the only reason my teachers passed me at all was because I was a complete and total annoyance, constantly sassing my elders, demeaning my classmates and generally being unruly; like a four-eyed Bart Simpson. To fail me would have meant another year of putting up with me and no one was going to willingly volunteer for that, so I squeaked by year after year with a grade-point average just cunt hairs above failing. As time passed and the curriculum became increasingly more confusing to me I was forced to reach into my wallet and hire fellow students to do the work for me. It's a funny thing that I would end up being a paid professional writer late in life because for all my 15 years of schooling I never wrote one thesis, term paper or book report. So if you find one on eBay just know it's a forgery. I may have signed my name at the top but that's about all that I can take credit for. In my first of many failed attempts at college I actually dropped out of my Intro to Writing class a week before exams because my professor assured me even a perfect score on the finals couldn't save me from repeating the class. It's not to say I'm a complete dunce, just that I had little focus. I assumed that I would be a factory worker or on a construction crew like all the other men in my family and just chose not to pay attention to studies that weren't applicable to a blue-collar life. Instead I passed the time taking acid, smoking weed and getting drunk behind the dumpsters on the far side of the football field.

There were a few subjects that held my interest: math and history, mostly. Generally, though, I pretty much tanked everything; the worst of all for me was science. I could not make heads or tails out of any of that shit. Periodic tables, dissections, organisms; it was all French to me. Luckily I shared a desk with a sexy, intelligent cheerleader who smelled of fresh flowers every day of the year. Sometimes if the wind is right I can still smell her. She was kind enough to take pity on me and give me every answer to every quiz; she'd always pick me as her partner knowing I'd have no chance without her. She was an angel with a bad perm and freckles and she refused to take any payment for her services. I offered her drugs, alcohol, even to take her on a shopping spree for clothes and shoes but she would have none of it. She enabled me to pass and did so out of the kindness of her heart. So you can understand why I got so emotional when she was killed by a drunk driver as she crossed the street only two weeks after the school year ended.

SPECS Appeal 9

KICKASS.COM • DIR: ANDRE MADNESS • RATING: 10

I'm supposed to wear glasses. I'm supposed to but I don't. I've been wearing them since I was 4 and I'm over them and contact lenses just feel weird in my eyes. I'm slowly going blind and sitting here staring at this computer screen isn't really helping matters.

People are always asking if I'm nearsighted or farsighted because when they try my glasses on they get a headache. The answer is: I'm neither. My right eye has 20/20 vision. The problem is with my left eye; it's lazy, like me, which means in my younger days it would squirrel around in my head uncontrollably like a goldfish or a broken cuckoo clock. Try as I might to look straight ahead my left eye would always be pointing north or south, east or west. Anywhere but where was intended. You'd think I'd be embarrassed by it but I wasn't.

I hadn't entered school yet and had never heard the taunts of evil children. I also thought it was kind of cool. I felt like a wild and zany cartoon character, and so I'd act like one, bouncing about, giggling and hitting the cat over the head with a hammer. But the doctor told my mother that I'd be blind before long if some kind of corrective measures weren't taken. He suggested surgery.

Mind you, this was the 1970s, not the futuristic world we live in today. There was no laser surgery. Back then they used a scalpel and sliced part of your eye off and hoped it didn't get infected and fall out of your head. My mother, being a more practical person from a simpler country, refused to let such torture happen to her little boy and insisted on alternate means.

The doctor explained that if there was some way where we could get me to stop using my right eye completely it would strengthen my left eye and force it to focus on what my brain commanded it to do. They spoke about me as if I wasn't in the room; but I was smart enough to understand what was going on. As they debated the options I practiced keeping my right eye shut for long stretches. It was much harder than I'd thought. Then I tried covering my eye with my hand. They came to a decision. They would take duct tape and cover the right lens of my glasses, giving me no choice but to use my left eye.

I thought the idea sucked. I'd rather be cartoony and blind than a dork with taped glasses. So I made a suggestion: "Can't I just wear a patch over my eye like a pirate?" The adults looked at me strangely. They had just assumed that making a small boy wear an eye patch would be very traumatic. They never considered that with my penchant for playing dress-up I'd actually enjoy it. And so on my first day of school, as other kids were crying about leaving their parents and holding on to Mommy's leg for dear life, I strutted through the front door and right into my class dressed as a pirate: eye patch, tooth colored black, hook made of aluminum foil and all. And every kid there thought I was the coolest guy on earth.

Wax Dat Juicy Booty

EBONY PRODUCTIONS/STONEYCURTISXXX.COM • DIR: DUST • RATING: 9

It was difficult choosing which film to review from Ebony Productions because all of them had the most amazing titles. In the same box as *Wax Dat Juicy Booty* was also *Phat Azz Titties,* whose box cover boasted 120 minutes of "Boom Booty's & Boobies," and another amazing disc called *Phat Buttz Drain My Nutz!* You can see my predicament, can't you? I generally like to write my reviews based on the titles, without having to actually watch them, but in this case I was torn. I couldn't possibly review all three; I don't have that many stories about having sex with black women that I can remember. I was then forced to turn over the boxes to see if maybe one of the synopses could win me over; what I found was an exam in ebonics that I clearly failed. This is what it said on the back of *Phat Buttz Drain My Nutz!*: "Chyanne sho' know how to work doze cheeks 'n' please dat meat. Jersey Montana's fine ass be as big as her name, and she don't hesitate to use dat shit!" What does that even mean? I have no idea. Neither does my spell-check. I just went to run spell-check and my laptop let out a whimper. *Phat Azz Titties'* summary was rather amazing in its own right: "Candace shakes da house, Niya's tight coochie vs. Byron Long's monster bone when he goes balls deep in dat shit. Vida's vagina get stretched by Sylvio's seismic salami." Seismic salami . . . I couldn't make that up. But as good a term as that might be, *Wax Dat Juicy Booty* had the three best lines of all. First, "Big bootied Lisa get her fina azz taken to the carwash and stretched by Sylvio." I don't even know what "taken to the carwash" means, but I know I want to do it to my wife. I keep asking if I can take her to the carwash but she just ignores me. I think I'm going to have to "take her to the carwash" without her knowing, if that's possible. The next great line is "Hypnotic grinds dat phat booty, then goes freakazilla on big black beef." Again, I don't know the exact definition of "freakazilla," but I'm just going to assume it's a lot of fun. The wordage that really did it for me, the line that truly put *Wax Dat Juicy Booty* over the top, was "Ashley's booty blings and bounces when she be gettin' freaky on Ace's weenie." Isn't that fantastic? I wasn't even aware that bootys could bling. It shows how little I know, I suppose. What blew me away was the use of the word *weenie*. Here we have three box covers full of black vernacular and then they go and use a completely Caucasian word like *weenie*? Could there be a whiter word in the English language? Who even uses the word *weenie* any more? I doubt even young, suburban crackers use that word. And that's how I knew *Wax Dat Juicy Booty* was for me; it appealed to my whiteness.

Cum Fart Cocktails

REDLIGHTDISTRICTVIDEO.COM • DIR: JAKE MALONE • RATING: 8

I am a man, like any other red-blooded male, who likes to fart. I am not special or unique; I simply like to smell my own ass. I derive pleasure from the loudness, tone and stench of the music my lower extremity makes. I like disrupting the silence of a chilly fall afternoon with the sound of my ass trumpet and knowing I made that sound and it is good. But I do not fart in front of my wife. Never have. It stems from my oafish father, who was sub-Neanderthal at best, and his callous, uncontrollable ass. He once tried to spark a fire in our living-room wood-burning stove by throwing a coffee can's worth of gasoline on the flames, to give you an idea of what we're dealing with. He set the room ablaze. He also liked to beat women. And he farted whenever and wherever he liked without a shred of concern for who was in his vicinity. As a result I have never farted in front of any girl I've ever been with. I just don't do it. I am programmed to take others into consideration before unleashing my toxic gases. But it is especially difficult with my wife; she has amazing hearing. I'd leave the room and go into the bathroom, turn on the fan and let out five or six bars and she'd yell, "What? Did you step on a duck?" Then it got cartoonish, with me having to go farther and farther away from her to mask the sound. Once I went out into the backyard in a thunderstorm, with the winds spinning with a fury and the dog barking at the moon, to let out my semiautomatic *brrrap brrrap brrrap* and still out the window I heard, "What? Did you step on a duck?" Then I tried taking a walk down the block but she still heard me and said it again. I tried driving my car a half mile down to the river to unload a few rounds. When I was done all was quiet and I thought to myself, "Finally." I drove home content in knowing that I had finally found sanctuary, a place where I could be alone with my farts, but when I walked through the front door I heard, "What? Did you step on a duck?" come from the kitchen. I am at a loss. I feel as if I've tried everything and that I've tried too much. I should stop fighting it and just share my ass noise with her yet something inside me won't allow it. Instead I'm building a music studio in our basement. At least that's what I'm telling her. It's really a fart bunker. I woke up one morning and told her that I wanted to be a rapper. She said, "That's nice, honey," and went about her business. I often tell her of some stupid occupation I'm considering such as an astronaut or hibachi chef or sumo wrestler or poet; I can see why she wouldn't take me serious. Little does she know I have spent $12,000 of our money on music equipment that I'll never use or understand. I've built a special little fart bunker and fully soundproofed it, all in an attempt to keep her from hearing me break wind. If this doesn't work, if I hear one more mention of that goddamn duck, I swear to fucking God . . . I'm going to build a spaceship from old car parts and go fart on the moon.

Cum on My Tattoos

BURNINGANGEL.COM • DIR: JOANNA ANGEL • RATING: 9

I've been waiting a long time for someone to do a series dedicated to women with tattoos. Of course, I was hoping that that someone would be me, but what are you going to do? I'm just happy that Joanna started Burningangel.com and is turning out tricks for people who love women with tattoos. It has been a void that has needed to be filled since the dawn of time. My only problem I have with this title is that it completely contradicts my theory that any woman with tattoos takes it in the ass, since there is only one anal scene in the entire film. I stand by my theory and still firmly believe that all of the girls featured in *Cum on My Tattoos* do in fact take it in the ass in their private life. Perhaps they're just giving their asses a much-needed vacation. That's understandable. Everyone deserves a break. My wife's ass is pretty much on permanent vacation except for those few days of each month when her vagina starts spitting blood, then her pussy tags out and her butt gets off the hammock. It's a great life, I suppose. Working only three or four days out of the month. I'm jealous. I wish I could be on permanent vacation. I think I'd sell my house and travel the world. I've always wanted to go to Poland and see if all the jokes were true. I'm part Polish, did you know that? It's why I make really easy tasks seem so difficult at times. Do you know why the Polacks were so easily defeated by the Nazis in World War II? Because the Nazis marched in backwards and the Poles thought they were leaving. Fucked up, right? Have you ever been to Australia? I think I'd like to visit there as well. When Bart Simpson went it seemed like so much fun. I like how the toilet water spins the opposite way when you flush. I also like that everyone is drunk all the time. I could get used to that. From there I'd take a train to Taiwan. I think it's Taiwan where the girls in the strip clubs shoot Ping-Pong balls out of their vaginas and you can pay them to put glass or razor blades in their pussies. I don't think I could get off on it but it's just one of those things I'd like to see before I die. Like the Pantheon. Or the Coliseum. I'd like to have a pretend sword fight with my wife in the Coliseum in front of a crowd of thousands. But there would need to be a wager. What do I have that's worth anything? I guess I could offer to come out of retirement and go back to work if she won. And if I won? Her ass must trade duty with her vagina and be available to me 27 days a month, allowing her vagina the rest it has earned. I think that's fair. And so it shall be. A duel! En garde!

F to the A

VERTIGOVIDEOS.COM • DIR: MARTIN DEL TORO • RATING: 9

Baseball is referred to as America's pastime, as you well know, but to be completely honest, I'm not a huge fan. It's not that I hate the sport, it just moves too slowly for my liking. I'm more of a basketball man. I like fast-paced action, constant scoring. Baseball makes me want to do drugs, get wasted, numb myself and just stare. I've never once watched more than 20 minutes of a baseball game on television in my life. I just don't have the patience.

Seeing a game firsthand is better but only because of the crowds. At Yankee games I get the cheap bleacher seats in the outfield that overlook the other team's bullpen and I laugh as the children spit and throw sodas on the opposition's pitchers as they prepare.

One main rule in New York is not to wear the opposing team's apparel to a game. If you do, it will get ugly. To soccer fans this rule is obvious, but in baseball New York is the only city you need to worry about. I've seen games in many other towns with a Yankees hat on my head and never got more than a "Nice hat, jerk," which is easily silenced by a hard stare and simple question: "How would you like it if I fucking came over there and knocked your fucking teeth down your throat?" The answer is usually never spoken, but it's understood that the correct response would be "I would not like it very much at all. My apologies." Most other sports towns' fans in the United States are pussies. New York, New Jersey and Philadelphia fans are a different breed. It's like they're wild beasts who haven't been fed in weeks. They will eat you alive. Once, in the late '60s, the attending Philadelphia Eagles fans, all 50,000-plus of them, booed Santa Claus at halftime. I recall going to see the Yankees play the Cleveland Indians and some elderly man behind me was wearing an Indians cap. Late in the game the Yankees were behind by six or seven runs so the crowd turned on the old man and beat him bloody. I don't know if the man died or not but he was carried out on a stretcher. Those are obviously die-hard baseball fans.

I'm the same way with basketball. Once at a Nets/Celtics game I made a sign that said, "WILL SOMEONE PLEASE STAB PAUL PIERCE!" It was psychological warfare. Pierce had been stabbed repeatedly outside a nightclub years earlier. Me and my sign made the back cover of the *New York Post*. So I can understand when someone loves a sport so much that they would do just about anything to let people know. You take the one girl in this DVD, for instance. She must have been born and raised on baseball. Perhaps her father was an ex–professional ballplayer. Maybe her brother played for the Mets. Maybe she played softball all her life. Baseball must be in her blood— I mean, what other reason would there be for having the large end of a baseball bat rammed up her ass repeatedly on film?

A Train 4: Urban Anal Assault

SINCITY.COM • DIR: COREY JORDAN • RATING: 9

I was a naive and trusting teenager who thought himself invincible. It was back then that I thought it was a good idea to start selling weed to my fellow college students. Being business-savvy I found a place where I could cop huge amounts of dirt weed for very cheap: Harlem.

Here I was, a skinny, bleach-haired kid on a skateboard walking around 125th and St. Nick's looking for bud. My being there always seemed so normal, so safe. I mean, I listened to Biggie Smalls and Wu-Tang Clan; that gave me an all-access pass to anything black, right?

I wish I could have a picture of my big doe eyes from the first time I went uptown and met my first dealer, a woman named Flo, to compare with a photo of the very suspicious-looking me who eventually gave up selling drugs after being robbed at gunpoint one too many times.

Flo was mid-40s, and looked like that rapping black chick on the first season of *The Real World*. She saw me both as a cash cow and defenseless bunny in a pen of starving wolves. As soon as I stepped onto the street more than 20 dealers were asking what I needed. Overwhelming. What to do? How do you shop around for weed? Are you allowed to compare prices? Is it okay to ask one dealer to match another's offer? It was like I'd discovered a hidden city of Elven car salesmen.

Flo walked up and hugged me and kissed me on the cheek. She saw that I didn't know how to decide so she made the decision for me. We walked a block or so making small talk about how I've been and my family. Before I knew it I was heading up a stairwell, then into a low-income apartment with children scurrying about and a 20-pound bag of weed sitting on a coffee table beside a scale and a 9 mm pistol.

I hadn't noticed either of the men on the couch until they cocked their guns and pointed them at me. It all happened fast. But Flo sorted it out. Smoothed it over and I somehow walked out with a half pound of brown rat weed for $350. Flo walked me to the train and kissed my cheek goodbye. And warned me to be careful.

Spanish Harlem

VIDEOTEAM.COM • DIR: ANDRE MADNESS • RATING: 6

As long as the kids in Harlem knew I was buying from Flo I was safe. I started noticing things I hadn't before: kids in alleys, undercover cop cars, thugs following me. Still I was protected by Flo and her crew. I was doing a few thousand dollars a week with her. She wasn't going to let her cash cow get hurt. Then one day I got off the train and Flo was nowhere to be seen. It was the first time I truly felt afraid for my life. A woman approached me. "You're Flo's boy, right?" "Yeah," I responded. "Where's Flo?" "Flo got got" is all she said. I found out later she'd been shot twice in the face two days earlier. This new woman led me to her apartment. She reluctantly hooked me up with the same deal I was getting from Flo, $300 for a half (Flo dropped the price after six months of me getting a half pound a week). As I left she locked me out and waved goodbye. I was on the streets of Harlem, crotch full of weed, alone. That day there were no undercover cops, the only people following me were the two men I'd seen standing outside the dealer's building. One was wide and round, impossible to get away from if he got hold of me. The other was long and slim with a stride twice as quick as mine. The stupid kid I was thought they'd never follow me onto the train platform. Wrong. Before I could think of another plan I was backed against a pillar with a gun jammed into my chest.

"Give us the weed and you won't get hurt," the skinny one said as he pushed the gun hard into me. I tried lying. "I don't have any weed." "Don't fuck with us. I'll kill you right here."

I felt a breeze, then I saw a train coming. I tried to inch toward the track. "Don't you fucking move. Run the shit." The train slowed, stopped, then the bell of the opening door rang. Without a second thought I said, "Fine."

I reached under my coat, grabbed the corner of the bag and ripped off a handful of weed. I took a deep breath, waited for that door-closing bell to ring, handed them what I had in my hand and darted onto the train. It took them a second to notice they weren't holding more than a quarter ounce but by then it was too late. My train was pulling away, and I was flipping the bird.

Under Pimp Arrest

SMASHPICTURES.COM • DIR: MR. JOHNSON • RATING: 5

My neighbor keeps dying, like, two, three times a week. It's rather annoying. Every few nights I'm woken up by ambulances next door. They cart her ass out on a stretcher, oxygen mask on, with nary a blip coming from the ECG machine. But by two o'clock that same afternoon, they bring her home again. I think she's faking and just likes to take rides in the ambulances to hear the siren's DOOOO-REEEE DOOOO-REEEE DOOOO-REEEE.

I can understand that as you get older and older and eventually go senile, you revert back into a child in nearly every sense. You shit yourself, you scream for no good reason, you talk to yourself, you don't know your name, you have no control over your farts.

So ambulance rides for an 80-year-old make sense, but it's driving me up the wall. Especially at 5 a.m. I go outside in my underwear now and I poke her. I ask the paramedics, "Is she really dead this time?" Thinking I am a family friend they tell me they think she'll be fine.

"Fuck," I say, "can't you take the long road to the hospital? Maybe if she doesn't get there in time she'll die." They laugh. I tell them I'm not kidding, then they look at me in disdain. "What?" I ask. "You have to be sick of coming here every other day. Just kill her and let's get it over with already."

They are mortified and wheel her past me. I yell at the flashing lights as they pull off, "If you bring her back here one more time, I'll kill her myself! I swear it, I will!" Still, like clockwork, she's back in time for her afternoon soaps. That's the problem with health care in

America: They don't regulate it. I can't even afford health insurance, so if anything were to happen to me and I did need an ambulance I'd be fucked. A ride in an ambulance for a person without health care is $3,000. That's just the ride, before seeing any doctors. But the elderly get free health care and can take all the ambulance rides they want at no charge. I think that we need to instate a cutoff date like once a person hits 80 their health care is terminated and passed down to an infant who needs it.

We tell the old person, "Listen, you're great and all but you've overstayed your welcome and you need to go out into the mountains and die already. Enough is enough." It's forward-thinking ideas like this that keep me believing I'd make one hell of a president. Health care reform aside, it would obviously help immensely with the US's overpopulation problems. I don't know exact numbers, but I think it's safe to say we have a whole lot of old people in this country that we could easily do without and I tell you what, if this old lady next door wakes me up one more time by pretending to die, I'm going to set my plan in action without the okay of any legislature.

Surprise, I Have A Dick

COLOSSALENT.COM • DIR: LUCIO FLAVIO • RATING: 5

Yesterday I picked up a hitchhiker on the way to the train station. I have a certain level of respect and understanding for hitchhikers. For many years I was one. It's rather fun to think you can walk outside, throw up your thumb and get a ride somewhere. But with all the craziness in the world these days less and less people are inclined to pick up strangers. I feel obligated to pay back all the rides I was given in my youth. My only criteria for picking up hitchers are they can't be wet (one never knows if it's water or urine), they can't look like they smell (I shouldn't have to suffer through a nice gesture. If someone is going to make me vomit because of their odor and pos-

sibly leave a stench behind, I can't be bothered), they cannot be bigger than I am or look like they could overpower me and lastly, they
can't be holding anything (no paper bags, no boxes, nothing. For all
I know there is a knife or a gun or a decapitated head in the bag and
it will be pointed at my throat). The fellow I picked up Thursday was
dry (save for the rain that was beginning to fall), clean-looking, short,
skinny and empty-handed. When I pulled over he thanked me for
stopping, which is required etiquette for hitchhiking. Turned out he
was going to the train station too. But as soon as his ass hit the
bench seat of my 1972 El Camino he broke rule No. 1: Ease into the
situation and make the driver comfortable. Instead of asking my
name, where I was from (not that I ever answer those questions hon-
estly) and how I was doing, he instantly began telling me about himself and his world of woes. I can't stand that shit. I don't go for
people pissing and moaning in my ear. I've got my own problems.
I'm fighting with my wife-to-be over air-conditioning; I could give two
fucks about this guy's life. In the first mile I heard, "Yeah, I was fucking standing there for two hours waiting for this guy to bring me my
check. Asshole. I worked all week for this guy. Forty hours and he said
he'd pay me today and drive me to the train station. People are scum-

bags, man. Last time I do a favor for anybody. I would have been standing there all night if you didn't stop." I tell him the train station is only four miles from where I picked him up, even at a slow pace he could've made it there in under two hours. He ignored me and kept on about this guy who owed him money. So I pulled over, looked him dead in the eye and told him to get out of the car. "WHA? Why?" he blurts out. "Because you don't shut the fuck up. I'd have taken you all the way if you'd just kept quiet and let me listen to my music. Now get out and walk." He stepped out, slammed the door, and I pulled off. He looked stunned as he threw his thumb up in the air.

 ## Cindy Crawford's House of Anal

DEFIANCEFILMS.COM • DIR: CINDY CRAWFORD • RATING: 9

As I was walking into the men's room of my brother's restaurant, Sayreville Bar, I heard a man say, "Good to hear from you, John. Thanks a lot." Then I heard a cell phone close. The man was standing at the urinal with his penis in his hand. I assume he had his penis in his hand. I didn't see his penis but he was at the urinal so by simple deduction I must assume his penis was in his hand. There is the outside chance that he was one of those free-spirited pissers who don't hold their peckers when they urinate and just let the thing fly as it may, like a wild fire hose on the loose in an old cartoon. I am not a free-spirited pisser. I am an adult. I hold my dick when I piss. Mostly because I am afraid it might fall off. Or someone will steal it. I'm not sure what those two thoughts are based on and I do not wish to dwell on them any further. So I was saying, the guy was standing there with his dick in his hand . . . unless he wasn't pissing at all and he was faking just so he could stand in front of the urinal in the men's room and get some alone time, but I doubt that completely. There is only one urinal and one stall in my brother's restroom and just as I hear the guy say, "Good to hear from you, John. Thanks a lot," and hang up, I walk past him into the stall, unzip my pants, pull my dick out and say, "John, huh? Yeah. I like to call my penis Randy sometimes. So that when I'm at home and my wife catches me touching it I can say, 'I'm feeling little Randy tonight.' And it's, like, a double entendre. Funny, right?" And with that I leaned back on my heels, stuck my head past the partition that separated us, smiled and waited for a reaction. It came swiftly. He put his penis away, I'm not even sure if he was done pissing, zipped up, scowled and stormed out. I guess if I had to choose my favorite place to fuck with people on the planet it would have to be men's rooms. Granted, I love to fuck with people anytime, anywhere, but men's rooms create a natural uneasiness. Men don't like being too close to other men, and they like it about a million times less when both have their dicks in their hand and one strikes up a conversation. I think my favorite maneuver is walking into a men's room and seeing a pair of feet in a stall, taking a shit. No matter how bad I have to piss I turn around, giggle, shut the lights off and walk out, leaving the guy stranded in the dark to wipe his ass blind and make a judgment call as to whether he got it all. That one doesn't get old to me. The cell-phone guy was off the cuff; I doubt I'll ever get a situation where I can use that one again. Best part was after I left the bathroom (I don't wash my hands, by the way, so yeah, that was piss you touched when you shook my hand) and went back to the bar the guy was talking to my brother. He points at me and says, "That's the weirdo right there." My brother just laughed, "That's not a weirdo, that's my brother."

How I Bluffed My Way
into Old Porn

I went through a major George Costanza phase in my early 20s in terms of jobs. I worked on Wall Street for a day before they realized I knew nothing about the stock market. I was an editor for a Disney publication for two weeks until it became apparent I was signing off on anything that came across my desk and had no idea who any of the characters in *The Lion King* were. I loaded boxes at UPS for a spell, and even did time as a waiter at an IHOP (I got fired for punching a customer in the face after he threw a boiling cup of coffee on my chest). The most ridiculous job I ever held down was copy editor/ghostwriter/ad designer for a series of gay porn magazines and three straight porn publications aimed at a more mature audience. Have you ever seen *Over 40*, *Over 50*, or *Over 60*? How about *Black Inches* or *Latin Inches*? Or *White Inch*? Yes, sir, for three long weeks I was at the helm of all those stellar titles. And I had no clue what the hell I was doing. I was a 21-year-old college dropout, addicted to cocaine, with no computer knowledge, who lied in his interview like a seasoned criminal. "Are you fluent with Quark and Photoshop?" Oh, sure. Isn't everyone? "What school did you attend?" I was a double major at NYU, graduated top 10 percent of my class. "Do you have a problem with sexual content, gay or straight?" Fuck, no. All my friends are gay and I love it!

So I got the job, and an $85,000 salary plus benefits. I was the king of the world. To celebrate, I bought myself an eightball and a blowjob. Then I actually had to do some work. For three days I was trained by the girl I was replacing. When I asked her why she was quitting, she simply said, "Give it a week and you'll understand." As I met the cast of characters I quickly got it. There was the flamboyant gay editor who could barely speak English, let alone use grammar correctly; the standard office whore; and a bitter old copy editor who had been with the company for decades. His office doubled as the storeroom, and every time he saw me he screamed, "I hope you know *The Chicago Manual of Style*! We don't use that pussy New York one!"

For those of you who don't know, copy editors have their own shorthand, a series of symbols used to indicate paragraph changes, spelling corrections and the like, sort of like those red marks found all over your papers in school. If you already knew that, then you're smarter than I was back then. We'd get the proofs back from the printer and I'd attack them with a red wax pencil, circling misspellings and then drawing a line from the word to the margin with a big note that read, "THIS WORD IS SPELLED WRONG." When I was done, the proofs looked like the beach after we took Normandy. The publisher was like, "What the fuck is this shit? I thought you knew copy editing." I told her I was just kidding around and said it would never happen again, not even knowing what I'd done wrong. Luckily my friend's wife Debbie, who worked with me, knew I was lying and helped me through it all.

This was the first job I ever had where I had to check proofs. I was 21, I jerked off to *Hustler* and *Penthouse*, and I thought every girl in a magazine was supposed to be airbrushed. I knew nothing of lower-tier porn. So when I got proofs of a layout with some girl with zit-covered ass cheeks, I circled them red. The publisher told me, "We don't airbrush those, people like those." The next week I got a spread with a 50-year-old lady spreading her asshole with a hemorrhoid dangling out. I again circled it and again was told to leave it be. There was also the layout with the girl and her visible tampon string that "people like." I was so confused. I hadn't hit my real deviant sexual peak yet. I thought I was kinky because I stuck baseball bats in girls' pussies. I began to think something was wrong with me since I didn't find tampon strings, zits, and hemorrhoids sexy. When the most disgusting pictorial ever showed up on my desk to be corrected, I didn't touch it. I figured I had a lot to learn about fetishes, and looking at these photos of a gray-haired 77-year-old (I wish I was kidding you) on her knees reaching around and fingering her pruned asshole, I just assumed, "People like this." My instincts were right but I still got chewed out. "Are you fucking blind?" the publisher asked. I twisted the arm of my glasses in my hand to emphasize that, yes, my vision isn't exactly 20/20. She threw the pages down on my desk. "Now tell me what's wrong with this photo." I went with the obvious answer. "It's a 77-year-old fingering her ass?" "No," she said, "people like that. She's wearing Nikes! We can't have name-brand logos in the magazines. We'll get sued. Christ, already! I might as well do your job for you!"

I was losing my mind. I felt like I was walking on thin ice with cement shoes. I didn't know what I was doing, and I was way too slow. When they asked me to correct something in Quark, I looked the word up in *The Chicago Manual of Style*. Debbie told me it was a computer program and opened it up on my desktop. I took one look at the toolbar and started to cry. You don't bullshit your way through Quark. Nor do you try and write gay copy when you don't understand homosexuality. There I was, staring at some oiled-up and shaved Latino in camouflage holding his rod, trying to write a quirky yet steamy quip to accompany his photos. I closed my eyes and pictured myself fucking a big-assed Puerto Rican girl from behind to the tune of "I want to throw you down on the bed and spread your ass cheeks and slip my thick cock in and out, in and out." The English-as-a-second-language dropout of an editor screamed, "No, no, honey. You need fires. Make it hot and more dirty, like this." He began typing over my shoulder. When he finished, a full five minutes later, he pointed at the screen and proudly said, "There." To this day, I still have the page printed out. Here's what he wrote: "Ass fuck me stud, I so hungry for mouth fuck. I eat cock sandwhich, eat an ass, baby I horny to make pony ride on face." (Again, I wish I were kidding you.) Aside from the creative pointer, he also gave me a xeroxed glossary of key terms that supposedly "drive queers ca-raaaazy." Here it is, in case you ever need it: "puckered asshole," "clean-shaved," "big bear," "steaming load of man juice" and, of course, "uncut." I had to use "uncut" in everything I wrote. That was the rule, regardless of whether the guy in the pictures was clearly circumcised. Believe it or not, in my short stay on the job, I became really good at writing gay fiction. The job even helped me become more accepting of the gays. For the loose-cabooshed editor's birthday, we threw an office party and had soda and cake, and we all signed a card. I wrote, "Edwardo, if you were five years older and I was four years younger, I'd be so up on your shit." After that day he was much nicer to me, and his pants always seemed a bit tighter in my presence.

Then one day, proofs for all 10 magazines arrived at once. I arrived for work early, as I'd been doing for some time, trying to actually learn the job, but the proofs were there before I was at 7 a.m., along with a note that read, "We need all of these by 11:00." That was it. An impossible task. It took me an average of five hours to proof one magazine because I was so terrified of being found out. I stormed into the publisher's office and said, "This is too much. No one can pull this off. I either need a raise or an assistant." I was praying so hard that she would agree to get me an assistant, then I could make them do all the work—perhaps even have them show me what I was supposed to be doing. Instead they offered me a $10,000 raise. So I quit, knowing that sooner than later I'd have a nervous breakdown. The coroner might say it was a result of $85,000 worth of cocaine, but God would know it had more to do with uncut cocks, Civil War–widow centerfolds, and *The Chicago Manual of Style*.

CHAPTER 3
"Even the Losers Get Lucky Sometimes"
(My poor wife)

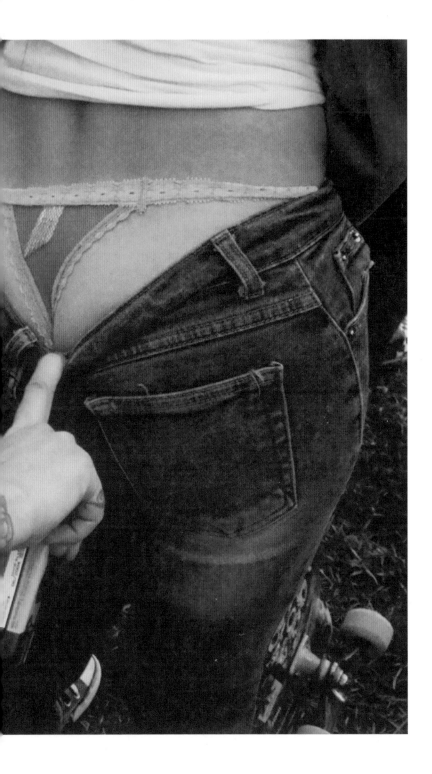

My Girlfriend's Cock

REDLIGHTDISTRICTVIDEO.COM · DIR: CARLOS SAFADO · RATING: 5

I got engaged to Crissie, my lady of many years, on 25 June 2004, for those who want to mark it in their diaries. It was all quite romantic. Despite what one may think of my various perversions I'm quite a sweetheart. Ask any girl I haven't fucked over, they'll tell you the same. For me, the hard part was toning down my sentiments and coming up with a memorable way of popping the question on short notice. For months leading up to asking for her hand I was making lists of ways to do it: taking her to Hawaii and asking her on a deserted beach; pulling over on the Jersey Turnpike and popping the question in front of a bright refinery; hiding the ring in her food; and so on.

When I actually picked up the ring I expected to let a month or so pass and allow the perfect plan to come to me but the moment I actually held it something came over me, like in *Lord of the Rings*, and I couldn't stop thinking about The Precious. The ring was on the fringe of my every thought and within days I couldn't take it anymore. I was worried she'd find it, or, worse, I'd lose it before we could insure the damn thing. "I have to give her this thing, already, it's driving me mad," I thought.

That's when I learned of a small cruise ship near my home that went around Manhattan and the Statue of Liberty, with dinner, dancing, booze and the whole bit. So I lied to her and told her a car was coming to take us to a formal dinner in New York to discuss my screenplay with some bigwigs at Miramax. I think lying is acceptable, and marriages based on lies are the only ones that really have any chance of success. The lie is the cornerstone of life, is it not? So I fooled her. I fooled her into thinking we were meeting Harvey Weinstein and I fooled her into marrying me. Now I'm engaged and I don't feel any different. Not about her, nor life or anything. I'm not sure if I am supposed to, but I don't. Yet when I saw the title of this transsexual DVD I began to wonder, "Is that what I am? My girlfriend's cock? Have I just relinquished my identity?"

Then I went and brushed my teeth, as that's what I do when I feel insecure, and as I spit out a clump of excess toothpaste I caught my sad brown eyes in the mirror and realized I was kidding myself. I never had an identity to begin with. I've been a nobody since the moment the air hit me in the delivery room and an engagement ring doesn't change that.

On Location Portugal

SCORELAND.COM • DIR: LOUIS LAWSON • RATING: 8

I'm getting married on July 1, 2006. I'm very excited. I'll finally be able to call my woman my wife and have the title become official. Right now I call her my wife because I don't like the term "fiancée." It doesn't roll off the tongue the way "wife" does. I don't know if it's because it's a multisyllable word or because it sounds too French but I hate it. FREEDOM FRIES! I rarely use it, and when it leaves my lips I get mad at myself.

Lately, I've begun making various arrangements for the wedding. Yesterday I chose my ring, last week we decided on our wedding party. We're currently trying to figure out what we're going to do for a band. Crissie wants to make things easy and get a typical wedding cover band. I, on the other hand, want to hire Ghostface to do half the evening and a fellow by the name of Big Elvis to do the other half. If you're not familiar with Big Elvis he is an amazing Elvis impersonator from Las Vegas, with the voice of an angel, who happens to weigh 450 pounds. I love him. One thing we have both agreed on is that our honeymoon will be one month in Portugal. That's right, folks! The Nieratkos are taking a European Vacation. Come check us out. One month only, we'll be touring the countryside. Come next July you can find us anywhere from the Algarve to Oporto. I thought it would be funny to tell you we made our decision to go to Portugal based solely on this DVD; that after seeing the crystal-blue water and white sand of the Algarve beaches as a backdrop to these massive-breasted women frolicking about we made up our minds. "Thanks, Score! Portugal, here we come!" But no. That is not the case. This film just conveniently came as I was explaining to Crissie how serene the south of Portugal is. I tried to use the film as an aid in my sales pitch. "Look past the big tits and you will see an amazing honeymoon waiting for us." "But the tits are so big, they take up the whole screen," she said. I tried to fast-forward so she could see the large, rocky cliffs that line the beaches, but she was right, it was difficult to see much more than the massive mammaries. I found a few frames where the breasts weren't as prominent and I paused them and used a laser pointer to explain what she was looking at. Granted, video or not, she didn't have a choice.

Chunky School Girls

SKIN TIGHT MODELING • DIR: GRIP JOHNSON • RATING: 3

Remember back in school when it was cool to tell fat people just how fat they were, right to their face? Those were the days. No matter how bad you felt about yourself you could always walk into class and say to the cow next to you, "God. You are so fucking fat. How do you live with yourself?" After that it was just a matter of time before they started to cry and instantly the world was a better place. The world seemed so different then. And for as small as my town was it somehow produced an endless supply of unsightly creatures to help with any self-esteem issues a growing boy might have.

There was this one girl whose stomach hung down below her twat, completely covering her snatch. Me and my friends call it a gunt (gut/cunt), I don't know what you'd call it. She was the easiest target. It wouldn't take more than a few seconds of well-timed insults regarding her weight for her eyes to well up with tears before the dam broke. Oh! How we all laughed at her loud, cowlike sobs.

What I don't understand is at what point making fun of the ugly stopped being chic. Personally, I'm not one to follow trends so I have continued to indulge in mocking the eyesores of this world. Yet my friends, friends who once pointed their fingers along with me, now are "shhhh"-ing me as if I'm doing wrong. I'm doing this world a service. If more people spoke their minds maybe the fat would do something about their appearance. My biggest fear is marrying a beautiful girl, going to bed, waking up 10 years later and finding she's become too obese to get up. Have you ever considered murder? I think under such circumstances a husband should be allowed to kill his wife.

Do you think if I wrote in my prenuptial agreement that if my wife allows her weight to exceed 135 pounds I reserve the right to kill her, that it would be legally binding? It's no different than euthanasia, really. If the person agrees to premature death, I shouldn't go to jail for killing them. It's kind of like buying a car, I suppose. You invest in something that is going to hold up over time. When that car's appearance and performance fail to meet basic standards and is no longer worth keeping around, isn't it the owner's responsibility to dispose of it, for the safety and consideration of others? If and when my future wife breaks down and no longer has that new-wife smell that I fell in love with, I should be able to dispose of her as well.

I wish things were how they used to be, when you could say, "You fat pig, if you don't stop crying I'm gonna slice your neck," and not get arrested for it. And if she went and slit her wrists, so what? It's not your fault. Why is everyone so uptight nowadays? I blame the Taliban.

The Wedding

VIVID.COM • DIR: BO EDWARDS • RATING: 9

In the eyes of the church and those of the court I am still not married. In terms of commitment and love, I feel as if I've already made my vows but there are still formalities I must tend to before it is official. Have I ever told you my mother is a total God-fearing Catholic from the old school? She is, and for her sake I make certain concessions to keep her happy. At the moment she's especially pissed at me and hasn't spoken to me in days.

My brother and his wife recently asked me and my gal, Crissie, to be godparents to their newborn second child, Ethan. To do this you need to prove you are a practicing Catholic worthy of the responsibilities that come with the title. My relationship with God is my own and I don't wish to discuss it here or with anyone, including my mother, which translates to her that I no longer believe. For me and Crissie to get the necessary papers we went and visited our church secretary. I insisted to both Crissie and my sister that it didn't matter if I attended church or not, if I wrote a check big enough they'd grant us the certificate. I was correct. I haven't been to church in a great many years but my mother, in the hope of saving my soul, has been turning in my weekly donation envelopes, so when I told the secretary my name she responded with, "Oh, I know you, you come to church each week, I see your envelopes all the time." I said nothing, she handed me the certificate. I asked for a second for Crissie and she obliged. No questions asked. To be a dick and prove my point I went to my mother's house and hung our certificates on her refrigerator with cute magnets of ladybugs. And the trouble began, unbeknownst to me, as my mother is completely passive-aggressive. My brother called the next day and explained how everyone in my family was pissed at me because I lied to the priest to get the forms. I told him I hadn't even seen the priest and I didn't lie. I was prepared to lie but didn't need to. The next day was Ash Wednesday.

Mel Gibson's controversial film *The Passion of the Christ* was released and I celebrated by renaming the day Ass Wednesday and having Crissie stamp her butt on my forehead, informing her that was how I'd get the brown mark on my head. She thought it quite funny but caught herself mid-laugh for fear of my mother hearing her. Not the fear of God, mind you, fear of my mother.

No Man's Land 39

VIDEOTEAM.COM • DIR: REN SAVANT • RATING: 9

Lesbian videos are a big hit around our house but good lesbian videos are hard to find. Generally the girls who are in girl-on-girl videos don't like girls and it really comes across that way. There's nothing worse then watching a girl pretend to lick pussy when you can clearly see she's not even making contact.

No Man's Land 39 won me over when Crissie pointed out a position she'd never seen before. One girl's on her back with a strap-on, then a second girl climbs on top of her and rides the strap-on, then a third girl, also wearing a strap-on, comes behind the second girl but rather than fucking her ass she actually starts fucking the first girl who is lying down. Hope I'm not confusing you. If so, it's fine. I was confused for a moment too. The point is, Crissie turned to me and said, "I want to try that," and friends, there aren't many maneuvers left that can elicit that response from her. But I've got kind of a situation on my hands now. It's hard enough finding one girl to pair her up with due to her very high standards and very low tolerance for filthy whores, so finding two girls who fit the bill to reenact this scene is near impossible. I wish life were like casting a movie, where I could just call some agencies to track down talent. "Listen," I'd tell them, "we need someone young but not too young, who is knowledgeable and experienced and able to ad-lib. They should be in good physical shape and well-stacked on the top end. Hair color and ethnicity aren't as big of a concern as a clean bill of health. We need six months of documentation showing blood tests, checkups and everything else. The most recent tests should be no older than two weeks and we'd like written confirmation from a doctor that the person is in good health and is a good candidate for lesbian sex. Let me know what you come up with." Once we've come up with a number of prospective bodies we'd have them come by my office for Crissie and I to meet, greet and inspect. After some basic questions (How old are you? Do you like anal?), we'd have them undress, do a little dance, then give us a solo audition to see how they work firsthand. We'd thank them and tell them we'd get back to them. From there we'd go home and study notes and photos to see which applicants best suited our needs. If only life were that fucking easy, I wouldn't have to try and find ways to persuade my fiancée to lick a blowup doll's crotch.

 ## The Reincarnation of Betty Paige

METROINTERACTIVE.COM · DIR: ROMAN PORNANSKI · RATING: 10

I got my first tattoo when I was 17 but didn't really appreciate the art form until I'd turned 21 and could drink legally. Most likely it was in some smoky shit-hole biker bar that I began to realize it was possible to literally and figuratively wear your heart on your sleeve. That's when I really got into not only getting tattooed but observing and appreciating tattoos of all kinds from the typical (butterflies, suns and yin yangs) to the silly (Yosemite Sam, pictures of ham and eggs) to the religious and so on and so forth. And when you fall in love with tattoos it automatically changes the image in your head of what sexy is. The hair gets blacker, the bangs get chopped, the thighs wider, the tits bigger, the clits pierced, the arms sleeved with ink, and suddenly without knowing it you realize that if she doesn't look like Betty Paige you really don't have time to bother with her. This feeling or fetish or uncontrollable desire or whatever you want to call it really manifested itself when I landed in Ohio. If I went on one date I went on 20 and aside from a pair of thick-rimmed glasses, varying tattoos, and minor discrepancies in pubic-hair trimming they were all the same girl: a Betty Page clone. Since then my tastes have changed drastically. My fiancée is the polar opposite of the woman I have just described but I will always hold a soft spot in my heart for that girl, for that look. So I thank Metro Interactive and Darla Crane, the busty beauty in this DVD who stars as the Betty Page look-alike, for making this film and allowing me to reminisce over days long gone from the comfort and safety of my own home without fear of "Is this stripper going to break in my apartment tonight," or "If I don't go over there will she really kill herself," or "What happened to my television set and my wallet?" I do have one concern that I should probably express since I know my fiancée, Crissie, is reading this and many times I find it easier to broach a subject on paper, in the public forum, rather than one-on-one. Is that healthy? Well, this is one of those times. She has been watching this DVD on her own and has really been enjoying it, which I think is great because it means we both find Betty Page sexy and 6 times out of 10 we differ on which porn stars we think are hot. And if she were to come home with a black Betty Page wig for when we play dress-up I wouldn't make her return it. But recently she has been talking about getting her first tattoo. She's brought it up a few times in the past but as of a few months ago, when I made her kiss a napkin and had an artist tattoo her exact lip marks right above my penis, she's been bringing it up more and more. I don't want to dissuade her, I have no right to because I don't exactly run it by her before coming home with something new tattooed onto my body. It's just I don't want her tainted, if that makes sense. Her skin is still clean and pure, I look at her as an angel and something inside me tells me it should be criminal to allow her to deface something so perfect. Unless it's a pussy or nipple piercing, then I'm behind her 100%.

Bella Loves Jenna

CLUBJENNA.COM • DIR: JUSTIN STERLING AND JENNA JAMESON •
RATING: 8

She rolled over and woke me from a dead sleep to tell me about her strange dream. She does this often enough so I wasn't really annoyed. Generally she'll just stare at me allowing her psychic powers to wake me, but this night she turned on all the lights in the room and poked my neck, "Hey, baby. Baby, are you awake?" "Yes," I said through a venomous laugh, "of course I'm awake. I'm just doing the crossword puzzle in *The New Yorker* at 4 a.m., in the dark, waiting for you to talk to me." "Are the lights too bright? I turned on the lights, do they bother you?" I pulled the blankets over my head and told her it reminds me of solstice in Alaska, then I asked what it was about. "What?" she asks, pretending that this is not a routine we've mastered over the years. "Your dream. What was it about?" I enjoy hearing her dreams, they are always twisted and borderline insane and I envy them. I am a man without dreams. My mind is put to rest as soon as my eyes close, for those short hours from night to sunrise I'm a blank slate. Or so it seems since I am unable to remember my dreams aside from the reoccurring one where I'm shot outside the movie theater, but that one grows less and less frequent as the years pass. If anything I get snippets, fractions of scenes from my subconscious, non sequiturs from my psyche that don't add up to much at all: a coffee cup with lipstick about the rim, a cameo by Sean Penn, a Chinese rice box full of maggots. Therefore I'm delighted when she shares whatever her mind whips up in the wee small hours of the night. "We went back in time," she started. I loved it already. I wanted to stop her before she got too far along so I could go and make some popcorn and really settle into the story. "Do you remember that porn chick Belladonna that you took a photo with in Vegas? The one your friend Chris likes even though she sucked off a transsexual?" "Yes, of course. What did she do, that evil slut? Did she go back in time and try to rescue Hitler and we had to stop her?" "Uh . . . no. We went back in time and we met her when she was younger. She was fucking all these guys, like a whole football team at once. Afterwards she'd cry and cry. She hated herself. It was very sad." "Sounds boring. Is that all you've got?" "Well, you and I got into a big fight. I wanted to talk to her, to tell her she needed to stop doing what she was doing, that she was better than that, that if she kept on she'd end up on camera in some $20 motel with two dicks up her ass, wondering how she had gotten there. But you wouldn't let me say anything to her. You said it wasn't for us to meddle with the fabric of time. That by changing just one aspect of Belladonna's life it could send the whole world into a downward spiral that it could never recover from." "That's ridiculous, I was probably just joking." "Yeah, you were. As soon as you said it you started laughing, and said that you just wanted her to suck that tranny's dick or else no one would. I thought that was really funny."

Silvia Saint's Private Collection

PRIVATE.COM • DIR: VARIOUS • RATING: 10

Hitler is a cock-blocker. Actually, his secretary is. There I was in bed with this amazing blonde piece of ass, dick rock-hard, ready to do terribly filthy things to her naked body. I'd been thinking about it all day, the entire fiendish act. A full eight-hour shift on the job passed quickly with the aid of depraved mental images. Customers with questions were ignored as I stared into the future, seeing the sweat flying, smelling the scent of unbridled passion. Then, just as I was about to pounce, I recalled I had rented a documentary on Hitler's secretary, Traudl Junge, called *Blind Spot: Hitler's Secretary* and that the film was due back first thing in the morning.

Junge was but a teenager when she met the Führer, naive and impressionable, searching for the father figure she'd never had. Strangely, some 50 years after the fact, her bright blue eyes seem just as wide and uncertain as if three years in the Nazi leader's secret bunker hadn't affected her at all. She danced back and forth between believing the man was a genius—a kind, nurturing man—and accepting he was indeed an evil, evil monster. The "documentary" was really nothing more than a series of interviews, there were no photos or footage of the diaries she kept from her time in Hitler's service. No stock footage from the era or anything aside from her tale to keep the viewer reading the subtitles. I found myself nodding off until the final 30 minutes, when she focused on the eerie last three days when Hitler asked her and the other women to leave the bunker, to leave Berlin and Germany, when Eva Braun refused, swearing she'd never leave him. The others vowed to stay as well. Junge discussed their bunker wedding, Adolf's last dictation where he declared to the dying end that what he had done was with Divine Providence, that his goals were just. I saw the uncertain emotion in her face, torn between love for the man and love for humanity. She struggled to absolve herself for aiding such a madman; her final words to the director, just as the film was due to premiere, were that she had "begun to forgive myself." Oddly, her words inspired me and I turned to the sleeping beauty by my side and reached for her. Stone cold she said, "You want Hitler's secretary so badly, you can rewind it and jerk off to her."

Outnumbered 2

REDLIGHTDISTRICTVIDEO.COM · DIR: ERIK EVERHARD · RATING: 8

I only got to see this DVD once and as the title indicates there are many woman getting fucked by very few men, a fantasy all men wish to be a part of but one that doesn't film very well, at least not to my satisfaction. Picture a scenario with 10 women, three men and only one camera. Tell me how, with all that touching, one camera can possibly catch all the action. It can't.

Certainly double anals are impressive but visually they are sickening. If filmed directly from behind the men, which they usually are, all you can see is two sets of nards rubbing frantically against each other causing a four-ball pile up, a sight I can live without, thank you.

Crissie was rather fond of this porno, which is just more reason for her to be angry with me this week. I am very good at coping with her menstrual cycle, and generally I know not to rock the boat for the days leading up to the rising of the red tide, but this time around I chose Hitler's secretary over sex with her the night before the blood came. To make matters worse I put *Outnumbered 2* into the rental case for the documentary on Hitler's secretary, and returned it to the video store. It took a day for me to realize I still had the documentary, a fact that annoyed Crissie to no end: "Well, if you were going to keep the movie you could have fucked me the other night," as if I'd returned the wrong video on purpose. When I called the store to explain the mix-up the manager told me they had indeed received the wrong film. I laughed it off, I mean it's a funny situation, don't you think? The manager didn't agree and told me, "The film you returned was very inappropriate." His righteous, accusing tone quickly brought my blood to a boil. "Listen, pal. I don't want your shitty DVD," I said. "It wasn't even that good, it's not like I was trying to steal *Caddyshack*. How about I just come up there and give you your movie back and I grab mine and we can be done with this?" "That's not possible," he informed me. "This is a family establishment. Maybe you've noticed we do not carry offensive films in our store. Your film has already been discarded. We have also charged your account for the movie you kept." So that's that. Now I'm the "porno guy" every time I go to my video store.

Plumb and Dumber

PLUMPRODUCTIONS.COM • DIR: ANTHONY SPINELLI • RATING: 7

You know what else is dumb? The video store has caller I.D. so whenever I call there, whoever answers laughs and without covering the receiver says to their co-worker, "Hey, the porno perv is on the phone." I really need to find another video store. Of course I always seem to ask for videos that have titles that can be misconstrued as porn titles like *Cocktail* or *Jackie Brown* or *Saving Ryan's Privates*—I mean *Saving Private Ryan*—which forces a giggle from the other end of the phone and an, "Uh, we don't have adult movies, sir" from some zit-faced teenager who makes less per hour than I spend per beer. Depending on my mood I'll try and explain, "No, you little shit. *Cocktail* with fucking Tom fucking Cruise," but that only gets me transferred to the store manager, who will never forgive me for "trying to double-cross him" for the Hitler documentary. It's all bullshit. The thing is I live in a suburban area where video stores aren't very common. I can't think where another one is in my area. If I knew I'd gladly go there because these big corporate family rental places have no real selection aside from bullshit blockbuster movies like *Pearl Harbor* or some bullshit Jim Carrey movie; finding a documentary on Hitler's secretary was like finding an original Picasso at a garage sale. Let me ask you something. Can I get in trouble for writing down violent thoughts, if by chance they miraculously happened? I began thinking about this yesterday after watching the Lakers destroy my Nets. As the Lakers walked to their locker room at halftime I yelled at Shaquille O'Neal a few feet away, "I hope your plane crashes and you all die." Now, if their plane were to crash, without any help from me, am I liable? At the moment I'm thinking, "Fuck that video store. I hope the place burns to the ground." Let's say that tonight as I sleep the place does catch on fire, can I be arrested? There's no law against wishing ill will on someone, is there? I hope not because there are a lot of people I want dead and

I would hate to read in the paper that they were brutally murdered in a way that I hoped they would be and then have to worry about fleeing the country or a life in prison. I don't think I would fare too well in prison. I don't particularly like the company of men that much. Especially when I'm showering, which is definitely when I would get gang-raped because I have really awful balance. If I want to scrub my lower legs and the soles of my feet I need to prop myself up against the wall with either my shoulder or my head and even then I nearly fall over and most always drop the soap. It's not a good quality for a prison inmate. Not to mention I go through severe separation anxiety from my girlfriend if she even leaves the room to piss in the course of the night. The other day I called her school and had her pulled out of class so I could hear her voice. "What are you doing?" I asked. "I'm in the middle of teaching class. What's the matter? Is everything okay?" "Oh. Yeah. Everything's fine. I'm just lonely. Can you come home so we can hang out and play Monopoly or Connect Four?" "Sure," she said. "I'll be right there." But she was just lying to get me to leave her alone.

The Perfect Secretary

ADAMEVE.COM • DIR: NICK ORLEANS • RATING: 11

From the ages of 17 to 19 I worked for Disney in a high-rise Manhattan office building. I'm still not sure what I did there, something with comic books, I'm just not sure what. What I do know is that working in that environment, surrounded by sexy, married, mid-30s professionals in their work attire and office skirts, gave me a two-year-long boner that 10 years later comes back at the mere sight of a long pair of legs poured into a pant suit. Back then I was a snot-nosed kid living off ramen, showering weekly, changing my clothes even less frequently; my dirty thoughts of forcing myself on one of those high-paid white-collar dolls were justified to me as a means of balancing out the universe, leveling the playing field between lower and upper class.

Sadly, I never acted upon my desires. Instead, I try and force my wife to dress in the garb that I still find so alluring. It's not often that I hand over my credit card freely; shit, it's rare that I buy her anything at all. I mean, she has me, what else could she possibly want? A new coat? I'll keep her warm. A new car? Where could she be going? I'll drive her. New sneakers? People survived centuries without any footwear at all and it was good enough then, it should be good enough now. The only time she has an open invitation to max out any and all of my Mastercards is when she is shopping for outfits of my liking. I'm more than willing to shell out for a closet full of blouses, professional-looking pants and/or dress skirts with matching blazers. Are they called blazers if they are for women? You know what I mean, though, the jacket. I like when the stockings match the blouse and are connected with those clamps. The girders? Or gardners? Whichever, put them on my bill. I understand the importance of accessorizing, so I'll even go so far as to buy an authentic pearl necklace. And glasses are an absolute must; possibly two pairs, one to wear and another for her to chew on the end of one of the arms in a seductive manner.

Not that I have any complaints in life, but if my wife could dress like that around the house all the time, it would ensure that I'd live out the rest of my days a happy man. Nick Orleans knows that. That's why he made this movie specifically for me, to appease me while I try and find some money to buy a house that my wife can actually walk around in. In the meantime I must wake at 6 a.m. and sit at the commuter parking terminal, watching all the fine women waiting for their bus to Manhattan, and pretend.

Secret Suburban Sex Parties

ADAMEVE.COM • DIR: NICK ORLEANS • RATING: 9

I need to buy a house. I've been wanting to do it for some time now but haven't had the money. I've been waiting on a multimillion movie deal to go through for years. But who isn't? I'm hoping I'll be able to get a house sooner than later. It's not like I really need a house, I've been sleeping in my office for years and haven't really minded it. But recently me and my girl moved into my mom's house to help her out while she gets knee surgery. My mom is great and is never a hassle, it's just that our sex life has taken a bit of a kick in the balls. When I was commuting back and forth between New Jersey and Los Angeles we'd always get hotel rooms and have loud, animalistic circus sex but now we are forced to use the mute button on ourselves; cringing and worrying if the bed so much as creaks once. It's like being in high school again. It's not that my mother doesn't know we're fucking down there, it's just rude of us to be blatant about it. Also I bought this amazing sex swing off eBay nine months ago, when we were looking at homes, but because of our living situation it still sits in the box. Can you imagine my mom knocking on our door and seeing that rig hanging from the ceiling? Or worse yet, what if it cracked a board in the ceiling and brought the whole floor above us crashing down. How the hell would I explain that? One thing that I've decided when we get our house is we are going to have a fuck chamber. It will be connected to and only accessible through our bedroom. No one will even know it exists. It will have wall-to-wall mirrors on the walls and ceiling. The swing will be in one corner, a comfy love seat against one wall, a gynecologist chair in the middle of the room with stirrups and restraints and a large, sterile, stainless-steel doctor's closet to house our ever-growing collection of dildos, vibrators, plugs, corks and contraptions. Another key reason we need our own home is that we're unable to have sex parties at my mom's house. I think that's why I'm so in love with this DVD. Director Nick Orleans has managed to compile some of my favorite domestic fantasies onto one disc to tide me over until we get some real estate and start having girls sleep over every night. Each of the six scenes is straight-forward, perfect and to the point. There's the panty party, bache-lorette party, breakfast party, going-away party, lingerie party and birthday party; all very self-explanatory. At the panty party a bunch of girls try on panties, ultimately getting naked and finger-banging each other and fucking each other with toys. After they are all good and turned on and drenched in their own fluids the boyfriend (me) comes home, finds the girls, pulls his dick out and starts getting love from all three.

That should be my life. It should be everyone's life, but the differ-ence is I can have it be my reality. I just need to get a goddamn house. And a video camera.

Busted!

STARRPRODUCTIONS.BIZ • DIR: ELIZABETH STARR • RATING: 7

We've been looking for houses lately with no luck at all. Everything is either too big, too small, too old, too expensive or too run-down. One that we looked at last Sunday was most defi-nitely a crack house. In the driveway sat a tireless automobile resting on cinder blocks beside a basketball rim that was bent so it faced the ground. On the front porch were nearly two dozen pairs of worn-out sneakers and boots, none of which matched. A small child answered the door, looked us up and down, then went back inside, leaving us looking into the house for nearly five minutes before a middle-aged crackhead came to the door. "What do you want?" he asked. We told him we'd come to see the house and he perked right up. Inside smelled of a combination of death, dog shit, burning hair and crack. All the windows were covered over with tarps; with no light for us to see by, we bumped into everything in our path. The homeowner did, at one point, lift a tarp to reveal his sprawling backyard. Instead of looking out the window I scanned the room and found a number of children hiding in the corners, shielding their eyes from the sun. You could almost see the filth and disease floating in the air. He then led us into the master bedroom, which had a mattress on the floor and three ragtag baby cribs. I began to think that they were producing children and reselling them on the black market to support their addiction. Next to the master bedroom was the garage, which was converted into a playroom/paint-huffing den. On the floor sat an outdated videogame system and a number of aerosol paint cans. The toxic odor in the room burned my eyes. A small child lay on a tattered couch, eyes crossed. I told him we'd seen enough. "What about the upstairs? Don't you want to see the upstairs?" he asked. I told him, "Your house is fucked. You're lucky I don't call the police on you." With that we went to our next appointment. I had an awful feeling in the pit of my stomach. I wish it was from seeing the atrocities in the previous house but I knew it was from the cheeseburger sub I ate earlier. I doubted I could see one more house without shitting myself. Two houses later I was certain I'd soil my pants. Two houses after that I had no choice but to use the bathroom of the house we were looking at. I assumed it would be fine. The house was empty. The owners having already moved out, no one would mind. As Crissie went on to check out the master bedroom I snuck off and did my business. But when it came time to wipe my ass I realized there was no toilet paper. I weighed my options: don't wipe and smell like shit all day; use my T-shirt and see the next three houses shirtless; jump in the shower and rinse off; or call for my wife in hopes she might have some napkins in her purse. I opted for the latter. A knock came at the door: "Are you okay?" I told her, "I need your help. Get in here!" The door swung open but instead of seeing Crissie it was some middle-aged woman in a sundress. In unison we yelled out, "Who the fuck are you?" Turned out she owned the house and she was none too happy to see me shitting in it. Next thing I'm getting hit with a broom and being chased out the front door with my trousers around my ankles, excrement smearing my ass cheeks.

Nina Hartley's
Guide to Threesomes

ADAMEVE.COM • DIR: NINA HARTLEY • RATING: 7

I've begun looking into buying a home and I refuse to get one with a pool. I know it's only a matter of time before my wife finds herself a young, strapping pool boy. I'm also trying to avoid homes with plumbing, electricity and cable TV for similar reasons. I do want a room full of mirrors to have sex in. I guess I'm an egomaniac in that sense. I like to look at myself while performing my dirty deeds. It is also the only reason I'm marrying my wife, Christine, in the first place; it's quite exhilarating to be able to call your own name in the throes of passion. I would preferably like to be able to call my own name and that of another woman's, but my lady is ultra-picky when it comes to inviting girls into our bedroom. She basically insists it has to be either Pamela Anderson or Savanna Samson. I've begged her to be a bit more realistic with her selection and she's mildly attempted to compensate.

The other night we met a cocktail waitress at my friend's bar, a brunette with a petite figure, narrow "fuck-me" eyes and a pleasant disposition. Crissie took to her and they began chatting it up. They even casually kissed goodnight. On the cheek. We've been back to see her twice since but nothing really has come of it. I have no idea how to broach these topics with women and sadly my wife's not putting forth much effort either. She's the one with the rapport with the girl; she should ask her to dinner or whatever it is that gets the carpet-munching ball rolling.

It's quite frustrating. I have less than a year until my actual wedding day and I'm ready to tell her I'm going to postpone the festivities if she doesn't make nice with a girl soon. Two nights ago I introduced her to a stripper I knew and she said she wasn't her type. I told her she needn't fuck that stripper but she better fuck someone, and soon, because I'm losing my patience.

Party at Butts Place

SEYMOREBUTTS.COM • DIR: SEYMORE BUTTS • RATING: 8

The box reads: "It started off as a housewarming party and it turned into a 24-hour bun-scorcher!" I finally bought a house; it isn't quite ready to be shown yet but I think if and when I do have a housewarming party I would like it to "turn into a 24-hour bun-scorcher" as well. I'm sure it won't. I'm not that lucky. And more importantly I'm dead broke. Since becoming a homeowner I feel as if I've moved into the poorhouse. We barely have money for the mortgage. Our trips to the grocery store are brief, with little more than ramen, rice and wine in our carts. We have implemented money-saving rules that have severely compromised our lifestyle. The first one is: Learn to see in the dark or use a candle. In an attempt to keep the energy bill low I have insisted we not use lights at night. A bylaw of this rule is that the bedroom door must always stay open because once after a long night of drinking I awoke at 4 a.m. and had to piss like a racehorse. I jumped out of bed and sped to the bathroom in the dark but the door was shut and I ran smack into it, knocking myself out cold. I ultimately peed all over my new hardwood floors; so you can understand the reason for such a rule. Also, in the winter I would not use the heat, rather I had seven layers of blankets on the bed to keep us warm. Now that it's getting to be summer I have put a ban on all air-conditioner use; I have a stack of paper plates in each room to be used as hand fans. We don't have cable television and won't get it until after we're married, if ever. Actually we don't have a TV whatsoever. The worst and possibly the grossest money saver I've implemented is that I don't allow Crissie to flush the toilet unless she makes poops. If it's only piss I tell her to wait until the end of the day, and multiple pisses, before flushing to conserve water. I say, "If it's yellow, let it settle. If it's brown, send it down." There are times in the stifling heat that the entire house smells of urine but that's just how it is because we're broke. It can be quite embarrassing when unexpected visitors stop by. The other day Crissie's mom stopped by for lunch and went to use the bathroom. She returned to inform us, "I think someone forgot to flush." I apologized. Then she walked into my office and saw the stack of porn that I had on my desk to review. She went white. Again I apologized. She ignored me, got in her car and went home. Crissie turned to me and said, "We need to buy you a bin to keep your porn out of sight." I simply asked, "With what money?"

M.I.L.F. 4

HEATWAVEVIDEO.COM • DIR: COOL BREEZE G • RATING: 4

I'm not sure if this is a New Jersey thing but doesn't every circle of friends always have that one mom who is always trying to get in her son's friends' pants? In high school it was this Puerto Rican kid's mom. I felt awful for him. I think she slept with every friend the kid had, except for me. I thought she was disgusting, brown trash. Recently divorced with high hair, low expectations, floppy pancake tits, saggy ass, yellowed cigarette teeth, and unsure of who the kid's dad was. She sickened me and she knew it, which caused her to ignore me completely when I came around, which was fine. Oh, but the stories. She was in her mid-30s and I know a few pairs of 16-year-old boys that double-teamed her. Have you ever had sex with a chick who had kids? It's kind of weird. Especially when the kid keeps asking for cookies in the middle of it. I hate that.

Lately I've been checking out a lot of pregnant girls with wanting eyes. There's something very sexy to me about a petite woman with child. I like how that little belly juts out so cute, almost supporting her newly enlarged milk-filled breasts. Do you think my biological clock is ticking? I think my lady would look very good with a baby belly. Sometimes I daydream about lying on a grassy knoll in the country, rubbing her tum-tum while drinking from her delicious breasts. How awesome would it be if black girls made chocolate milk

when they were pregnant? Mmmm, chocolate. I wonder if lactate is like sperm in how it takes on the taste of things you've eaten over the course of the day? I hope not. My girl's a vegetarian, so it wouldn't be too exciting. If she ate bacon that'd be different. Mmmm, bacon milk. I hope my wife can shoot her milk far. That would be fun, I think. Like at the dinner table, when I say something stupid like, "You know what?" and she says, "What?" and I say, "Chicken butt." And instead of her saying, "You're not funny," she just pulls out her tit and shoots me in the face from across the table. And the kid will love that. He'd laugh and laugh. Do you need to squeeze the tit to make it shoot? Or is it controlled mentally like some X-Men shit? I'd prefer the squeeze option because I don't think it would be fair to give my wife sole control over the tap. What if I can't sleep and want some milk or what if I'm bored and she's not in the mood to let me play with the sprinklers? I think by rights I should be allowed access to the milk whenever I like. Fuck X-Men tits. And do you think that in the early stages of pregnancy the woman's belly-button hole ever gets deep enough to fuck? I'd fuck a belly-button hole without thinking twice. And when the baby is born is it weird to have sex with it in the room, like if it was sleeping? How does that work? Because I don't see myself getting a separate hotel room on vacation for my newborn, so is it cool if we do it while it's sleeping? I should really write a book on this kind of stuff because all I ever see in the parenting section of the bookstore are books on teething and potty training, like any parent-to-be is concerned with that shit.

Lewd Conduct 15

ANABOLIC.COM • DIR: MIKE JOHN • RATING: 8

In terms of things in this life that we actually have some say in, is there anything worse than a lame fuck? I'm serious. There's nothing you or I can say or do to stop war or change the economy or teach women how to drive properly but in the bedroom poor performance is inexcusable and should be dismissed immediately. I'm very happy to say that at this point and time I am having the best sex of my life. My woman understands my needs, but doesn't compromise her own. She likes hot, freaky, circus sex but thankfully has never asked me to shit in her mouth. And she doesn't mind me sharing our love life with you, my friends, because when she is with her friends she does the same thing. A few weeks back her and a few of her girlfriends had a discussion about all things sex. Most were in agreement that anal sex is one of the best ways to spend a Sunday morning, all except for the young bride-to-be. At 22 she is about to marry and was sickened by the thought of any scenario that varied from the old "okay-get-on-top-okay-now-me-on-top." She referred to the type of sex that my girl and I have as "whore sex," a term that I have since fallen in love with and added to my daily dialogue. I no longer ask my girl if she'd like to hump, instead I say, "Who wants whore sex?" like a father about to take the kids for ice cream. Can you imagine how boring it must be to sleep with a person who refers to just about all sex acts as "whore sex"? The non-sinner said that she enjoyed romance, and that if she feels like her fiancée isn't being sensual and romantic she'll stop in the middle of it all and call it quits; sometimes it even makes her cry (okay, issues!). She also isn't into giving blowjobs. "I will, but not all the way," were her words, meaning she won't suck him off to completion and when the poor son-of-a-bitch does nut it's always inside her snatch, never on her tits, her ass and definitely not on her face. Once he came in her mouth and she spit it out like it was poison. She also feels sex toys are dirty and unnecessary. Are you turned on yet?

The other day the girls had a bridal shower for the psuedo-nun. As a gag my girl got her a little vibrator appropriately called "My First Vibe" and a cock ring for the fiancé. Even without a name tag on the gift the bride turned to my girl and said, "You are so kinky," laughed, then said, "What am I suppose to do with this anyway?" holding up the vibrator in confusion. "And what is this? Some kind of bracelet?" she said, holding up the cock ring for her mother, grandmother and aunts all to see.

Pleasure Island

PRIVATE.COM • DIR: ANTONIO ADAMS • RATING: 9

Hawaii was a fantastic vacation from my usual life of leisure. I spent three glorious weeks in the sun working on my tan; another week or two and you'd think I was Wesley Snipes. As it is, if I don't continually smile at night people can't see me. I'm that dark. The point of my stay was to document a skateboard trip; I felt the best way to do that was by buying an enormous amount of drugs and alcohol and lying on the beach and ogling camel-toe. I'm a master of the long, discreet stare. What I do is lay my towel just below the hottest girl on the beach, in perfect view of her covered pussy. I then proceed to lie on my stomach and act like I'm reading a book for hours, all the while imagining what's under those bikini bottoms. Sometimes it's sexual (what's does it feel/look/taste like), but once the drugs take effect it always becomes more of a hiding spot for my mind, much like a child with action figures. The sun burns so bright the world gets hazy. I get tunnel vision. The dehydration causes delirium. I begin to think I'm held up inside the vagina, looking out, like a camper in a sleeping bag. The only sounds I hear are the constant squawks of the gulls flying about. Going in the ocean seems like a good idea yet my legs cannot function even on a basic level. I fear I might drown, even in the shallowest of pools. Where are the lifeguards? I think I need an ambulance. Is it possible to drown on land? I crush up an orange pill, not sure what it is. I've lost all order within my drug collection. I had too many bottles in tow whenever I traveled. I was afraid of being stopped at customs so I've since consolidated them into two main bottles, the first being pills that affect the body, which must be what I'm on. The second bottle is strictly mental, those that shut off the brain completely for anywhere from one to twelve hours. I had both bottles with me on the beach but couldn't figure which was which. When sober I had thought up a brilliant yet simple way of distinguishing which bottle was which but at that very second, drooling into the sand, eyes rolling back into my head, I couldn't tell my ass from my elbow. I decided it best to just take a nap and hope that if and when I woke up my brain and body would both be in sync again. I pressed my luck and chose the smaller bottle full of tiny tic tac size meds. I dumped them out into my hand but missed, spreading them all over my towel. I scanned for the tiniest pill available. Rule of thumb: The smaller the pill the bigger the bite, plus it takes less time to digest and kick in.

When I awoke, the sun had been replaced by the moon and I was all alone on the beach. I'm not sure how long I'd been out but my gamble had worked. I was totally coherent. The next day I flew my girl in and we had sex in the ocean, which I thought was impossible, and she tried to give me a blowjob underwater and nearly drowned. The photo is hilarious.

Love Is in the Web

PRIVATE.COM · DIR: KOVI · RATING: 7

I 've never pursued ass on the Internet. Supposedly it's quite easy to find loose women in your area who are eager to put out, I've just never looked for them. I think it's just the fear of opening my front door to a 300-pound manatee looking for love that turns me off. Friends have insisted there are as many sexy lusting ladies as there are obese pigs, but I'm not buying it.

A sexy woman can walk out her door, whistle at the first person that passes by and say, "Excuse me, sir. I have a pussy that needs fucking," and she could be bent over within seconds. Fat people do not have that option. Fat people can only turn to fatter, more ugly people for love, and even then their chances are slim.

I always wonder what it's like to live that kind of life, the kind where you haven't got a snowball's chance in hell with any woman. Would I sit at home watching my smut and imagining an entire universe where I am king, where the most delicious women only yearn for me? Can you imagine? I wonder if that's what the fat and ugly are thinking when they look at people like me and Pamela Anderson. I bet in their heads they're thinking, "That guy wants to fuck me until my pussy starts yawning. He wishes." I bet they see me and take a mental picture, which they take back to their fortress of solitude to pleasure themselves to while eating biscuits and staring in the mirror with a bag over their head.

Their kind sicken me. We should quarantine the fat and the ugly. Environmentalists are so concerned with beautifying the lands, but I say fuck the forests and the landfills, let's start with the real eyesores. Put all the grotesque in a pen and let them cuddle all they want, just get them out of my sight. Or better yet, we could invite them all to a super-great party, with pie and beer and their favorite singer, whoever that is, Barbra Streisand most likely. We'll tell them that to get into the party they all have to take a group shower but we won't tell them that the shower really isn't a shower. Instead of water toxic gas comes in through the vents. This is brilliant. Once they've been thoroughly "cleaned," we could make soup, sorry, I mean soap, out of them, like in *Fight Club*. Hold on . . . I have to write this on my hand so I remember.

Okay.

You know, I had a funny anecdote to go with this video that had nothing to do with slaughtering the unsightly and I can't remember what it was.

Ah, yes. My brother-in-law is really into finding and fucking hot chicks off the Internet. He does really well for himself and he's a rather good-looking fellow. There was this time when his father was looking for something in his room and came across a number of naked Polaroids he had taken of himself, I suppose to e-mail to prospective gals. Supposedly the photos had him in all sorts of unnatural poses, sporting a stiff log in his hands. The father, instead of putting them back where he found them and pretending he'd never seen them, called down to his three other children, "Hey, guys! Get up here! You have to see what I found." They all had a good laugh at his expense. To prevent the photos from being misplaced they stuck them to the refrigerator so the brother could find them when he came home. It made it very difficult for me to prepare a sandwich.

Stocking Secrets #5

SMASHPICTURES.COM • DIR: KIRA EGGERS • RATING: 10

I asked Crissie if she had any funny stories about wearing stockings or pantyhose and she said, "I know a joke about pantyhose. What do pantyhose and New York have in common? Flatbush." I couldn't help but laugh. Isn't that retarded? That may be one of the worst jokes I've ever heard, yet I was pretty impressed that she had that one stored up her sleeve ready to go when I needed fodder for a stocking review. Then she said, "One time I was getting ready for dance class and I put on tights and as I bent down to pull them up they exploded. Completely blew out the crotch and I fell back and landed flat on my ass." I like when she tells me embarrassing stories of her childhood or any stories for that matter. Except when they involve boys or boyfriends, then I stop listening and just get jealous. Stupid, isn't it? For 25 years of her life we didn't know each other and yet I somehow expect her to be this untouched virgin. In my head I lie to myself and try and convince myself that I'm the only person she's ever been with and the fact that she gives amazing blowjobs is just one of those natural talents that God has given her, like throwing a baseball or being able to jump real high. Sometimes when she climbs into our sex-swing harness upside down and swings from her ankles I just say to myself, "Oh, she must have been in the circus when she was younger." In a sense I suppose it's good to not know everything about her, it enables me to make up little lies to protect my ego. Like when she gives me handjobs while she's driving the car I think, "I bet she used to drive 18-wheelers for a living. That's probably why she's able to multitask so well while driving." And when she gives me blowjobs underwater without coming up for air I just assume that she was probably a mermaid before I met her. She used to live under the sea with King Neptune breathing underwater just as I do above. I mean, what other logical explanation is there if she wasn't a mermaid in her past? That she's Aquaman's sister? I've met her brothers, she's not. I would know. The truth is my virgin fiancée once lived under the sea as a mermaid until she got bored and joined the circus where she was a trapeze artist for a number of years until deciding to hit the open road and do some soul searching as a truck driver and eventually ended up in New Jersey as a dance teacher and my little princess. Which by my account makes me the luckiest boy on earth.

The Masseuse

VIVID.COM/CLUBJENNA.COM • DIR: PAUL THOMAS • RATING: 9

Prior to last Christmas the only massages I'd ever had were from Asian massage parlors or ex-girlfriends and they all seemed to end with handjobs. So I found it kind of strange that my future mother-in-law would get me and Crissie a day at the spa, which included an hour-long deep tissue massage. "Did your mom just buy me a hand-job for Christmas?" I asked Crissie. Sadly, she explained it wasn't that kind of massage. Not that I needed a handjob massage, I was just curious as to what Crissie's massage was going to be like. I was hoping some hot little masseuse would take her into a dark room and turn her out with sounds of the sea playing over the speakers. Instead we had shitty back massages, which were made infinitely worse because we had two total loons administering them. Crissie's masseuse complained to her for an hour straight about her deadbeat husband who she was currently separated from, who liked to beat her stupid with a broomstick and had been cheating on her for a year with the neighbor and who she suspected had inappropriately touched their 6-year-old daughter; all the while kneading at Crissie's spine. Mine wasn't much better. I have a tattoo on my left arm of Our Lady of Guadalupe, on my right I have St. Michael. People see them and assume I am overly religious where in reality I am just a fan of that type of imagery. I grew up with my grandmother and she had reli-gious statues and paintings everywhere in her house and I'd lose hours of each day staring at them. My masseuse decided she was going to get all born-again Christian on my ass while trying to loosen the knots in my back. Five minutes later I had to tell her, "If I wanted a sermon I'd have gone to church, so how about you shut the fuck up and make with the back massage." She gasped, fell silent and made a tsk-tsk sound, then went back to working my back with all the strength and fury she could muster as if she was going to somehow work the devil right out of me. She fucked my back up so bad I

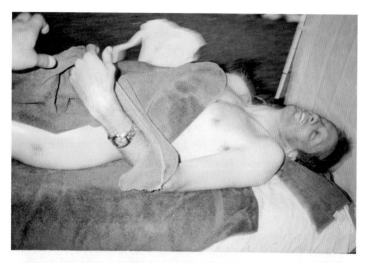

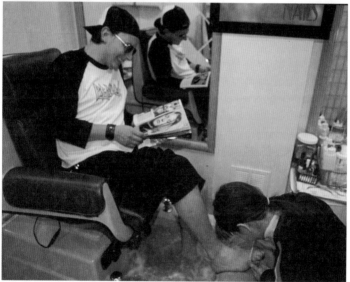

couldn't walk normal for a week. We've since completely given up on back massages, with and without handjobs. Now Crissie and I get pedicures when we need to relax because the Koreans can't speak English.

Stocking Fantasies 2

SUBURBANAMATEURS.COM • RATING: 10

That sexy blonde on the cover's name is Natalie Heck. She's made some dirty movies and I think I have a little crush on her. Ever since we met in London for a photo shoot I've wondered how I could get my wife and Natalie to put on a private show for me. I'm certain she's probably been thinking the same thing. Just kidding. She probably believes I'm a buffoon (which isn't far off the mark) because of my bumbling antics in her presence. I don't know what it is about women but they reduce me to nervous energy similar to Kramer or Jerry Lewis. I often wonder how I was able to keep my composure long enough to rope my wife. Of course, now that I have her entrapped I have returned to my goofy self when in her presence. I recall showing Crissie the photos from the shoot and having her ask me if I got a hard-on. I laughed. "Are you serious? I'm a professional," I told her. The reality is I was so scared having the attention of three lovely women directed at me that I thought I was going to soil myself. Sexual arousal was a distant thought. I, of course, wanted to see Natalie naked and play with herself (like she does in this film) and I subtly informed her of these desires in a nonspoken manner in which I chain-smoked, drank excessively, smeared cakes on my face and hit myself in the head with pots and pans. Needless to say I didn't lay much groundwork toward a ménage à trois with Crissie and Natalie that day. But as I said, I have thought about her quite a bit since. I even asked *Bizarre* publisher Will Watt where he found her. He referred me to an adult modeling agency in London. Turned out Natalie is willing to do more than pose and just look pretty. She's also willing to do masturbation and girl-on-girl porn. The fact that she won't suck or fuck cock on film tells me she truly is a classy woman. So I got to thinking because, you know, that's what I do. I plot and I scheme. Constantly. I may not look like a very smart man but neither did Hitler. It's the awkward, dim-looking ones you need to worry about. Anyway I came up with a plan. If Natalie is for hire for doing girl/girl scenes then why don't I just fly Crissie and I over to the U.K. and pay Natalie to do a "scene" with my wife? Naturally I'd film it, to keep things on the up-and-up. I have a number of directing and producing credits under my belt; I am essentially a filmmaker, I just have never shot porn outside of my home. How much can she charge per scene? $1,000? $2,000? I think my happiness, I mean, my wife's happiness is worth that and more. What do you think? I'm not proposing anything illegal, am I? Hope not, because I think this is one of the better plans I've thought of recently. I mean, my wife is always saying she'd like to go back to London.

Cum Inside 2

DIGITALSIN.COM • DIR: DILLION DAY • RATING: 11

Recognize that sassy lass on the cover? Yes, it's my dear Natalie Heck again. A few years back my buddies Will Watt and Alex Godfrey flew me over to London to do a photo shoot with three lovely ladies of my choice. That blonde firecracker that is pictured on the cover just happened to be one of the girls. Natalie Heck is her name and her website is www.natalieheck.co.uk. Isn't she dreamy? Years have passed since we did our shoot together and I can't get her out of my head, like that Kylie Minogue song. Every time I see a photo of her I picture myself and Crissie rolling about in the hay with her, making sweet circus sex to each other. I think I mentioned to you in the past that I planned on hiring her services to make a private video that would include her, my wife, a rubber chicken and a number of blunt objects. Well, after poking around on her site I found a rate card and it seems like my little plot may just become a reality when Crissie and I visit London next year. On the "About Me" page it states that she'll do a photo shoot with toys for 60 pounds per hour, and 75 for video. The same prices apply to girl/girl softcore. That being said, I would gladly pay double that for hardcore video. It seems more than worth it. Since discovering these facts I immediately went to my editor Alex Godfrey and *Bizarre* publisher Will Watt and said, "In the name of science and journalism I beseech you to fund a private photo and video shoot with my wife and darling Natalie Heck. Please refer to the attached rates." Will promptly responded, "If Crissie goes for it, we'll fund it. However, we have to have Crissie's consent in writing before taking this any further! Call it a wedding present to you both or maybe just you? Young Natalie is certainly a game girl. I'm thinking hotel room, nice bathroom, lots of bubble bath, two blondes go hardcore? We'll also video it for the website, too." Most likely I will refuse to put the hardcore action in print or on the website. I share everything else with you all, some things I must have for myself. Maybe I'll allow you to see the footage of us jumping on the beds and getting drunk, maybe even a photo of a kiss, but that's it. The rest is up to your imagination. If my superiors feel that is not enough, that they're not getting their money's worth, then I will pay for it out of my own pocket. Despite what I told you about being broke. Because I can live without heat or electricity, I can go without food, I don't mind stewing in my own piss but this is something I cannot live without.

It's Your Wife

EROTIC CITY ENTERTAINMENT • DIR: TOMMY GUNN • RATING: 8

"Hey, guess what? I fucked your wife." I love saying that to people, even when it's not true. It's almost as fun as spitting in someone's face. Another one I like is, "Have you kissed your wife today? Oh yeah? How's my dick taste?" That type of devastating humor always makes me laugh. Usually I'll just say it to guys I don't know, guys who are trying to be the biggest dick in the bar. I'm not a fan of loud, obnoxious people when I'm drinking. I like to drink in silence, save for the sounds of Hank Williams on the jukebox. Playing pool is acceptable but talking is strictly forbidden. Each time I open my mouth to speak is one less opportunity for me to put alcohol in it and I don't like that. If I wanted to talk I would have stayed home, poured a beer and picked up the telephone. Instead I chose to go out and pay inflated pub prices because I enjoy the atmosphere. It has nothing to do with needing the company. Anyhow, my point was I generally save my sharpened tongue for those that disturb my drinking. If I happen to actually see someone whose wife I had fucked I tend to panic. I try my best to avoid eye contact or having to make conversation. Not for fear, I'm just not much of a fan of awkward moments and when it comes to dealing with any man whose wife you've slept with it's always awkward. Even if you did it before they were married, even before they met. Isn't that strange? I understand it and can relate to it but it's still odd. I hate everyone that my wife has ever dated, slept with or even spoken to on principle alone. It's what men do. We're idiots but it is our way and any man that does not harbor ill will toward his woman's previous suitors more than likely is a homosexual. Or a candidate for membership in the porn community. There's a lot of that in porn, husbands allowing their wives to fuck on film, sometimes even serving as director on the set. I have difficulty understanding the depths of the love in such a relationship. How can one stand idly by as two men simultaneously fill their wife's ass and pussy with their cocks? It's madness, I tell you. Once I found a homemade sex tape of Crissie. I threw it in and found Crissie getting fucked by some random guy from behind. All I could see was his faceless ass and dick laying into her. I was enraged. I wanted to kill him. Until I realized the man having sex with her was me. But even then I was still pretty pissed at myself.

Loaded

DIGITALPLAYGROUND.COM • DIR: NIC ANDREWS • RATING: 7

So my wife took me to see that show *Stomp* for my birthday, you know where they bang on shit and call it music. I had seen part of the show once before, about 10 years ago, at a performance in Central Park hosted by my former employer Disney (which is a story in itself). What I saw summed up the entire show; they banged on garbage with garbage and made trash noise. I wasn't impressed. But I was young and uncultured so when Crissie gave me the tickets at Christmas I feigned interest, saying I'd always wanted to see the show in its entirety. And I did because I felt I hadn't given the show its fair shake. Seems I wasn't such a dumb kid at 17 because at 29 I was falling asleep within 20 minutes of the show starting. Not even the incessant banging could keep me awake; it was more a soothing white noise easing me off to slumber than a racket worth paying attention to. After a while I couldn't take anymore and I excused myself to take a piss. After pissing I saw a man smoking outside and decided to join him. As I finished my cigarette a chain of events began that I had no control over, as if I were a pawn, being pushed down a dark path by a higher power. First I noticed San Loco Taco next door. San Loco is my favorite taco stand. The food is often lackluster and I have repeatedly seen cockroaches on the walls but I have a soft spot for the place and I make it a point to eat there whenever I'm on the Lower East Side. I went in for a taco then thought, "Maybe I should get a beer," but that particular San Loco didn't serve beer. So I didn't order any tacos and went next store to a French restaurant but their bar was too packed and I couldn't sit so I exited and went to the next bar but that one was too loud and I was trying to escape any noise. It was like the story of Goldilocks and the three bears because the third bar was just right. The owners were dressed as monks and the patrons were forced to keep their voices to a whisper or be thrown out. I ordered a double bock, dark as night, thick as negro hair, and began to drink as many as I could in rapid succession. Within 10 minutes I'd finished three pints and I was well on my way to intoxication. I figured another 10 minutes and I'd be primed to sit through some more bang-bang-banging. Then I met James and he threw a wrench in my plans; he slowed down my entire forward progress just by introducing himself and saying hello. He said he was from the South and that people in the South were more courteous and that he was just trying to be friendly. I tried to explain to him that I wasn't trying to be rude but I had to be back inside the theater before anyone noticed I was gone. Just then the phone rang: Crissie, asking where I was.

 # House of the She-Wolves

PRIVATE.COM • DIR: SUZI MEDUSA • RATING: 6

I answered the phone, said I'd be back in five minutes, then quickly muttered something about having a drink, then hung up. "Bartender, line me up one more for the road," I said, and he did as he was told. My plan was to put that last one down, run across the street, take my seat, kiss my wife on the cheek and space out for the remainder of the performance. "Did I tell you I was a baggage handler?" the stranger who was talking at me asked. What an odd thing to offer up, I thought. I'd never met a real-life baggage handler. I bet he has tons of stories. Next thing I know he is showing me the flare signals used to bring an airplane into the terminal. They were basically what you'd think they were, no big secret: left, right, forward, back. Then he showed me his left pinkie or rather where his left pinkie should have been. He said he had it ripped clean off by the door of the luggage cart. "I didn't even bleed," he told me in his redneck drawl. I once knew a girl who had her pinkie torn off in a car accident. I was fascinated by her warped hand, as I was James's. I don't even remember the particulars of his tale, just that he no longer had his tiny finger on his left hand. But he did have a watch on that hand and I noticed the time and it was far past the 30 minutes I allotted myself to get drunk. Then Crissie called again. You could hear her teeth gritted together with contempt as she asked, "Bay-bee? Where the fuck are you?" "I'm coming right now, sorry." I slammed the rest of my bock, paid the man, said goodbye to the fingerless fellow and ran like a puma back to my seat in the theater. I tried to put my hand on Crissie's thigh and lean in to give her a kiss; she turned her fully loaded eyes of hate on me, cocked the hammer back, squared up and pulled the trigger unleashing two pissed-off bull's-eye shots to my heart. I knew I was fucked. I didn't even try and lie. I told her I went and had a drink. It's funny how the performers on stage never seemed to stop making noise until Crissie yelled out, "YOU WENT AND HAD A FUCKING DRINK? ARE YOU KIDDING ME?" You'd think they timed that just right so it was dead silent for everyone in the house to hear her. Now not only was she looking at me with disdain but so was the rest of her family, the rest of my row, the entire theater, all the performers on stage, the ushers. I bet even the ghosts of shows long gone were looking at me with disapproval. I waited for the actors or musicians or whatever the hell they consider themselves to start back up but no one moved; they just kept staring. I threw my hands up and lied, "It was only one drink! It's my birthday! Can't I have one drink?" Still no one diverted their eyes. "OKAY! OKAY! I'M SORRY," I cried out. "I WAS BORED. I COULDN'T TAKE THE BANGING! ALWAYS WITH THE BANGING! DON'T YOU DO ANYTHING ELSE BUT BANG? BANG! BANG! I GET IT ALREADY WITH THE GODDAMN BANGING FOR CHRIST'S SAKE! CUT THE SHIT!" And that's when everyone started booing in unison.

Photographic Mammaries Volume 4

CLUBPLATINUMX.COM • DIR: BRANDON IRON • RATING: 9

I don't remember many things. There are years, mostly from 1998 to 2003, that I have very little recollection of. I think it has something to do with the great amount of drugs I consumed during the course of those years; not to say I haven't been on a steady diet of drugs since 1993, it's just that during those years it was as if I was trying to break some sort of drug users' world record. I have been drug-free for two years now but my sobriety has done nothing in the way of returning those memories to me. All I have are the second-hand recollections of friends and strangers and photographs I don't remember taking. You wouldn't believe how often I bump into someone and they try and get all nostalgic like, "Do you remember that time you vomited on that stripper's crotch while she was on stage?"

or "How about that time you pissed on that woman's leg on the dance floor?" All I can do is smile and let them know that although they will cherish that moment for the rest of their lives, that they feel we had a shared experience, I have zero memory of the incident. It's rather sad. I feel like a man with no past, like I have amnesia or I've been brainwashed by the Gestapo. A few months ago I was going through photos for our wedding website that we're putting together and I kept coming across pictures that blew my mind. I'd look at them and say, "I met Mike Tyson?" "I've been to Mount Rushmore?" "When was I in Paris?" "I caught a marlin?" It's as if I've missed a life's worth of adventures. How does that happen? I sit now and I look at photos of myself, hopped up and inebriated, and I tell myself that from now on every picture I take I will write down the exact date and time and the story behind it. I've been good about it too. I have this Polaroid of Crissie and I and a Chinaman that was taken the night before her 30th birthday in September. There's a sushi/hibachi place near our house that we frequent. I can't pronounce the name correctly so I call it Orangutan. If you tell them it's your birthday they come out with a cake, sing a funny song and make you dance for a photo. We fake at least two birthdays a month there. Usually I make my Chinese-eyes face, this time I opted for something a bit more festive. The note I wrote to myself in my notebook was: "Took Crissie for hibachi on her birthday." We got seated with two lipstick lesbian couples. Crissie thought they were strippers at first, then they started kissing and she asked me, "Did you hire them for my birthday?" Sadly I didn't. Note to self: Next year hire Crissie lesbians for her birthday.

Milking Mamas

SCORELAND.COM • RATING: 8

M y wife told me about this woman in her Pilates class a few months ago who has a faded rose tattooed on the small of her back with the words "Frankie's Girl" etched below the flower. What I gathered from it, or rather what I can recall from the conversation, since I forget a great many things, is that Frankie's Girl had big tits but as big tits are prone to do they began to sag. Naturally she went and had them upgraded, lifted or whatever the term is for when you have your existing melons tuned up but not enlarged. She came back to class and let everyone know she had the alterations made. A week later, or maybe it was a month, she decided her big tits just weren't big enough. Perhaps Frankie helped her come to that decision but who can say since none of us have ever met Frankie. Either way, she was getting implants. She disappeared from class for a spell, then returned with two new, larger bags neatly tucked under the flesh of her breasts. I asked Crissie how they looked; she didn't seem impressed. I suppose Frankie's Girl wasn't impressed either because

before long she was having them removed. Some time later I was given the update on Frankie's Girl's tits but I was either half asleep or fully drunk so I missed it. At present time I'm sorry to say I cannot report on her tits with any certainty. I'm not sure if she now has small tits or just smaller. I can't even say if she has any tits left at all at this point. She may be flat-chested for all I know. Or worse, concave. Can doctors do that? I'm sure there's a fetish website already up and running for enthusiasts of the concave-chested. The latest news on Frankie's Girl, the reason I brought her up today in the first place, is that I'm told Frankie's Girl no longer wants to be Frankie's Girl anymore. Turns out Frankie's got another girl, on the side, that none of us were aware of. Do you like how I included myself in the sum of the knowing members of the steamy, gossipy Pilates housewives? As if I could bend like that. Frankie's Girl told Frankie last night that she wasn't his girl anymore. They were done. Through. Kaput. Would you believe that he felt his cheating was justified? Why, you ask? Turns out the woman he's sleeping with is his boss's wife and he's only doing it out of revenge because he had asked for the evening off on the night that his mother died so he could be with her at her deathbed since he knew it was her time. But the boss refused to give him the night off work, denying Frankie the chance to say his goodbyes to his momma. How's that for some reality?

 ## Joanna's Angels

BURNINGANGEL.COM/VCAPICTURES.COM •
DIR: JOANNA ANGEL • RATING: 12

The moral of the story, friends, is never get someone's name tattooed on your body unless they are related to you or they're already dead and have no chance of breaking your heart. Wino Forever? Although I am lucky in the sense that I could tattoo my wife's first name on me without care because we both have the same name, yet I would not. As much of an egomaniac as I am, and as

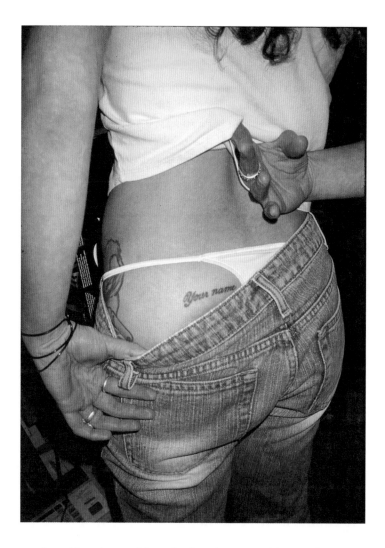

much as I love her and love the fact that I am able to call my own name during sex, I would never have her name put on my body. If we were to ever separate, why would I want my own name on my body? Granted I do forget many things but the day I can't remember my own name is the day I take a long walk off a short pier. Instead, in an act of love far deeper than writing her name on me, I had her kiss a napkin and then had her lips tattooed right above my dick, which is far sexier than any group of letters. When I worked for Larry Flynt I ran across this porn star in the elevator. We chatted it up as we ascended. Her and I shared a moment back in the '90s when I was on the set of her first film ever up at Big Bear Mountain. I handed her sex toys as she went about her business. It's a bond we have that I believe can never be severed. I noticed as we arrived on the ninth floor that she had a man's name on her arm with a line-drawing outline of a heart around it. I asked whose name it was. She told me it was her current boyfriend's. I laughed, then told her I had my grandmother's name on my chest. "Do you know why I put my grandmother's name on my chest?" I asked her. Not waiting for a response I told her, "Because she'll always be my grandmother." She didn't get the joke. At least not then. Months later she figured out what I had meant . . . when she had his name covered over.

Very Very Bad Santa

LOADEDDIGITAL.COM • DIR: MICHAEL ADAM • RATING: 9

When I was more of an international jet-setter, traveling the world and reporting on the skateboarding lifestyle, I would always call ahead to the various towns I was visiting and arrange it so there were drugs waiting for me at the local skate shop in exchange for large boxes of pornography. One such time in Utah, where they can't get quality porn because by law all porn in Utah must have the penetration scenes edited out, a kid with his leg in traction traded me his prescription and three refills for Dilaudid in exchange for a box of smut. On one hand I felt bad because he was clearly in pain and needed the painkillers for valid reasons but on the other hand Dilaudid isn't easy to come by and my addiction far outweighed my empathy. I did offer him a chance to renege on the deal, asking him if he was 100% certain that he could survive the pain without the drugs. He assured me that he had never seen more than half the sex acts on the DVDs I'd sent him and those sights were more than enough to get him through the tough times. That was good enough to put my caring junkie mind at ease. He took me to his home to get the stuff and that's where I witnessed the most brilliant collection of "father and son with Santa Claus" photos I'd ever seen. The kid was actually no kid at all, he was probably mid-20s and from the time of his birth his father had taken him to get 8 x 10s of him and Santa at Sears. But his father really knew how to spice things up. Both he and his dad, from age zero to 25, had donned camouflage outfits, from head to toe—boots, pants, sweatshirts, hat and gloves, as well as face paint—and took their guns to town and sat themselves on ole St. Nick's lap for posterity's sake. I was floored by the volume and continuity of the work. To see twenty-five framed 8 x 10s on one wall chronicling the kid's entire existence nearly knocked me over. Right then I knew, I had to rip off their idea and make it my own. 25 photos in the same outfit is a bit redundant so to build off of their concept Crissie and I have decided that instead of camo we'll pose with Santa in our Halloween costumes starting next year. So there will be one photo of Elvis and Marilyn Monroe and Santa sans offspring. The following year, after the birth of our first kid, you'll see Batman, a moo cow and a sexy stewardess with Santa. The following year? Who knows? Perhaps Hitler, Dracula and Bride of Frankenstein with Santa. Maybe us and two kids as KISS. The possibilities are endless. We're hoping that our children carry on the tradition with their kids, and the generation after that and so on and so on. Maybe someday, a hundred years from now, when Crissie and I are long since dead, there will be enough images to be collected into a coffee-table book. Perhaps that, in addition to being the greatest monosyllabic writer of our generation, will be my legacy. I suppose there are worse things to be remembered for.

Pink Clam

VIDEOPIX.COM • DIR: FRANCIS HEALY • RATING: 5

The phone rang in one of the other rooms. I couldn't tell which one. We had just moved into our new house, really, and I still needed to figure out the acoustics of the house. When the first ring sounded it had that echo that one gets in a restroom but it sounded further down the hallway. Maybe the kitchen at the end of the hall. It rang a second and third time. I had no intention of getting up to answer it. I was in a mood and didn't feel like speaking to anyone unless the conversation was going to end with a blowjob and I knew Crissie was ironing clothes so that wasn't going to happen. I knew she'd answer the phone, though. She is a pleasant woman, always in high spirits, with a perpetual smile on her face, always willing to talk to anyone who speaks to her. I always found it odd that her and I get on as well as we do, what with her liking people and I, in general, detesting humanity. I'm still waiting for it to prove itself to me. Or perhaps it's that I'm happiest when I'm miserable. In the end I will bring Crissie down and she too will be miserable one day. But before it gets to that point I knew she'd answer the phone. The fourth ring cut off midway and she said, "Hello." Then I heard her tell the person I was home. Then she called my name. "Tell them I'm not home," I yelled back. "They already heard you," she said. "I don't care, tell them I'm ill. I'm not speaking to anyone today." "I don't know what his problem is, he doesn't feel like talking," she explained to the person holding the line. "Can I get your name and have him call you back?" She paused, then asked what it was regarding. I knew it was most likely a business call, not a friend. She wouldn't have been so formal with a friend. Crissie's voice rose, "Excuse me? He did what?" Great, I thought, what the hell did I do now? "Listen, lady, he's a married man!" she shouted, making sure I heard her quite clearly. Whatever was happening, I knew my chances of getting a blowjob were out the window. More then likely I'd be the one on my knees before the day was done. "Don't call my house again, you bitch" were the last words I heard before the receiver smashed down and she began her march toward my office. I could not for the life of me think what the hell I could have done to get myself in trouble this time. I'm a good man. I have never been unfaithful nor have I ever lied to my woman, the woman who was about to give me a verbal lashing any second. Perhaps it was a fan calling. A female fan looking for some hot action. Don't laugh. It is possible. Its not like I'm very hard to track down. If that were the case then there was no reason for me to be worried. I cannot be held responsible for the wild desires of total strangers.

Pick Up Girls

BADSEEDDVD.COM • DIR: BRETT MAVERICK • RATING: 7

She kicked open my office door and it nearly came off its hinges. The room shook. Things fell from their shelves. I think I saw the lights flicker. The gust of air that came with her entrance sent me back in my chair. "What's your problem?" I asked. "I'm in a shit mood." "Go fuck yourself," she suggested. "I bet you were in a good mood yesterday." I tried to think back to the events of the previous day. Nothing stuck out in my mind. I ran some errands, got new screens for the gutters and took some old music to the record store to trade in. I remember being happy with the offer the cashier made for the old disks; the amount would just about cover the tab I'd racked up for the fifth and sixth seasons of *Seinfeld* on DVD, the seventh season of *The Simpsons*, the Bruce Springsteen boxed set and the enormous 6 x 6' print of Elvis I wanted. So I suppose in that sense she was right, I was in a good mood the day before but was unsure if admitting it was wise at the present moment, without having any information on the battle I had just been volunteered for. I instead played dumb. "What was yesterday?" I asked. "Yesterday was when you went to the record store," she explained. "Yeah. So? So what? You knew that?" I said. "No, I knew you went to the record store," she agreed. "I just didn't know that you gave some girl your fucking phone number at the record store." I had no response. I was dumbfounded. I truly had no clue what the hell she was talking about. I stammered like a fool, "I-I-I . . ." and she began to cry. I tried to wrap my arms around her to console her but she smacked me off. "Okay, this doesn't make any sense," I offered. "I didn't give my phone number to any girl at the record store. I sold the CDs, I picked up some DVDs and shit and I came home." "Then tell me how she knew you were at the record store and got our home number?" she asked. "How the hell should I know? I don't know what to tell you. I didn't speak to anyone other than the cashier. You know I don't talk to strangers. They annoy me." "That's who it was," Crissie said. "Who?" "The cashier. She said you gave her your phone number yesterday. Did you give her our number?" I had to think about it and the truth was I had, but not with any sexual intentions, it was meant to be used as reference of some sort. "Yeah, I did give it to her but it's not what you think." "I can't believe you, you're such an asshole." "No, no, no. You've got it all wrong, baby. I've been duped. This is a setup. I'm an innocent man." I started to giggle because the words sounded like such a bad spaghetti Western that I couldn't help but laugh, which only pissed my wife off more.

Evil Pink 2

EVILANGEL.COM/ENTERBELLADONNA.COM •
DIR: BELLADONNA • RATING: 8

She picked up one of my Elvis busts, the one of Young Elvis, my favorite one, and pitched it at my skull. I'm a real sucker for the young, skinnier era of Elvis. He was a truly handsome man. Had he tried to bed my wife at that time chances are I'd have let him. Hell, I'd probably let him have my ass too if he wanted. The ceramic head whizzed by my ear, just inches away from hitting my eye, possibly permanently blinding me, and shattered into pieces upon contact with the wall behind me. I jumped up out of my chair, screaming, "Whoa, whoa, whoa, you goddamn banshee!" I roped her up before she could break any more of my shit or hurt someone. "If I wanted to fuck someone else, do you think I'd give them our home number?" I asked. And just like that she stopped wrestling and tried to hear me out. "Are you going to be calm?" I asked her. She stood there waiting for my explanation. "Okay, I sold them the CDs and then this girl rang up all the stuff I wanted to buy. And she forgot to ring up the Elvis print and that was supposed to be $25 so I told her she'd forgotten it. She was already about to cash me out and she looked at me, then looked at the picture, then the register and then looked back at me and said, 'Don't worry about it.' So I thought she was just lazy, that she didn't want to re-ring my order. I thanked her and I told her she was a sweet girl and that was it. I grabbed my bags in one hand and stuck the print under my right arm and was about to leave. Then she said, 'Sir, can I have your name and phone number . . . for the store records?' I just figured they needed it because they had just paid me out a sizable amount of money. That's all. I mean she wasn't even cute. I'm telling you, I was not trying to pick up on the damn cashier." Crissie looked even angrier than she did when she stormed in. "That little bitch," she said. "She can't do that. That's illegal, right? At the very least, it's inappropriate." I felt vindicated and wanted to be a bit of a prick so I said, "You really can't blame the girl. It's not her fault. I am an amazing example of masculinity. I can't imagine she sees a specimen such as myself very often." "Don't joke," she said. "I'm pissed off." I pulled her close, set my hands on her ass and kissed her neck and said softly, "I think you owe me an apology." "I'm sorry . . ." she said. I whispered, "I think you owe me something else, to make up for the way you treated me." Then I made the blowjob face, you know, where you stick your tongue hard into the side of your mouth to make it look like there's a penis pressed in it. "Actually," she said, stepping back from me, "I was thinking more like we should go down to the record store and file a complaint with her manager and get her fired. This is bullshit. She should not be allowed to steal customers' information like that. Her boss needs to know about this. What if she's some kind of maniac?" "She's not a maniac. She's just a young girl who had the hots for an older man and she acted on her urges." "I don't give a shit. It's sketchy and I'm not going to let her get away with it. I'm going down there and you're going with me."

5 People You Meet in Porn

HUSTLERVIDEO.COM • DIR: JEROME TAYLOR • RATING: 8

So we went down to the store to confront the girl. She wasn't working and her manager was on lunch break. "What do you want to do?" I asked Crissie. She, of course, wanted to stay and wait to speak with the manager. "Come on. I've got things to do. We'll come back another time. I don't want to waste my afternoon in a record store. I'm liable to spend all the money I made yesterday." But she wasn't budging, so I took to looking at the new DVDs. Did you know they just released a two-disc special edition of Elvis's globally televised comeback performance from Hawaii called *Elvis Aloha From Hawaii*? It has all sorts of never-before-seen footage as well as his sound check from the day before and the short set he did for fans at the after-party. Once I saw that I got a serious boner and basically went into shopping mode. "Cris," I said to her, "I'm warning you, the longer you keep me in here the more money I'm going to spend. So if we're a little short with this month's mortgage payment there won't be anyone to blame but yourself." She kept her eyes fixed on the front door of the shop, ready to pounce on the girl if she showed up. I hadn't even told her what she looked like. I thought to myself, wouldn't it be funny if Crissie attacked the next female to enter the store and it turned out to be the wrong girl? How amazing would that be? But you know that wouldn't happen. Not that Crissie isn't a scrapper; it's just that women don't make those mistakes. They have a sixth sense about things. There was no doubt in my mind that if that girl had come through the door that Crissie would know it was her, without having a description of her or even hearing her voice. It's just one of those amazing superpowers that comes from possessing a vagina. Why is it that women get all the good superpowers? Like flawless memory? Where men's superpower is being able to forget anything of importance with great ease, women get shit like producing and shooting milk and knowing which condiments will remove which stains from clothing. It doesn't seem fair, I thought, as I leafed through the LPs. Then it happened. The worst possible scenario. I looked up to see Crissie at her post and then felt an awful rumble in my belly. My stomach tightened. My neck stiffened. My ass cheeks cinched and clenched together. The burrito I'd eaten earlier wanted out and there was nothing I or anyone else could do to stop it. "Oh. No," I said to myself aloud and with those words I let out a silent but very wet fart. I did my best to keep from letting out another as I dropped whatever I was holding and quickly made my way over to Crissie. "We have to go and we have to go now," I told her. She said she wasn't leaving. I said she didn't have an option. Again she refused. I can safely say I've never laid a heavy hand on my wife for any reason but in that moment I was forced to put my hands on her shoulders and squeeze with all my might and tell her, "We're leaving now." With all my attention focused on her shoulders, it let my ass's guard down for a second. That's all it took. The burrito shot from my anus with the spray and strength of a geyser. And I was defeated. I relaxed my grip, my head dropped in shame. I turned toward the exit and told her I'd be in the car.

Porn Fidelity 2

PORNFIDELITY.COM • DIR: KELLY MADISON • RATING: 9

I laughed when I opened the manila envelope containing the second installment of Kelly Madison's *Porn Fidelity* series. Porn fidelity, I thought to myself, isn't that a bit of an oxymoron? Then I read the front cover that states, "We're redefining the institution of marriage" and assumed that it meant that their new definition permitted husband and wife to hump whomever they liked. That was not the case. It was on the back cover that their new definition became perfectly clear. It read, "This is a continuing, personal sex scrapbook of our life together, meeting, sharing and fucking girls. Not your average marriage, not your average couple . . . and not your average sex video." I pondered that for a moment. A married couple both in pursuit of bringing women home into their bedroom. I liked this new definition. I liked it quite a bit. I turned to Crissie to tell her how this fantastic couple was changing the meaning of everything we held sacred and how we should get on board while stock was cheap. She didn't respond, so I repeated myself, only louder, "THIS FANTASTIC COUPLE IS CHANGING THE MEANING OF EVERYTHING WE HOLD SACRED. WE SHOULD GET ON BOARD WHILE STOCK IS CHEAP." Still she did not respond. So I turned the light on and gave her a shove. Still nothing. If there's anything in this world I hated it was having to repeat myself and the fact that she was ignoring me pissed me off to high heaven. I laid one hand on each of her shoulders and started shaking her violently, asking, "Do you hear what I'm saying? Damn it! Why won't you answer me?" Finally she opened her eyes and looked at me and asked what my problem was. I told her there was no problem. Actually, it was less a problem than it was a blessing. She didn't seem to understand what I was saying and her eyes kept shutting for long periods of time. Again I shook her, "Don't you close your eyes at me! This is our life we're talking about!" "What time is it?" she asked. The alarm clock said 4 a.m. I told her it didn't matter what time it was, if she cared about me and our future together she would sit up and say yes to this new definition of fidelity. Friends, I'll tell you what, my woman must really love me because she sat right up and said, "Yes. Whatever the hell you're talking about, yes. Just leave me alone and let me sleep." Just like that my heart was full. I danced, like a little girl or a butterfly fresh from its cocoon. I ran through the house without my feet ever touching the ground. At the stereo I put on something festive at full blast, Diana Ross's "Love Child" I believe it was. In my office I marked the date and time on my calendar: 4:15 a.m. February 7th, 2006, 12 days before my birthday. At my fancy dictionary I flipped to the page marked "M," using the magnifying glass I searched for the word *marriage* and with a red marker crossed out what had been written. Then I ran to the window to get my first glimpse of my new world, a world where both Crissie and I were on a constant hunt to bring home female game, as if we were lion hunters in the wild, but it was still dark out and I couldn't really see anything.

Cousin Stevie's Pussy Party: Anal Mimosas

COUSINSTEVIE.COM · DIR: COUSIN STEVIE · RATING: 9

L ike I've said before I'm not much of a scholar but I can't help but believe that champagne enemas are as old as man himself. It seems like since the dawn of time man has been sticking champagne bottles up their women's asses and loving every minute of it. What's amazing to me is the fact that society has never tired of the act. Over the centuries hair, dress and speech have changed dramatically but one constant that is woven into the fabric of society is the champagne enema. Why is that? Perhaps it is simply the festive nature of the beverage, perhaps not. I don't know. It doesn't matter. Whatever the reason, I raise my glass to Adam and Eve in thanks for creating such a cherished tradition. Granted, I myself have never tasted an anal mimosa but there is nothing that would indicate that I would dislike it. I love champagne, enjoy orange juice and relish the taste of a woman's ass; how could I not like it? I particularly enjoy a good, stiff mimosa first thing in the morning. Especially if they're free. Everything free always seems to taste better. I recall a trip to Hawaii many, many years ago with my wife all hopped up on goofballs and hooch. Many details are hazy but one thing I'm certain of is for one glorious morning we lived it up, free of charge, at the Royal Imperial Windsor on Waikiki Beach. We'd just eaten a lovely seafood meal and watched the sun set at Michelle's, our favorite restaurant on the island, and gotten fall-down drunk. The bill was excessive, as is expected when you order two whole uncooked lobsters to use as puppets to re-create the scene from *Stir Crazy*, with Gene Wilder and Richard Pryor, when they first enter the jail. And wouldn't you know it, I didn't have my wallet on me. I asked the valet to bring my car around, which hinted that I might have been trying to skip out on the bill and prompted the entire staff to walk me to the vehicle; waiter, host, busboy, owner and even the chef. I tried my best in my drunken state to explain, "My car is in that wallet. I'm leaving the woman behind." One of them, the biggest one, gripped my shoulder. He had massive hands. The biggest hands I'd ever come across. Hands that could make a basketball feel like a golf ball. He should have been in the *Guinness Book* for those hands. It didn't even feel like he was holding only my shoulder; it felt as if my whole body was in his grasp like King Kong. My rental car was brought around but the driver refused to give me my keys. "I'm not trying to run out, goddamnit! I just need my wallet!" Lucky for me my car was in that wallet and I was able to pay and not have my ass handed to me by Hawaii's service industry's finest.

Butt Pirates of the Caribbean

SEYMOREBUTTS.COM • DIR: SEYMORE BUTTS • RATING: 9

W ait. I completely missed the point of that last story. I was talking about free mimosas and I got sidetracked. Okay. So I paid
the bill at the restaurant and we stumbled out the front door. The
drive back to the hotel was a blur as was the wild night of passion that
ensued. What I remember quite clearly is waking up the next morning and learning all of our belongings had been stolen. Everything:
camera, camcorder, clothes, dirty socks. "Hold on," I said to Crissie,
"who the hell would steal dirty socks?" Just as I asked she yelled from
the bathroom, "This isn't our room." She pointed to the unopened
toiletries beside the sink. I stuck my head into the hallway; across the
hall was room 1321. Our room. We had slept in 1320. I went over to
1321 and there were all of our things just as we'd left them the night
before. "How the hell did that happen?" I asked. "Door must have
been unlocked. We were drunk," she suggested. As she dressed I
watched her bend over to put on her pants and wondered how we
could take advantage of the situation. To just sleep in the wrong
room is a draw; we paid for a bed either way. There's nothing gained.
I checked the mini bar. Unlocked and stocked. I grabbed a pillowcase
and emptied the contents and ran them across the hall to our room.
Nieratko 1, Hotel 0. Still I felt I could somehow exploit our folly more.
So I called room service. "Yes, hello? Hi. Can I get two egg-white
omelets with every vegetable you have, four orders of shrimp cocktail,
six lobster tails, do you have oysters? You do? I'll take two dozen, a
pot of coffee, extra creamer, a gallon of orange juice, two bottles of
champagne and some glasses to mix mimosas. Also can you bring
hot sauce for the omelets and some extra napkins?" "Will that be all,
Mr. Davies?" the voice asked on the other end of the line. Mr. Davies?
There was still a name on file for the room. Could it be Ray Davies of
the Kinks? Either way, I was going to get away with it. "Yes, that'll be
all," I said. I hung up and instantly began to worry that Mr. Davies

might show up or worse they'd realize Mr. Davies had checked out, smell my scam and send up security. I could be in jail before noon. What do I do? What do I do? Women and children first; "Crissie, go back to our room and wait by the door for me." Off she went. I sat on the edge of the bed trying to formulate a plan. Then I began to sing, "If my friend's could see me now, sitting in Ray's hotel room." Nothing came to me, so I opted to get out of there while the getting was good. I ran across the hall: "I can't do it. It's too much pressure. I'm all panicked. I don't want to go to jail for a couple omelets. I need to calm down. Crissie, give me the bag with the valiums." "I don't have the bag. You had the bag. Last I saw you were crushing them up and using them as sugar in your coffee with dessert last night." Fuck. I must have left them in the other room. I ran back across the hall. I turned the place upside down and finally found them. As I went to exit the room a knock came and the door swung open. "Mr. Davies?" "Uh . . ." The longest silence ever. "Here is your breakfast, sir." I signed it to the room and wrote him a hundred-dollar tip. I waited a few minutes until he'd gotten in an elevator before wheeling the cart across the hall. The rest of the morning we enjoyed our free mimosas and laughed at the constant knocking on the door across the hall for Mr. Davies to open up and give them a different credit card.

Big Booty Moms

EVILANGEL.COM • DIR: JUSTIN SLAYER • RATING: 8

I'm considering not getting married. I have less than three months to go and I'm thinking about backing out. I'm not nervous or frightened or any of the typical forms of neurosis that kick in right before tying the knot; it all has to do with the dwindling size of my wife-to-be's ass. For Christmas I purposely bought her a half dozen pairs of jeans a few sizes too small. My hope was that her amazingly thick non-white-girl ass would protrude like a bookshelf in the jeans and they did. It was as if she had two asses in the pants. Looking at the massive buttocks I fell in love with her all over again. If I didn't notice her blonde locks, I'd have thought I was looking at the back-door of some Nubian ghetto princess. My eyes welled up with pride. I looked forward to our long life together. Images of us dancing in a field like in the film *The Sound of Music* or *National Lampoon's*

European Vacation filled my head. I never doubted that I was marrying the right woman but her ass in those jeans, with the seams ready to burst, reaffirmed it all. Then it happened. She started to cry. So I started to cry too, thinking we were crying tears of joy for the same thing. "I know, it's beautiful," I said. "It's the most beautiful ass I've ever seen." She tried to gain composure and asked, "What are you talking about?" "Your ass," I said, "in those jeans. It's a work of art." "No," she answered, "I'm fat. I can barely fit into these pants." "No, no, no," I told her. "I purposely got the wrong size. They're ass jeans. They're not for you, they're for me. I mean yes, for you to wear but for me to enjoy. You know, just around the house." My words did nothing to make her feel better. Instead she stood in front of the full-length mirror sobbing. "I don't understand," I told her. "A big ass is good. It's what boys like. It's the American Dream: to marry a white woman with a black woman's ass. It's like . . . I don't know . . . you're like a, a, a sexual Minotaur." Wrong choice of words. It's as if someone took a sledgehammer to the valve that controls her tear ducts. A geyser shot from each of her eyes. I literally had to go into the garage, dig out my fishing equipment and put on my wading boots and grab the wet/dry vacuum to suck up the eight inches or so of water that was filling up our bedroom. And I'm a man. I don't know what to say to women, or anyone for that matter, when they're crying. "See," I said. "This is why I don't buy you anything. You're completely unappreciative." She told me to fuck off. So I did, with an ice-cold frosty barley pop. A month or so later she stopped crying and without my authorization decided to take it upon herself to lose the weight to fit into those ass jeans; missing the point completely. We all know the first two places a woman loses weight is her ass and her tits, neither of which I'm willing to part with. Well, to make a long story short, Crissie now fits easily into the aforementioned jeans and looks like she has half an ass and I'm really not sure if I should marry her now. You can see my dilemma, can't you?

Dirty Dykes

DEFIANCEFILMS.COM • DIR: AURORA SNOW • RATING: 9

Okay. This is going to come off rather chauvinistic but oh well. My wife's job in the family is to cook for me and keep the house clean and wear very little, other than six-inch heels, while doing so. Granted, she works very hard as a dance teacher, sometimes putting in longer hours than myself, but that's the way things are. Everyone has a role in life and hers is to tidy up after me. I would help if I knew how but I don't. I'm rather useless with a mop or broom. I'm liable to hurt someone or myself. My department is taking out the trash, occasionally washing some dishes and paying the bills. Doing laundry, windows, scrubbing toilets or tubs, making beds, dusting or folding are all tasks that are beyond me. Crissie has the vagina and the experience so I defer to her. And she really seems to enjoy it. Just last night she was set to go into Manhattan to drink with a friend who was visiting from out of own but canceled so that she could clean the house for when I got home from my trip. Admittedly she has some obsessive compulsion toward cleaning, which works in my favor. I'm surprised that she doesn't walk behind me with a dustpan and hand broom. I've been on the road for a week now and at about 2 a.m. each night I call home to check in on her to make sure she's alive. I left her a loaded 9 mm Beretta on the nightstand and a baseball bat by the front door for safe measure but I still worry. Each night she's been balls-deep in housekeeping. Be it vacuuming (we don't even own a carpet), polishing china (china that we have never used), itemizing my receipts (by date and category, alphabetically) or washing my soiled boxer briefs, it's as if she's possessed. "Need to get this cleaning done. Must get clean. Can't get the dirty off." She sounds like a rape victim. "Are you okay?" I ask. "Dirty, so dirty," is all she says. "You really should get some sleep," I tell her, but she refuses. I've considered telling her to go see a doctor but then I thought about it and is it really so bad? Sure, she's sleep-deprived and that can't be healthy, but my home has never looked better. My only real concern is that I wake up one night tied to the bed covered in ammonia with her scrubbing my flesh away with a steel wool pad repeating the word *dirty* over and over. Because I don't know if you can tell from the photos, but I have really nice skin. Nearly flawless. In 30 years I've had all of four pimples. I can't grow facial hair so my skin is as soft as a baby's bottom from a lack of shaving and I'm Portuguese, a culture blessed with good skin. I don't want to brag but there have been a few times that casting agents have stopped me on the street and told me how lovely my skin was. And as I told my wife, them being homosexual and accidentally putting their hands on my ass does not change the fact that strangers are taken aback by my perfect skin. If this writing thing doesn't pan out, I always have that modeling career to fall back on and I'm not trying to have Crissie blow it because she's losing her mind.

Housewife 1 on 1

NAUGHTYAMERICA.COM • DIR: BRETT BRANDO • RATING: 7

Okay, so I had a brief MySpace.com addiction but I've got a handle on it now. I'm not sure what happened but I lost my passion for it. For a time there I was spending hours of each day scrolling through scantily clad photos but I hit a brick wall and it all seems rather dull and uninspired now. Yet there's still one aspect of the site that keeps me entertained when drunk, bored out of my mind or waiting for the lay to get home from work to cook me dinner: the "browse" option. By clicking on browse you are able to look through complete strangers' profiles while modifying your search by gender, age, location and, most importantly, by sexual preference. What I like to do is set the browse option to female only, for ages 25 to 35 (anything under 25 can be too immature). I mark women who are either swingers or looking for a relationship or divorced (divorced women shouldn't be shunned simply because they had an unsuccessful marriage). Next I click on the box marked bisexual or gay, then I type in my zip code and start a search of all lesbians and bisexuals within five miles of my home. Then I click away and pretend, pretend that if ever my wife comes around and gives me the one and only sexual act that consumes my every waking thought on a daily basis it would be with one of the sexy ladies I am looking at. She doesn't know that I do this, of course, because I've given up bringing up the topic. I am resolved in the knowledge that it will be the one experience I will die without ever knowing. It kills me. So to make do I often visit my lesbian land of make-believe and check out random women named Bambi, Sheryl, Sonia, Bebe and the like, picturing myself entwined with them and my wife in a loving embrace. Sometimes when I'm extremely bored I'll Google the zip codes of faraway places like Chicago or Hawaii, apply them to the browser and think to myself, "If Crissie and I went on vacation, I wonder what kind of lesbians and bisexuals they have in Oahu or Illinois or Texas?" To say it's a fun and productive use of my free time would be a bald-faced lie. I'm well aware of how pathetic my actions are but what can I do? It's as close to a ménage à trois as I'll ever know. So please turn away, and allow me this indiscretion without mockery or distain. I don't know what to say. I am human and I need to be loved.

Sore Throat

OEVIDEO.COM • DIR: TONY T • RATING: 7

Crissie has had a sore throat all week so you know what that means: My hand is her new mouth. We have a little routine when she's sick. She says, "My throat hurts," and I reply, "I've got something to make your throat feel better," suggesting that somehow my penis and the fluids it produces would help alleviate her pain, perhaps coating her throat. Occasionally I'll mix things up by saying, "Maybe you need my special lozenge." (I don't want our life to get stale and predictable.) She generally does not acknowledge my joke, making it funnier for me because I then am able to repeat myself, at a higher volume. "HELLO! I said, I've got something to make your throat feel better. Didn't you hear me?" "Oh, I heard you." "Why aren't you laughing?" No response. "I said why aren't you laughing?" No response again. "Listen, lady. You don't know funny," I'm forced to explain to her. "I know funny. And that's funny." "No, it's not funny. And I don't want to speak, it irritates my throat." "You irritate my throat! With your lack of laughter." "That doesn't make any sense." "You don't make any sense. When I present a funny joke to you it is your responsibility as my wife to laugh at said joke." "Ha. Are you happy?" "Don't sass me girl. You're not funny." "Neither are you." "You don't know funny," I say again and walk down the hall to my office and slam the thick wooden door with a serious flair for the dramatic. This exchange happens every time she gets a sore throat without fail. It's sort of like our Abbott + Costello "Who's on first?" bit. Sometimes I wonder what my life would be like if I hadn't found a woman who could tolerate my over-the-top absurdity and ill-timed humor. What would have become of me? I'm certain eventually I would have been committed to a home. Society only tolerates funny people on stages or inside televisions. Being a funny regular Joe is unacceptable by normal standards. Today I went into the bank and the teller who always helps me with my money, a young girl, brunette, with a large collection of freckles, asked if I'd been exercising, insinuating that I was in fit shape. I said, "No, I've been eating with reckless abandon. I'm getting married and I must get ready to let myself go so when people see me on the street and say, 'Chris, you got fat,' I can say, 'No, I got married.' And it'll all make sense." She said, "That's awful" and directed her eyes to her left. I followed her eyes and saw that her co-worker was an enormous woman, just a few pounds light of being an elephant, wearing a wedding ring and looking at me in horror. "I wasn't referring to you." She ran off crying. "I wasn't." Fat people are so sensitive. For as thick as their flesh is, you'd think they'd have tougher skin. But do you understand what

I'm saying? Nobody likes a comedian in their everyday life. I don't understand it.

Hair to Stay

ADAMEVE.COM • DIR: DANIEL DAKOTA • RATING: 7

I hate hair. I've probably said that a million times but I can't stress it enough. Any hair not found on the top of one's head grosses me out. Sadly for me even the hair on my head has decided to vacate the premises. Anyone interested in cheap billboard space, call me. My forehead has drifted halfway to the back of my head and is available for your advertising needs. Can I amend my previous statement? I enjoy facial hair. The reason being that I really can't grow facial hair, at least not in any style or fashion. When it does grow in it's patchy and thin and somewhat of a Technicolor rainbow in various shades of black, brown, red and blonde. When my "beard" is fully grown in it looks as if I've given an earth-toned clown a blowjob. I've seen 9-year-olds with thicker mustaches than anything I've ever had. Still, I enjoy having hair on my face. Call it facial-hair envy. I often dream about being able to grow fantastic handlebar mustaches or a Rollie Fingers or muttonchops or a Fu Manchu. I know that will never happen without glue and borrowed fur but in a last-ditch attempt I decided on May 1 that I wasn't going to shave my face until my wedding day on July 1. Why? Mostly because I'm lazy and with all the wedding planning I wanted to alleviate my workload and decided to erase shaving from my "Stuff to Do" list, but partially I did it because my wife said I wouldn't. By the time you read this I'll already have shaven, gotten hitched and left for my honeymoon in Portugal. I'll have already forgotten that I ever wrote this sentence and have no recollection of ever having gone two months without shaving. My mind doesn't retain information for very long. I can't even remember where I was going with this. Isn't that a shame? Every day I'm supposed to be making these fantastic memories that I should treasure for the rest of my life and yet I forget things as soon as they happen. I think I have a mix of Alzheimer's and that shit that Mohammad Ali and Michael J. Fox have, what is that, Hodgkin's or some shit? Whatever it is, I think I have it because my hands twitch uncontrollably at times and it has nothing to do with the previous night's alcoholic festivities. I think it is a direct result of all the acid I did in high school. Is that possible? I'm no doctor, but that's my diagnosis. I also think I have a slight case of Tourette's because I blurt out awful things at very inappropriate times. Bitch. Fuck. Cunt. Do you think they could freeze my body in cryogenics at my age? Or do you have to be older? How does that work and how much does it cost? I'm considering asking my wife to get frozen with me after we get back from our honeymoon. I'll have them pin a note on my nose that says, "Do not thaw out until you've figured out a cure for everything. Especially erectile penis dysfunction." Not that I have a problem with that. It's for a friend.

European Hotel Confessions

TORRIDENT.COM · DIR: KELLE MARIE · RATING: 9

On the Fourth of July, 2006, three days after we get married, Crissie and I will be flying from Newark, NJ, to Paris, France, for two days, then on to Portugal for three weeks for our honeymoon. We couldn't think of a better date to arrive in France, a place that has such love and admiration for America, than the date of America's celebration of independence. To further strengthen our international bond with the French we've decided to make ourselves T-shirts with crudely drawn American flags on them under the words "FREEDOM FRIES!" written in French. We also plan on wearing berets, white gloves and drawn-on thin mustaches the entire time and painting our faces white like mimes. Have you ever heard of a better disguise? There's no way the frogs will treat us like tourists. They'll think we're

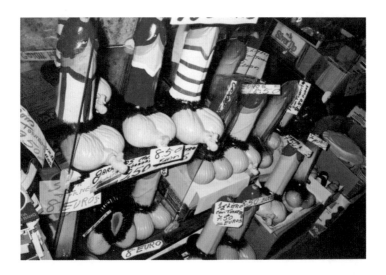

one of them. And that's when we'll get 'em! We'll pull their pants down in front of everyone and embarrass them. We'll reveal their small penises to the world and proudly declare, "Me American! Me have big penis! Me the world's asshole!" And everyone will applaud us because we are Americans and wherever we go, people love us. There's something about the way we wag our dicks in everyone's face that just turns them on. Boy, oh, boy! It's going to be a swell trip. Then Portugal. Portugal we're going to be a bit more low-key. We each have matador outfits that we plan to wear most of the trip unless we're at the beach, in which case we'll leave the capes in the car. My uncle has an apartment in the south, in Portugal's Algarve region, and my family still owns a farm two hours north of Lisbon. As a child I'd go there every summer for a month at a time. My fondest memory is after driving to the top of Serra da Estrela, Portugal's highest mountain range, we'd come to a clearing where gypsies had set up shop, selling their wares. Strangely, they only had two products for sale: goat cheese and porcelain penises. The goat cheese, as well as the penises, came in every possible size from extremely small and fragile to enormous and needing to be strapped to the roof of your automobile. It was quite bizarre. I'll be sure to take pictures and show you when I get back. The penises were all painted with bright red balls and heads and peach shafts and they were made into drinking glasses, water bottles, salt and pepper shakers—there were two soccer players or Mickey and Minnie Mouse having sex doggie-style and when you pull a string a penis raises. There were statues of policemen, firemen, chefs, astronauts and nearly every other occupation, without pants and with a penis attached to a string. I'm not sure of the meaning of it all and it strikes me as odd for a culture so sexually repressed to have such an economy based on penises, but who cares? It's funny. I have one coffee mug with holes all around the rim and a penis spout coming off the side, forcing you to drink off the dickhead. I bet you wish you were coming with us. But you're not. So stop your crying. I'll give you something to cry about.

Smother Me

BUTTMANMAGAZINE.COM • DIR: UNCLE D • RATING: 11

I misread the title and thought it was some sort of Oedipus film called *Mother Me*. Sadly, it is not. Instead it is scene after scene of women smothering a goofy-looking, pirate-bandanna-wearing Canadian's face with their asses. And although there is no sex in the film aside from a couple uninspired blowjobs, I must say, I really enjoyed it. I get immense personal satisfaction from burying my nose in my wife's ass. I just love the smell of it and the feeling of wearing a face mask made of butt. I've never had a full-on smothering session with her, but I think I may suggest it after seeing this film. I doubt she'll go for it. She gets kind of weirded out when she sees me smelling her underwear or when she wakes up in the middle of the night and I'm smelling her butt. I don't know what her problem is. It's not like I'm raping her; I'm not really even making physical contact. Her cat, on the other hand, recently moved into our home and that's an entirely different story. That animal violates me on a nightly basis.

He puts up this front all day of being timid and skittish. The moment I go near him he darts off. He won't let me feed him nor pet him. He plays the total 'fraidy-cat role but that all changes when the lights go out and me and my wife go to sleep. Like some sort of wrestler he gets all macho, stomping around the house, slamming doors with his tail. He climbs on our bed as we sleep and walks all over us with total disregard. He'll even stand next to my head and bat me with his paw and lick my forehead. I can almost hear him saying, "What? What are you going to do about it, asshole?" Of course, when I wake up and turn the light on and ask him what the hell he thinks he's doing, he looks at me with total contempt and fear, then takes off running down the hall. Eventually I get back to sleep and as soon as I do, he's right back to smacking me in the face. I wonder if he's mistaking Crissie's screams of passion for domestic abuse and thinks I'm actually hurting his caretaker. Maybe his pawing my skull while I sleep is his form of retaliation. I try to explain to him that sometimes when a man and woman come together in a loving way it sounds very violent, more so in our house than others. But the sounds he is hearing are a by-product of true adoration and affection. No humans were harmed in the making of our love. I just don't think he believes me.

Fine Women
& Fine Wine #6

MOTHER-PRODUCTIONS.COM/STARRPRODUCTIONS.BIZ • RATING: 9

I don't know a thing about wine. I know I like to drink it and it makes me feel good. I know I like Pinot Grigio with my fish and Merlot with my steak. After that I'm a complete dunce. You start swirling it in your glass, swishing it in your mouth and spitting it out and I'm lost. Have you seen that movie *Sideways*? With Paul Giamatti? The one set in California's wine country? I needed subtitles. I had no idea what anyone was saying for more than half the film. But it did make me thirsty, and if that was the point then it did its job. It actually prompted me, my wife, my brother-in-law and his girlfriend to go wine tasting in upstate New York. The idea actually spawned from a wedding that we were invited to in the area, friends of my wife. People I'd never met. I try to be open-minded but I'm a pessimistic, smug negatron by nature and when I read on the invite that the couple had reserved a campsite near where the wedding was to be held and that they'd be camping the entire week leading up to the ceremony "so anyone who would like to come join us for some quality time together in the woods, we'll be at Site 56," I looked at my wife and asked, "What kind of people are these? What kind of pagan festival are you dragging me to?" She looked at me with a blank stare. "Don't you find it odd that they are camping the week before their wedding? The week before our wedding I'm going to be a stress case, battening down the hatches and making sure everything is sorted. These people are hiding in the forest coating themselves in mud! Who are these people?" Needless to say we booked a room at the nearest two-star hotel; I practiced my fake smile in the mirror for the weeks leading up to the trip. A week before departing Crissie discovered a stretch of road around one of the Finger Lakes with over 30 vineyards just miles from the hotel, so we decided to stay the day after the wedding and get drunk off vino. Thank God we did because it was one of the most relaxing days I'd ever had, a stark contrast to the wedding day, which was the worst day ever. First off it was an out-door event, the heat was stifling and people were forced to piss and shit in steaming hot, unventilated porta-Johns. The beer, wine and spirits weren't chilled so it felt like you were drinking your own urine. There wasn't enough food for all the guests, not that there was much food to begin with. The entire meal consisted of a roll, roast beef and macaroni salad. Can you guess which of the guests was left unfed? You got it. Yours truly. I'm old-school when it comes to my wedding gifts; I give cash and I give lots of it. Weddings aren't cheap so I like to give enough to cover both our plates plus extra for a gift. But my gift must be earned and so I don't seal my card until after I am fed. If I'm fed well the card stays stuffed, like myself. If I'm shortchanged, then so shall the card. You can bet your ass that that day I was pulling twenties out of their card with the speed and fury of the gods.

The Best of Pregnant Girls Vol. 1–10

STARRPRODUCTIONS.BIZ • DIR: ELIZABETH STARR • RATING: 6

This really isn't the best of pregnant girls. These girls aren't very attractive at all. I've seen some really sexy pregnant girls in my day, and the girls on this disc do not rate amongst them. Me and Crissie have been talking a lot about having kids lately. I guess that's what you do when you are planning to marry. I personally want to wait a year or two after marriage before we start pushing them out. Crissie on the other hand wants to start making kids as soon as we get back from our honeymoon. She has two valid reasons in wanting to get the process started: 1) We're not getting any younger. If she had a baby today she'd be 40 when it turned 10 years old, 51 when it turned 21 and was legally able to drink. The second reason is more a health concern; she wants to finally get off of the birth control pill once and for all. She's been on the shit ever since she got her first period because she has these extreme, body-buckling cramps and the doctor said the pills would alleviate much of the pain. So she says. Maybe she was just a trollop at 10, who knows? All I know is that she hates taking them. I've eaten a few, they taste like tic-tacs; I actually like them but I'm not the one who has to take them day in, day out and bleed out my parts once a month. All things being fair, if I don't have to take them neither should she so I've agreed to let her stop taking them after we return from our honeymoon in Portugal. I told her we'd let nature take its course and if she got pregnant immediately, so be it. It was meant to be. Little does she know that for the next four years I'll be fucking her exclusively in the butt. So yeah, if she does somehow get pregnant, then it's a miracle child, just like our Lord and Savior Jesus Christ and it was, in fact, meant to be. But I wouldn't go placing any bets on it. If by some freak chance it does happen I told her, hell or high water, she was getting that kid to come out of her vagina. None of this C-section shit. I don't want my woman with a permanent war wound across her stomach, more importantly I know I couldn't handle being in the delivery room if they had to cut her open. A friend of hers had a C-section and her husband had to get taken out in a wheelchair. He said it was very surreal to see both sides of the sheet, one where the doctors were pulling and peeling her flesh back and reaching in like it was a goodie bag and the other with her head and arms, completely sedated with epidural, asking, "Did they cut me yet? What are they doing? What's happening?" I'm not a blood and guts guy. Haven't the stomach for it. I know I'd lose it and probably vomit all over my wife. So to save us all the hassle she's having a "natural" childbirth, even if that means she's hopped up on every drug in the hospital.

Over 30 and Dirty

ADAMEVE.COM • DIR: DANIEL DAKOTA • RATING: 10

By the time you read this my wife will have turned 30, and she's been miserable about it for the past two years. Me, I don't mind turning 30; it's just a number. With all my boozing and drugging I never expected to make it past 25, so any day I don't wake up dead is a good day for me. But she is a female and women put strange importance on age and, in turn, associate youth with beauty.

It's complete bullshit. I'd gladly take fiftysomething blonde Nina Hartley for a ride; like wine, women get better with age. Pointy hip-bones, protruding rib cages, sunken eyes and high cheekbones do nothing for me. I need a girl with some meat on her that I can hold on to, with light in her eyes for me to live by, and with enough experience in her fingertips to show me what she likes and teach me things I didn't know could be done without a rope and pulley.

I try and convince Crissie she is hands down the most gorgeous woman I've ever seen. She doesn't hear me. I think she might be partially deaf. It breaks my heart. Her turning 30 has a lot to do with my sudden longing for the ménage à trois. If she's making a big deal now, at 30, when her body is rock solid, then how is she going to react after we have children and her caboose is a little looser, her tits are hanging a little lower, her thighs are slightly wider? I know she'll want plastic surgery and that's fine, I'll get it for her. I'll fix whatever I break regardless of whether I want to or not. To me, those things come with motherhood. They're like battle wounds from war. You don't cover up a bullet hole with a tattoo. No, you wear it with pride as a badge of honor, proof you ran headlong into the shit and you came out the other side in one piece. That's me, though. I know she'll want no part of other women after braving natural childbirth. That said, I have a three-year window to make this happen before I plan on knocking her up and starting my little clone army to take over the world. It's really not much time.

The other day, I took a calculator and realized I spend a little more than four days out of each month on my cell phone. Isn't that awful? I can feel the brain cancer setting in as I type. So I don't know if I even have three years left. I could die tomorrow for all I know, and I will have never known the pleasures of my wife in a loving embrace with another woman. If I do die before she proves her love to me, could you be sure to tell them I want my headstone to read: "Hopefully They Have Lesbians in Heaven (Because I Couldn't Find Any on Earth)."

Navy Girls Love Semen

COLOSSAL ENTERTAINMENT • DIR: MARTIN DEL TORO • RATING: 8

What can I say? I'm a sucker for a good title. I don't even know if this movie is remotely good; I saw the title and was sold. I never even bothered to watch it. It could be all gay sex with men in sailor uniforms for all I know. Generally, when I choose a movie for its title it's because it sparks some sort of memory or anecdote in my head that is loosely related to the topic. But not in this case. I've got nothing. No navy buddies, no war tales, no adventures on aircraft carriers. Zilch. I have in my day been on a number of boats, if that's worth anything to you. On one occasion in Hawaii we went marlin fishing and I caught one longer than my own body. Took me an hour to reel him. When we gaffed him and pulled him in the captain, coked out of his mind, pointed to a bin and said, "There's a gun and a baseball bat in there. Grab one and either shoot him or beat his head in." For one brief moment I considered shooting the beast but I was three days into a five-day bender and the waves were throwing us to and fro; I knew if I pulled that trigger I'd shoot a hole in the boat and we'd sink and I'd drown. So I beat the piss out of that fish with an aluminum bat. I think Crissie has it on videotape somewhere. (I need to ask her about that.) That's really it for the boat stories. Sure, I've almost flipped a few and come close to demolishing a couple but the details are rather vague so instead I'll tell you that I threw Crissie a surprise birthday party the night after we had sushi with the lesbians. I like surprise parties. It really shows that the person who threw the party put a lot of time and effort into it. I'm mainly just saying that because the person in this case is me and I want to remind Crissie that sometimes I do actually do nice things. Rare as that may be. That night is a bit of blur as well aside from my friend Heather telling me her and her daughter Hannah went clothes shopping and saw a white-trash family and their child take a piss. The child had to go to the restroom badly but the store didn't have one. So they told the kid to climb into a clothing rack and to take a piss. And of course the kid did it—he had to go and mommy said it was okay. That, my friends, is why America is so fucked; we're taught at a young age to piss on everyone and everything.

My Baby Got Back! 36

AFRO-CENTRIC.COM • DIR: COREY JORDAN • RATING: 9

I have made many mistakes in my life. I have stolen, cheated, lied, coveted, gambled, drugged, whored and blown red lights. And that's just the tip of the iceberg. For many years I beat myself up over my errors, day and night. I have a handle on it now, and only obsess over the past once or twice a day.

It's easy to tell when it's happening because I begin humming extremely loud at a fever pace in an attempt to drown the thoughts from my head. After 30 or 40 seconds it passes and I go back to whatever I was doing. Sometimes it occurs mid-conversation; that's rather embarrassing. I'll be ordering dinner then start wondering why I wrapped those nunchucks around that girl's eyes when I was 11 to show her how much I liked her and the humming begins. "Yes, I'll take the prime rib, medium rare, with HMMM, HMMM, MMM,

MNNN, MMM . . ." I suppose it could be worse. I could have full-blown Tourette's. "I'll take the prime rib, cunt, bitch, whore."

On a professional level, I made most of my mistakes early on. Forgetting to file my taxes, not reading contracts, getting into bed with shady people and allowing myself to get ripped off; I did it all before I was 20, so the past 10 years have been smooth sailing as far as my career goes. Every once in a while, though, I will find myself making the most rookie error and not being able to do anything about it. I pick fights with people I'm interviewing, I call investors by the wrong name, I forget my tape recorder and so on. I interviewed sexy cover girl Ayana Angel in Vegas this past January and for whatever reason the tape recorder didn't work so I lost the entire interview. And every time I see her pretty face, I start humming like a madman.

What kills me was she was interesting, we hit it off, and most importantly, there was some unspoken sexual chemistry brewing between her and my wife. I mean they were talking hot and heavy about filthy, filthy things, which I found rather shocking since my girl generally doesn't go for black girls. Not that she's a racist or anything (that Ku Klux Klan outfit is from a Halloween party), and she has no set anti-black policy like Felix Vicious, it's just that she's never come across a black girl in real life who turned her on. Obviously she's attracted to your Tyra Bankses and Beyoncés and Oprahs, I mean, what's her name? Not Oprah. Catwoman. I can't think of her name. Anyway, there was my wife, in Vegas, putting the moves on this Nubian delicacy. I was very proud of her. I really thought we had a chance of going back to our room for a royal rumble before I ruined everything. Ayana had just finished telling us how she'd be willing to get fucked by Shaq, even if he did have a four-foot penis, and started to tell us about how when she's not doing porn films she's a high-paid escort back in Atlanta, Georgia, when I saw an opportunity to seal the deal with her and Crissie and said, "How much would it cost for you to fuck my wife?" She laughed at first, then saw I was serious and basically told me I blew it. "We were having a good time, I would have fucked her for free."

She then wrapped up the interview and we said our goodbyes, both she and Crissie annoyed at my stupidity. That's when I rewound the tape a bit to make sure I got it all and realized I didn't record any of it. And I hummed all the way to the bar. And the entire flight home.

 ## Animal Trainer 18

EVILANGEL.COM · DIR: ROCCO SIFFREDI · RATING: 9

I have two surefire comedic devices I employ that, for the most part, guarantee I get laid every night. I may have a deep, Barry White voice but I'm not much of a smooth talker. In my single days my approach to women was, "Hey, you want to get a pizza and fuck?" No? "What, you don't like pizza?"

I'm not good with pickup lines or seducing women into bed; women make me nervous. And uncomfortable. So yeah, my MO was either to drug them or offer them drugs in exchange for their hand on the pump. Or I'd win them over with oafish Jerry Lewis slapstick. That shit works; I can only imagine how many broads Mr. Lewis bedded down with. Have you seen my wife? Hot beyond comprehension. Have you seen me? Not so easy on the eye. I actually made a T-shirt that read, "I don't know what she's doing with me either." But I do know, sort of, and that is I'm a goddamn laugh riot. Especially in the bedroom. Like I said, I have two comedic stunts that have my wife spreading her legs for me on a regular basis. The first is humping her leg. Having her near me automatically causes a hard-on; I reinforce the issue by pressing it into her thigh and humping her leg like a rabbit in heat. She just laughs, occasionally saying, "You know, there is a nicer way to ask," then allows me to go about my business on her. The other method of attaining entrance to my lady's inner sanctum is even more childish and a backup for when the leg hump fails. While lying under the covers I reach down and remove my boxer briefs, tossing them across the room, grazing her face as I release to ensure she's taken notice I am completely naked. I cover my mouth in shock and say, "Oh, my God! My underwear fell off." This joke does not get old. She laughs every time. Once I believed it was my delivery that made her laugh because, well, I do it so well, but as time has passed I think she just laughs at my pathetic ways of trying to get

laid. I think she truly pities me like a sad, wet, lost dog. Which is fine by me, so long as I get sex.

I think in marriage you need to be able to laugh as much as love because when the love dies, you still need to be able to make fun of your partner. Then again, I'm not even really married yet so what the hell do I know? I know humping her leg and my underwear falling off is still working so I'm not going to mess with a good thing. But someday I'll have to think of new ways to get her in the mood. I've considered enrolling in clown school; clowns get more ass than any other profession, did you know that? That's why they're always smiling. Well, that and the cocaine.

Dirty Fucking Pictures

DEADMENHANGING.COM • DIR: ROD FONTANA & I.M. REAL • RATING: 6

I had planned on using this space to tell you about the many times we have tried to have our sex photos developed at Wal-Mart, only to have a photocopied note inserted in their place stating that due to the naughtiness of the images they refused to print them. This happened most recently when we went to Puerto Rico. I got the most awful sun poisoning known to man and asked Crissie to document my misery but instead of cropping my cock and balls out of the frame she shot a number of photos of me completely in the nude. We received yet another rejection note in the envelope with our returned negatives. Like I said, my intent was to tell you a number of such anecdotes about our amateur porn photography but then I flipped over the box cover to this DVD and spotted a young train wreck of a blonde woman with a Hello Kitty tattoo on her inner thigh and it reminded me of yet another missed opportunity to see my wife partake in lesbian sex. It was a few months back and I was waiting to catch a train back home from New York's Penn Station. As I stood splitting my time between watching the clock and critiquing the other travelers waiting for their trains a petite, bleached-blonde girl of 20 or so years of age approached me. "Where do you get your tattoos done?" she asked. I ignored her, assuming she couldn't possibly be talking to me; no one talks to me. I give off a certain leave-me-the-fuck-alone vibe that is quite effective. Especially against women. It's safe to say that I have never been picked up, hit on or advanced upon by anyone of the opposite sex ever. It has just never happened and since it was such a foreign scenario to me I didn't know how to react. She asked her question again. Like De Niro in *Taxi Driver* I responded with, "Are you talking to me?" She was and she smiled to indicate it. I instinctively responded to her flashing me her teeth by stating, "I'm married." "That's great," she said. "I was just wondering who did your work." Perhaps she wasn't hitting on me, I thought. So I told her of my friend J. Goldberg who owns Olde City Tattoo in Philadelphia and as it turned out that was where she lived. A conversation sparked and before long I received the most fantastic answer to "What were you doing up in The City?" "Oh, I'm a hardcore fetish model and I was doing a photo shoot." "How hardcore?" I asked. "As hard as it gets," she responded. I asked if she was into women and wouldn't you know it, she was. I told her, "I think my wife would really like you," which I didn't know for certain, since I still can't figure out what type of women Crissie is into, since she refuses to share that side of herself with me, but I hoped that Crissie would like her, for my sake at least. We exchanged e-mail addresses and said our goodbyes and I ran to my train with a bounce in my step, eager to tell Crissie I'd found us a girl to play with. I felt as I did as a child when I found a stray dog and I carried it all the way home to show my momma and ask if I could keep it. A few days later the girl sent us photos of herself in various compromising positions. As we scrolled through them Crissie had nothing negative to say, which is real positive in these situations. But the last photo showed the girl's bare legs, revealing that she had a Hello Kitty tattoo on her calf. Crissie turned to me, made a quizzical face and said, "She has a Hello Kitty tattoo," half asking, half telling. I just looked at her, already knowing what this all meant and responded, "What the fuck does that have to do with anything?"

Fuck the Teacher

COLOSSALENT.COM • DIR: MARTIN DEL TORO • RATING: 8

Have you ever had your heart broken? I hadn't, not until today. I never even knew I had one. Then a hot knife slid into my blood pump unexpectedly and I realized I was human. Red spilled onto my shirt and for the first time ever I felt pain. I looked down at the blade, then to the hand wielding it, then up to the face of the culprit and it made me cry. The face was my wife's. One month before I was to be married—exactly ONE FUCKING MONTH—I came to the cold realization that she had the power to do what no other woman had ever done to me: hurt me. Deep, emotional hurt. It crushed me. For years I'd been duped into believing that we loved each other so much that we did not possess the ability to hurt each other. That no matter what the world dished out, we had each other and no evil could penetrate that bond. But I was a fool, a fool for love. In life there are no perfect fits; not until they perfect cloning. There are only close fits, a fit that you must be willing to accept as the best hand you're going to be dealt and as I convey this to you, tears run down my face. A hurt like I have never known is all that I have to keep me and my bottle of wine company tonight. I suppose in life, just as in death, you must stand alone. What caused all this? You must be wondering, What could have happened to penetrate Nieratko's tough exterior? He must have caught her in bed with another man. Or maybe he learned she was previously married, or worse currently married? What if she were a serial murderer? A monster that stole, killed and ate newborn babies? It is none of those things. It is, in fact, a hundred thousand times worse. The root of our first knock-down, drag-out fight is air-conditioning for our wedding automobile. Isn't that the most pathetic and petty thing you've ever heard? We're fighting over air-conditioning. Before you go taking sides, let me present the facts and I'll let you come to your own conclusion that I'm correct. Back in November I bought a 1960 Cadillac Deville for the express use of driving it on our wedding day. "Does it have air-conditioning? It's going to be hot in July for our wedding," she asked. "No," I responded, "but I'll have it fixed." For months I tried to find an AC unit for the car with no luck. Finally, my mechanic located one but the price of the unit and the labor was $1,500. $1,500 I didn't have. I could not justify the amount since none of our cars have air-conditioning normally and we've dealt with it for years. On our wedding day we'd be in the car all of 30 minutes, and I would never use the AC again because I like my windows down when I drive. I told her we couldn't have air-conditioning. For a month we argued and finally she agreed to live without because we didn't have the money and what money we did have we needed for our new home. Now, with a month before we're to be married, in the wake of a constant shitstorm of requests, neuroses, insecurities and flat-out absurdities from her mother and my own she has decided to revisit the argument. Well, it's too late. Even if I had the money, which I don't, there isn't enough time to have the work done. So what do I do? I'm forced to hire a limo just so she can have her forced air. And I hope she enjoys it, because I'll be driving in my Cadillac. Alone.

Supersize My Snatch 2

STONEYCURTISXXX.COM • DIR: HARRY PALM • RATING: 8

Well, I compromised with Crissie on the car and the air-conditioning situation. If you recall, she insisted on renting a limo with AC and I so very much wanted to use my 1960 Deville for our photos. Here's what we did: I had someone drive my Cadillac to a nearby landfill and refinery industrial area near the church just for photos but our actual limousine was a 1965 black Lincoln Continental convertible with suicide doors similar to the one John F. Kennedy was killed in. It cost us a thousand dollars and guess what? The goddamn air-conditioning barely worked. We had the windows down most of the time. It would have been cooler in my Caddy. Yet to me it was worth every penny. Why? We used the Lincoln to reenact the JFK assassination with our wedding party. I had my buddy film me sitting on the back of the car with Crissie on the seat below me in Super 8 with the same exact camera as the Zapruder film. As we cruised along I waved to the guys and gals of the wedding party and on cue my head went "back and to the left, back and to the left." I collapsed into the seat and Crissie, doing her best Jackie O, started to freak out and climb out onto the trunk. It's all quite absurd and I think will make a fantastic close to our wedding video. After all the partying we fade to black and come back in with the assassination, then cut to credits. A sign of what is to come in our life? I doubt it. Unless Crissie beds down with some kind of serial killer, which I don't really think is very likely. But you never know. Stranger things have happened. Like during the wedding ceremony when Crissie put the ring on the wrong finger. Leading up to the big day she kept saying, "I'm a dancer, I'm used to looking at myself in the mirror. I won't put the ring on the wrong hand." And yet she still screwed up. It was partially my fault. Partially. I don't know my left from my right so when it was her turn to put the ring on me I offered her both hands. She just happened to pick the right hand, which wasn't the right hand. I tried to keep her error under wraps by blurting out at the top of my lungs, "HA! You put it on the wrong hand! I thought you were a dancer!" Everyone laughed. Except Crissie's mom. She rolled her eyes because she had warned and rewarned Crissie not to put the ring on the wrong hand. Unfazed, Crissie declared, "Let's try this again. From the top. Take two," making the priest reread the vows so that she could get it straight. I have all of Redd Foxx's and Richard Pryor's recordings and I can say that even so, I have not laughed and smiled as much as I did on my wedding day. It was like two 4-year-olds getting married.

Naked Ambition

BY CARLY MILNE • CARROLL & GRAF PUBLISHING

know this is a feminist book about successful women in porn, so
I'm not sure if it's acceptable to say that author Carly Milne is a
hot piece of ass. Is that okay to say? I'm really not sure what the sex-
ist etiquette is when it comes to feminism. Am I only allowed to think
dirty thoughts about man haters or am I allowed to voice my desires?
Or by speaking my dirty mind am I uttering the feminist equivalent to
the N-word? It's really sad that I live in a world where I am not sure
if complimenting a woman's body is kosher or not. I know I'm totally
objectifying Ms. Milne and I know how terrible that is but I feel it's
important that the world knows that the sassy photo on the back of
her book is neither air brushed nor shot from some magical camera
angle; my wife and I have met Carly and she is delicious. Well, we
assume she's delicious. I hoped we'd find out in no uncertain terms
what she tasted like but that did not come to pass.

Perhaps had I asked we could have learned the answer but the
truth is I am not comfortable around women. They frighten me. They
know something I don't and I don't like it. I get extremely nervous
and self-conscious around them. This book intimidated me itself.
Chapter after chapter of strong, no-bullshit women in the adult business made me shit scared to even crack the spine. Two weeks passed
before I got enough balls to read the first line. In some strange way I
felt like I was being ganged up on by the ladies who'd written about
their contribution to the new, feminist, forward-thinking porn. I don't
like feeling that way. I always do or say something stupid in those situations. My wife says I remind her a lot of Larry David in that sense.
For instance, some friends of ours just got married and they sat us at
a table full of feminists and lesbians. Not that there's anything wrong
with that. At some point the bride came and said hello and mentioned that she was not taking the last name of her husband. Soon
we were all involved in a roundtable discussion about adopting your

spouse's surname or not. One of the girl-on-girl couples asked me if we were married. I said we were not, that we'd marry in July, and I simply refer to her as my wife because I refuse to ever utter that French phrase that is meant to be used as a pre-wedding title. FREEDOM FRIES! Then I was asked if she would be taking my name. Without thought, I said, "Of course. She doesn't have a choice." Jaws hit the table. The women were enraged. You'd think I had personally extinguished 35 years of burning bras with my words. Then one of the more macho ladies puffed out her chest, raised her chin at me and declared, "I'd never force anyone to change their name for me." I replied, "That's fine." Then I explained to her that, "You don't need to worry about that because you're a lesbian and lesbians don't have the power to change last names. It's a superpower that comes with having a penis."

It was right about then that everyone got up and walked away from our table, not to return for the rest of the evening, leaving the entire table to me and my wife, which was awesome because we had, like, 12 pieces of cake.

Rocco Meats an American Angel in Paris

EVILANGEL.COM • DIR: ROCCO SIFFREDI • RATING: 10

Yesterday was nine years since my grandfather passed away. I went with my grandmother to his grave in monsoon rain and put flowers by his headstone. A long time ago I decided I'd be cremated when the good Lord takes me. I don't much care for the idea of decomposing in the ground and being eaten by worms and maggots. Even alive I'm not big on dirt. Standing in the rain, arm around my grandmother, water pounding down on my head and shoulders, I began to think about exactly where I'd have my ashes dumped when I'm gone. I think the job of the dead is to offer a sense of closure when they're gone and so I've decided, if she outlives me, to have my

wife take me and my ashes on a walk down memory lane. I'll insist that she go to Hawaii to our private beach and toss some remains into the sea where we took our first vacation together, then I'll have her fly to Paris to throw me off the observation deck of the Eiffel Tower, the first stop on our honeymoon. Next I'll have her go down to Algarve, Portugal, to drown me in the Atlantic, the second stop on our honeymoon. From there I'll have her randomly throw me out the window as she cruises the Portuguese countryside, reenacting the month we spent there after our wedding. From there she'll go back to New Jersey to a small Irish pub named McCormicks where I first saw her and instantly fell in love. I'd like her to dump me in the far back corner where I spotted her. After that, if there's anything left of me, she can go to the martini bar we went on our first date—when I first told her I was going to marry her—pour me into a glass and drink me down with some chilled vodka and toast a love that was more fairy tale than anything Hans Christian Anderson ever wrote. See? Even in death I'm a hopeless romantic. Do you think porn stars get misty-eyed in the same way? If so, then this DVD must mean the world to Savanna Samson because it was the first time she ever had sex on film. Long before she became a world-famous Vivid girl she went to

Paris and got fucked in the ass by Rocco; which to me, in a professional sense, is just like losing your virginity, I would think. It seems like as noble a rite of passage as there can be in the adult business. And I would think that's a very special day in a young girl's life.

Don't Kiss Me, Just Fuck Me! 2

NICKELASS.COM • DIR: NICK GREEN • RATING: 10

What did you think of the World Cup this year? I think it sucked. Portugal lost and that's really all that matters to me. Of course I was quite pleased that England lost, no offense to you, but it was either you or us. There's more to it than that. My sister-in-law is English so if Portugal lost to England me, my brother, my uncle and my entire family would never have heard the end of it and that in itself would be awful, but worse than that I believe that my happiness, both present and future, was tied to the outcome of that game. As we watched the tournament play out and watched both England and Portugal advance we came to the realization that the game would be played just hours before my wedding ceremony on July 1. No sooner did it hit me than everyone began calling me. In absolute sincerity family and friends asked if there was any way that I could push back the start of the wedding by a half hour to allow everyone to see the end of the game. I wanted to see the game myself but this was my wedding. There was no delaying it and especially not for football. I don't think God would buy that as a valid reason. The days leading up to the game/wedding had every male I know pissed at me for making them miss the end of the game. I knew then that if Portugal did not win that it would be a black cloud over my wedding day that would ultimately destroy any chance of a happy life together. Simply put: Portugal beats England we have a fairy-tale life together, England beats Portugal and we're divorced within a year. So instead of being nervous about exchanging vows or whatever makes people sweat

before they get hitched, I was worried that the sports gods were going to smite me. As the guests arrived at the church the outcome was still undetermined. Pachelbel's Canon played as Crissie started her way down the aisle and still no one knew who won. As she got halfway to the altar my Uncle John, with a wireless radio in his ear, belted out the loudest decree of joy. Some thought it was meant for Crissie and how beautiful she looked but most knew it meant Portugal had won. For those who were unsure he followed it with a church-rattling "Yeah, baby! Portugal won! 3–1!" With that the air got cooler, the mood lighter and the day just that much more perfect, and I was assured that I could expect a long, loving future with Crissie. The fact that I happened to be in Paris when France beat Portugal and those drunk Parisians refused to allow me any sleep as they celebrated was somehow acceptable to me. Portugal beat England on my wedding day . . . I can't be greedy.

 ## Oops, I Got Gangbanged Again!

KICKASS.COM • RATING: 8

N ot long ago I mentioned I was trying to con Crissie into bedding down with a stripper friend of mine. At one point I was even thinking of surprising her with two strippers doing a full-blown lesbian show in our living room as she walked through the door from work. Then I rethought that idea. It dawned on me how that picture might be misinterpreted by my wife: me on my leather couch, eating popcorn, drinking beer, throwing dollar bills at two naked women as they poke and prod each other's parts with fingers and various sex toys. "Yes, I know how it looks but I did it for you. This was a gift for you. Come on. Have a seat and enjoy yourself." I decided maybe a mellow photo shoot fueled by booze, accidentally leading into some girl-on-girl action was my best bet. A week before my wedding a bunch of my buddies took me to the club my stripper friend dances at and got me a slew of lap dances from every girl in the place; sometimes two and three girls at once. The place is butt naked and bring your own beer so there's really no need to have an active imagination. The girls are usually very open to perform any masturbatory or lesbian act you request. As I spoke to my friend I tried to lay some groundwork. "You should come down sometime. I'd love to take

some photos of you for my book." Which wasn't a lie by any means but I was hoping that after some drinks and some nude photos she and my wife might get friendly and . . . well . . . you know. Well, I can safely say that will most likely never happen. And for once neither my tactless plotting nor my wife's stubbornness is to blame. Not even my friend is to blame. At least I don't think she is. She seemed very much into it and told me to call her after we got back from our honeymoon but upon arrival back in Jersey I learned that she had been arrested for improper disposal of human remains. Turns out she had five human skulls and a severed human hand (floating in a jar of formaldehyde) on display in her home. And I guess that's illegal. Do I have some luck or do I have some luck? All I want is a little lesbian action in my life and I can't catch a break. If it's not one thing it's another. I haven't even bothered to tell my wife. Hello Kitty tattoos turn her off. I can only imagine her reaction to five heads in a duffle bag. Who knows? Maybe she won't find out and it can still happen once they let her out of jail. I know it's fucked up but I have to keep my options open. So what if she had skulls in her house? That does-n't make her a bad person. You can buy human skulls off the Internet. And the hand? I don't know, maybe she needed a hand around the house with the dusting and the cleaning. I don't really give a shit. I can look past just about anything at this point if it is going to help me achieve my goal of two women in my bed. I'll be honest, though, this skulls thing is so surreal that I'm thinking my wish is jinxed and if I ever were to have two women at once one of them would end up dead. And how the hell would I explain that? Me and my friend with her skulls lying in bed with my wife's naked corpse? "Officer . . . have you ever wanted something so badly in your life . . ."

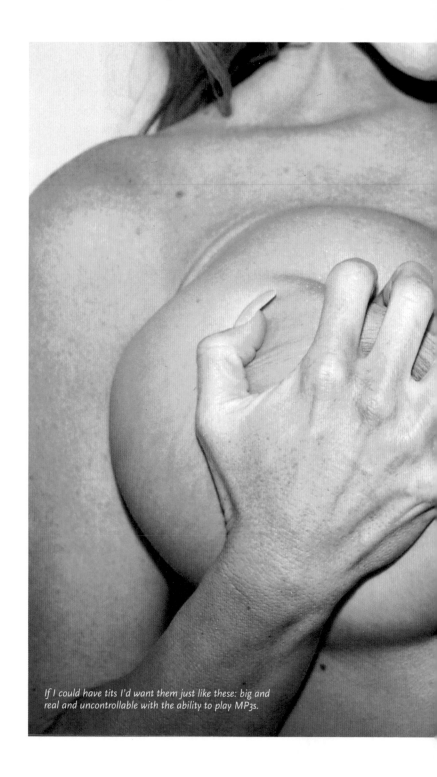

If I could have tits I'd want them just like these: big and real and uncontrollable with the ability to play MP3s.

CHAPTER 4
"Misty Water-Colored Memories"
(The photos)

(top) The Jersey Shore. (bottom) Rape has such a negative connotation.

I hate dirt. There was a period there where I wasn't showering for weeks on end. It makes me sick to think about it.

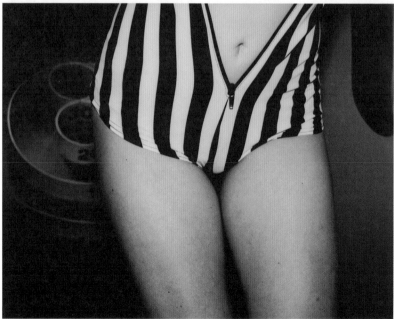

(top) Vice UK editor Andy Capper hard at lurk. (right) I think the most romantic Ghostface line is, "I'm gonna sell my guns and with the money I'm gonna take you to Vegas." (bottom) I have a skee ball machine in my basement.

I always laugh at those stories when people burn their house down and die because they fell asleep with a cigarette in their hand. Who does that? Grow up.

My friend Daniel Shimizu demonstrates why Asians are superior: they refuse to get tattoos without tits resting on their heads.

Porn star Kelly Madison. You can't tell from this angle but she has a lovely personality.

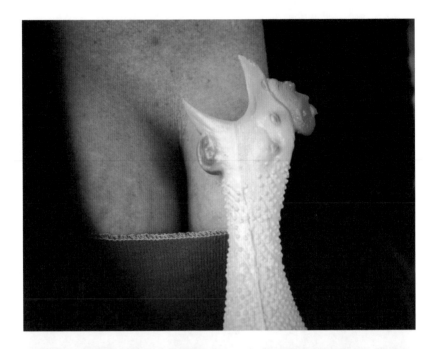

(top) I think the only thing I love more than women are rubber chickens. (Bottom) Thanksgiving at my in-laws' house is always a good time.

This is Mistress Rhiannon. She's my favorite person on earth. She's from Lodi, NJ, just like the Misfits, and she has 62MMM breasts. She has had so many surgeries that she has no feeling in one of her tits. She told me sometimes she burns it on the oven door and doesn't realize it until she smells the flesh cooking. I have a major crush on her and if I weren't already married . . .

Kut Master Kurt and his ex-girlfriend, chilling.

Sadly, this is as close to seeing my friend Amy naked as I've ever gotten.

Our honeymoon suite in Paris. Every time I
look at this photo it reminds me that
Portugal lost to France in the World Cup.

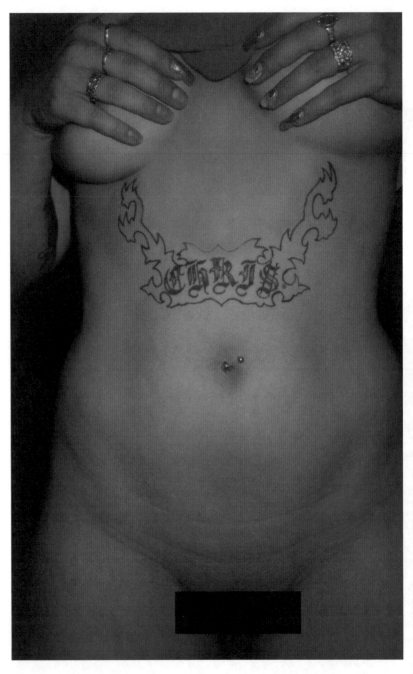

Two weeks after meeting this girl, Donna, in Arkansas she got my name tattooed on her belly. A year later she repeatedly attempted to commit suicide in my apartment in LA. I guess I have that effect on people.

I like those stories where people say they see the face of Jesus in a pool of melted chocolate or in the bark of a tree or a ball of pasta. There's something inspiring about them that always makes me hungry.

I married my wife for her ass.
Even when camouflaged it can't be hidden.

(top) I wanted to use this girl's amazing ass tattoos for the opening spread of an article I did on Oregon but I forgot how to spell it and the editor didn't care for my handwriting. (bottom) On the set of Shane's World 17. Where does one shop for a volleyball with a penis attached?

This is Gabrielle. Her breasts are utterly ridiculous.

I like to call this one "Hey! I saw your mom down by the pool."

My wife, on our honeymoon. I was going to show you a shot of her oiling up her breasts and say, "Normally I'd be hyper-protective of people seeing her topless but I know in 2 years her tits will get wrecked from childbirth so this is my only chance to immortalize her beautiful, natural breasts for all eternity." But then I thought, "I don't even know you."

JOHN DECKER

CHRIS NIERATKO

Chris Nieratko was born in 1976 in New Jersey, where he still lives today. His father was killed in Pearl Harbor. When he was 18 Chris got his first real job, working for *Disney Adventures*. It's been downhill ever since. Ten years ago he was getting drunk every night with pals from the skateboard magazine *Big Brother* and writing whatever came into his wasted head. When he became the editor in January 2000 they all started a now infamous group of idiots called *Jackass*. Chris ate eggs until he puked for the show but his love of pills and sleeping lent itself more to the literary world. His first job after *Big Brother* was editing a series of incredibly disgusting porn magazines until he was fired for making fun of them.

Chris has a BA in BS and continues to write for almost every magazine around including *Vice, Bizarre, i-D, Paper, Maxim, Farmer's Almanac, Skateboarder, Hustler, Vibe, Interview, XXL*. The rest of his time is spent managing NJ, his skateboard shop in his hometown of Sayreville, the boyhood home of Jon Bon Jovi. He truly believes Ghostface Killah is his father. This is his first book. For more of Chris Nieratko go to chrisnieratko.com.